THE
CONSTITUTIONAL
CONVENTION

THE
CONSTITUTIONAL
CONVENTION

A NARRATIVE HISTORY FROM THE NOTES OF
JAMES MADISON

Edward J. Larson
and Michael P. Winship

THE MODERN LIBRARY

NEW YORK

2005 Modern Library Paperback Edition

Published in the United States by Modern Library,
an imprint of The Random House Publishing Group,
a division of Random House, Inc., New York.

MODERN LIBRARY and the TORCHBEARER Design are registered trademarks of
Random House, Inc.

Library of Congress Cataloging-in-Publication Data

Madison, James, 1751–1836.
The Constitutional Convention: a narrative history from the notes of
James Madison / Edward J. Larson and Michael P. Winship.
p.   cm.
Includes index.
ISBN 0-8129-7517-0
1. United States. Constitutional Convention (1787).   2. United States.
Constitution.   3. Constitutional history—United States.   I. Larson, Edward J.
(Edward John)   II. Winship, Michael.   III. Title.

KF4510.M33 2005
342.7302'92—dc22   2005041649

Printed in the United States of America on acid-free paper

www.modernlibrary.com

2   4   6   8   9   7   5   3   1

First Edition

Preface

The curiosity I had felt during my researches into the history of the most distinguished confederacies, particularly those of antiquity, and the deficiency I found in the means of satisfying it ... determined me to preserve, as far as I could, an exact account of what might pass in the Convention. ... Nor was I unaware of the value of such a contribution to the fund of materials for the history of a Constitution on which would be staked the happiness of a people great even in its infancy, and possibly the cause of liberty throughout the world.

—JAMES MADISON

The more we used the notes that James Madison took at the Constitutional Convention in our own work, the more we came to agree with Madison's high regard for their historical worth. They have great value for anyone studying American history, government, and law. The Convention was also a wonderfully human event, full of intrigue and insight. Simply put, the history of the Constitutional Convention is both an important and a vivid story that bears retelling to every American generation.

Despite the ready availability of Madison's extensive record of the deliberations at the Constitutional Convention, and of other delegates' far less complete notes as well, the insiders' stories of that landmark episode in American history are not widely read. Those firsthand accounts are not very accessible for modern readers. They contain too much detail for readers to follow the underlying narrative easily, and anyone unfamiliar with eighteenth-century rules of parliamentary procedure might quickly become lost in the tangle of motions, votes, and maneuvers. Yet here were able debaters and crafty legislators forging one of the most significant political documents of all time. Their words, especially Madison's, tell the story better than secondary texts or commentaries.

Our goal with this book is to make the deliberations of the Constitutional Convention accessible to modern readers. To do so, we have edited out substantial amounts of material from Madison's notes that we view as extraneous to the main debates, occasionally substituted the notes of other delegates when these were clearer than Madison's, and added in extensive bridging material. In exercising our editorial judgment, we sought to preserve the Convention's fundamental complexity. Many people at the time, and since, have roundly criticized the compromises and other decisions made behind closed doors in Philadelphia. As much as possible, we let the delegates' arguments speak for themselves on these and other matters. To preserve the integrity of the historical record while still striving to make it readable, we have marked all of our deletions with ellipses or italicized commentary. (Our additions are in brackets when inserted within the body of Madison's notes.) Beyond this, we have freely used modern spelling and punctuation throughout, regularized Madison's erratic use of capital letters, standardized the records of votes, broken long passages into paragraphs, and written out abbreviations in full. Our goal in all our changes is to render the original text understandable today. As history, Madison's notes remain as relevant now as ever; as narrative, we hope they improve in our setting.

In closing, we wish to acknowledge the assistance that we received in preparing this book. Of course, our first thanks go to our students and colleagues at the University of Georgia, particularly legal historian Peter Hoffer. We also benefited from the suggestions of Susan McMichaels and two anonymous press readers. Ed Larson also wishes to acknowledge the inspiration that he received from the organizers and participants of a 2001 Liberty Fund conference on Max Farrand's *The Records of the Federal Convention of 1787,* particularly Barry Shain, Pauline Maier, Jack Greene, Kermit Hall, Judge Danny Boggs, and Judge Michael McConnell. Most of all, we thank our supportive and trusted editor at the Modern Library, Will Murphy; our production editor, Evan Camfield; and our copy editor, Steven Meyers. All these good people helped us greatly.

—E.L. & M.W.
Athens, Georgia
September 2005

CONTENTS

List of Delegates
Speaking in This Record

(in alphabetical order)

Delegate's Name	State	Signed Constitution
Abraham Baldwin	Georgia	Yes
Gunning Bedford, Jr.	Delaware	Yes
David Brearly	New Jersey	Yes
Jacob Broom	Delaware	Yes
Pierce Butler	South Carolina	Yes
Daniel Carroll	Maryland	Yes
George Clymer	Pennsylvania	Yes
William Davie	North Carolina	No
Jonathan Dayton	New Jersey	Yes
John Dickinson	Delaware	Yes
Oliver Ellsworth	Connecticut	No
Thomas Fitzsimons	Pennsylvania	Yes
Benjamin Franklin	Pennsylvania	Yes
Elbridge Gerry	Massachusetts	No
Nathaniel Gorham	Massachusetts	Yes

Alexander Hamilton	New York	Yes
William Samuel Johnson	Connecticut	Yes
Rufus King	Massachusetts	Yes
John Langdon	New Hampshire	Yes
John Lansing, Jr.	New York	No
James Madison, Jr.	Virginia	Yes
Luther Martin	Maryland	No
George Mason	Virginia	No
James McHenry	Maryland	Yes
John Mercer	Maryland	No
Thomas Mifflin	Pennsylvania	Yes
Gouverneur Morris	Pennsylvania	Yes
William Paterson	New Jersey	Yes
William Leigh Pierce	Georgia	No
Charles Pinckney	South Carolina	Yes
Charles Cotesworth Pinckney*	South Carolina	Yes
Edmund Randolph	Virginia	No
George Read	Delaware	Yes
John Rutledge	South Carolina	Yes
Roger Sherman	Connecticut	Yes
Richard Dobbs Spaight	North Carolina	Yes
George Washington	Virginia	Yes
Hugh Williamson	North Carolina	Yes
James Wilson	Pennsylvania	Yes
Robert Yates	New York	No

*Identified as "Gen. Pinckney" in Madison's notes to distinguish him from his cousin and fellow South Carolina delegate Charles Pinckney.

THE
CONSTITUTIONAL
CONVENTION

Introduction
The Road to Philadelphia

Then as now, Philadelphia summers were notorious for their heat and humidity. By 1787, the colonial capital originally laid out by William Penn over a century earlier had blossomed into one of the nation's largest cities and busiest ports, with approximately 30,000 people crowded onto the west bank of the Delaware River nearly one hundred miles upriver from the Atlantic Ocean. Although progressive by the standards of the day, with broad leafy streets and handsome brick buildings, Philadelphia lacked modern sanitation facilities and epidemics were a recurring threat. A stench often hung over the city during the dog days of July and August. No wonder many sophisticated Americans of that era preferred country life over city dwelling, especially in summer.

During the summer of 1787, Philadelphians had some highly distinguished visitors to share their misery: fifty-five delegates to a convention in the Philadelphia State House, where the Declaration of Independence had been signed eleven years earlier. The convention was called to revise the terms of the federal union for the United States. Those delegates comprised an impressive group of political leaders and nation builders. Thirty-nine had already served in Congress and seven had been state governors. Eight had signed the Declaration of Independence (while three had chosen not to), and fifteen had helped to draft constitutions for the states after the break with Britain. Over half were college graduates; thirty-four of them had trained as law-yers. The delegates came from as far away as Georgia and New Hamp-shire. They included plantation owners, farmers, and merchants. Most were born into America's colonial elite, while a minority had risen out of obscurity through hard work, ability, and good fortune. They were all white males; nineteen of them owned slaves. Their average age was forty-two years. The youngest delegate was twenty-six years old, while the oldest was the legendary Benjamin Franklin, perhaps the most famous of all Americans, eighty-one and in failing health. Gen-eral George Washington, idolized for his Revolutionary War service, had at first refused to come but changed his mind after worrying that his reputation as a patriot would suffer. Fortunately for all of them, the summer of 1787 turned out to be relatively mild—by Philadelphia standards at least—but still featured some very unpleasant days.

The convention was supposed to have started on May 14, but none but the most eager and well-prepared delegates had arrived by that time. One who had was James Madison, a thirty-six-year-old delegate from Virginia and ardent student of political history and theory. He had played a large role in bringing the convention about. Like all of the delegates who would eventually show up, Madison was in Phila-delphia because he believed that the United States had a government woefully inadequate to address the grave dangers that it faced.

Following their declaration of independence from Britain in 1776, the thirteen states had formed a "firm league" of "perpetual union" under the Articles of Confederation. However, it was a union in which, as the Articles guaranteed, each state kept its own "sovereignty, free-dom, and independence." The document took effect in 1781, after the thirteenth state finally ratified it. Under the Articles, the United States government was little more than a planning and execution board of foreign policy for a federation of thirteen otherwise independent re-publics. It consisted only of a single-house congress whose members were chosen annually by the state legislatures and in which each state cast a single vote. It had no independent executive or judicial branch. In contrast, by 1787 the innovative constitutions of every state except Pennsylvania provided for a two-house legislature and some form of independent executive and judiciary to provide internal checks and balances in its exercise of power. Congress could make treaties and de-clare war; and it was nominally in charge of the Northwest Territory, stretching from present-day Ohio to Minnesota, which was controlled in fact by Indians. It could not impose taxes, tariffs, or any other revenue device, however, and its financial ability to maintain a credible military had collapsed by the end of the Revolutionary War.

This arrangement initially made perfect sense to the states. When they ratified the Articles, they were in the process of collectively fighting for their independence from an oppressive, powerful monarchy, and their leaders had no desire to place themselves under another overbearing government. However, it quickly became evident to nearly everyone that the Articles of Confederation were an inadequate vehicle for guiding the fast-growing United States and its more than three million people through a treacherous world. Foreign countries slapped restrictions on American shipping and the United States could not retaliate. Spain encroached on territory in the American South while Britain continued to occupy forts in the old Northwest. Some desperate settlers in the rapidly expanding trans-Appalachian West hinted at forming their own states outside the Union or joining Spain. Although the Articles left the national interest of the United States heavily dependent on state goodwill, the states conducted themselves by narrow standards of self-interest. They regularly ignored federal treaties, including provisions of the peace treaty with Britain, and built trade barriers against products from other states. Struggling to pay off huge war-bond obligations, the states increasingly ignored the confederation's urgent pleas for money.

Almost as soon as the new government was formed, it became widely acknowledged that the Confederation Congress needed at least the ability to raise money and regulate commerce in some form. The states, however, fiercely jealous of their independence, had written into the Articles that any changes to them required the agreement of · all thirteen states. Even so necessary a revenue measure as an impost on imported goods floundered on the refusal of a single state, Rhode Island, to go along. The Articles did not work, and they provided no viable method for self-adjustment. By 1786, some Americans were speculating that the United States would soon split into separate regional confederations.

Thus, it was understandable that nationalists, people who wanted to strengthen the United States government, began looking outside the framework of the Articles for relief in the mid-1780s. Madison was an active supporter of a plan for an interstate meeting in Annapolis, Maryland, in September 1786, to discuss common commercial concerns. He prodded the Virginia legislature, of which he was a member, to invite all the states to send delegates to this convention. Some states were suspicious that the Annapolis Convention was a ploy to undermine the Articles. When only five state delegations showed up, those present, including Madison, adopted a report drafted by Alexander Hamilton of New York inviting all states to a larger convention in Philadelphia beginning in May 1787. The convention was to address all matters needed "to render the constitution of the Federal Government adequate to the exigencies of the Union." After five state legislatures appointed delegates to the proposed convention, the Confederation Congress reluctantly endorsed it "for the sole and express purpose of revising the Articles of Confederation." Seven more state legislatures ultimately named delegates to the convention. Only Rhode Island refused.

There was a consensus that the United States government could not function or even survive simply on the goodwill of the states. But Madison, as he considered the disarray of the American Union and what was needed to remedy it, reached a far more sweeping conclusion. The problem was not just that selfish states threatened the survival of the confederation. As he saw it, these states threatened the American Revolution's fundamental and radical goal of creating lasting republican forms of government, chosen by and accountable to the "people," in a hostile world of monarchies. Internally, the states exhibited the same ultimately self-destructive selfishness and pettiness that they displayed on the national scale. Madison had served in the Virginia legislature through much of the 1780s, and what he found there were not selfless patriots but narrow-minded politicians, concerned mainly with deal making and satisfying their local constituencies. Madison's plans to reform the state court system got nowhere and his effort to reduce British control of the state's shipping was gutted by local special interests.

More alarming, some state legislatures were taking the wishes of their constituents seriously in a way that Madison found profoundly dangerous. The United States went into a postwar depression in the mid-1780s. Farmers found themselves buried in debt and their farms heavily mortgaged. The value of hard currency soared under deflationary pressures from home and abroad—driving up the real cost of old debt. In an age when the United States had almost no banks, creditors were generally wealthy gentlemen similar in background to Madison. The American Revolution's rallying cry of liberty and equality had loosened such gentlemen's traditional grip on government. In several state legislatures, a new breed of politicians, often from lower social backgrounds, was passing debt-relief measures, most notoriously by issuing inflationary paper money. Such legislative action, Madison believed, was an attack on the rights of creditors and amounted to the few being plundered by the many. If the states were left to themselves, the liberty of these little republics, purchased with much blood and sacrifice, would degenerate into the "popular" tyranny of local majorities.

In the winter of 1786, Madison concluded that the United States, in order to survive, needed to be more than a federation of states with a "federal" government (as it was then called). It needed to have a national government that could break the power of the states to interfere with common interests. The diversity of local interests would be submerged in such a large government, Madison believed, and petty local tyrants would be too obscure socially to get elected. Instead, he hoped that national lawmakers of a suitably high social rank and the requisite education would unite around a broad understanding of the common good, which included the protection of the rights of property.

Republics, however, were extremely rare in the eighteenth century. They only worked, it was generally believed, on a small scale, like in the Netherlands or the then-independent Venetian Republic. Conventional wisdom taught that any national government with the power and force to control and defend a territory as large as the United States would have to be either a monarchy or a dictatorship, with little protection for liberty (it was rumored that some Americans were in fact concluding that the country needed a monarch). Madison was deeply committed to republican rule. How could this necessary national government be prevented from degenerating into despotism? Here Madison drew on the recent experiences of the states with their new constitutions. The government would have checks and balances in it. As in the states, a large lower house of the legislature whose members served for short terms and where the people were represented would be balanced by a smaller upper house whose members served for long terms and represented the wealthier and perhaps more talented and educated elements of society (many states had stiff property requirements either for the members of the upper house or for those who elected them). An executive and judiciary would provide checks on the legislature's power, while the legislature could impeach members of the other branches if they exceeded their constitutional authority. No faction bent on subverting liberty would be able to get hold of all the branches of government, Madison believed. Most important, in Madison's initial scheme, to protect national interests and private rights, the legislature would have the power to veto any state law. In sum, Madison concluded that the conventional wisdom was wrong: republican liberty could flourish only under a strong government that encompassed an extended territory and diverse population.

While Madison waited for enough delegates to show up in Philadelphia to make a quorum, with the aid of other Virginia delegates he solidified his ideas on the ideal republican government for the United States into fifteen succinct resolutions. Together, these resolutions became known as the Virginia Plan. Most delegates from other states would probably not have given the radical Virginia Plan a serious hearing if it had not been for developments in Massachusetts during the previous fall and winter. Unlike neighboring Rhode Island, which printed inflationary paper money by the basketful and made local creditors accept it, Massachusetts gave no quarter to debtors suffering under the twin burdens of deflation and depression. Quite to the contrary, the state legislature, dominated by wealthy merchants, raised taxes repeatedly to pay off the war bonds that those same merchants owned. It printed no paper money, imprisoned defaulting debtors, and strictly enforced foreclosure laws. To stop the foreclosures of their homes and farms, desperate debtors in western Massachusetts, under the loose leadership of Revolutionary War captain Daniel Shays, armed themselves and, in the late summer and fall of 1786, shut the county courthouses where their property was being foreclosed. The Massachusetts government, in preparation for the January 1787 sitting of the Hampshire County court in Springfield, sent a well-equipped army inland, funded by the creditor merchants, and the so-called Shays's Rebellion was easily put down with little loss of life.

Shays's Rebellion was the largest incident in a wave of backcountry agrarian unrest that was rippling across the United States. What made it particularly shocking, besides its scale, was that it occurred in a state that was supposedly well governed. Many Americans, particularly those with power and wealth, imagined Shays's Rebellion as a far greater and more deliberate menace to property and order than it really was. To their dismay, the Confederation Congress proved glacially slow and ineffectual in mobilizing against it, unnecessary though that mobilization proved in hindsight. To make matters worse, in the spring of 1787, Massachusetts voters chose legislators who were sympathetic to the problems of the rebels. The specter of Shays's Rebellion hung over the Philadelphia Convention and ensured that Madison's Virginia Plan would get a respectful hearing.

By May 25, 1787, enough state delegations had arrived in Philadelphia to make a quorum and allow the Convention to begin. Four days later, the governor of Virginia, Edmund Randolph, introduced the Virginia Plan. The delegates listening to him were men of the world, and they knew the United States needed to be able to defend itself and its interests against foreign powers. They were also men of property, and they knew that they would benefit from a government capable of spurring the country's economic growth and honoring its financial obligations. Moreover, as members of the country's upper class, they feared the swelling tides of popular hostility to their class that had penetrated the legislatures of many states. Finally, they were patriots: a third of them had served in the Revolutionary Army; some of them still bore the scars of the wounds they had received in combat. They wished to preserve liberty, property, and republican government from the manifold threats they perceived to them, both from within and without. They framed their solution to that desire within a shared intellectual universe shaped by Enlightenment political theorists, European law commentators, a century and a half of English polemical political literature, and a historical awareness stretching back to ancient Greece, all filtered through two decades of American political struggle and experiments in government.

Yet this group of delegates was also riven with mutual suspicions, conflicting economic interests, fierce state loyalties, and fears that the Virginia Plan would unleash a tyrannical monster that could destroy the very liberty it was intended to preserve. Madison understood that if the Convention finally approved a constitution with any resemblance to his fifteen resolutions, it could mark the beginning of an extraordinary, unprecedented experiment in large-scale republican government. Inspired by a keen sense of history-in-the-making, he decided to keep detailed notes of the entire proceedings. As he later described:

> I chose a seat in front of the presiding member, with the other members on my right and left hand. In this favorable position for hearing all that passed I noted in terms legible and in abbreviations and marks intelligible to myself what was read from the Chair or spoken by the members; and losing not a moment unnecessarily between the adjournment and reassembling of the Convention I was enabled to write out my daily notes during the session or within a few finishing days after its close.

Although other delegates occasionally took notes, including especially detailed ones by Robert Yates of New York, Madison's "journal" offers the clearest window into the interworkings of the Constitutional Convention: a remarkably insightful summary account of the deliberations in Philadelphia. We will let him take the story from here, with our additions in italic or brackets.

Record of the Convention

THE CONSTITUTIONAL CONVENTION *opened on a rainy Friday, May 25, 1787. Twenty-nine delegates were present from nine states. Because states set different voting requirements for their delegations, only seven states had enough delegates to vote: Delaware, New Jersey, New York, North Carolina, Pennsylvania, South Carolina, and Virginia. The Convention's major decision that day was unanimous: the delegates chose George Washington from Virginia, the most widely respected man in America, as president of the Convention. On Monday, May 28, the Convention worked out its rules, the most important of which was that all proceedings would be kept secret for the duration of the Convention. On this day, the first delegate from Connecticut arrived. Connecticut allowed one of its delegates to represent it, and so Connecticut was now voting. Massachusetts, which required three, also reached voting status on Monday.*

TUESDAY, MAY 29.
[IN CONVENTION]

On May 29, the aristocratic thirty-five-year-old governor of Virginia, Edmund Randolph, took the floor to attack the Articles of Confederation and introduce a series of resolutions for a new Constitution. The mandate of the Convention was only to revise and amend the Articles, but Randolph's resolutions, known collectively as the Virginia Plan (see Appendix A), would scrap them and substitute a strong national government with final authority over what had been semi-independent states. The government would consist of a national legislature, judiciary, and executive—each with the ability to check the others' power. The legislature would have two houses, or "branches," with the larger one (the "first branch") elected by the people and the smaller one (the "second branch") elected by the larger one. The national legislature could veto state laws it deemed to violate the national Constitution, and it would choose the chief executive, who could veto the legislature's laws with the aid of a Council of Revision.

———

Mr. RANDOLPH then opened the main business.... He expressed his regret that it should fall to him, rather than those who were of longer standing in life and political experience, to open the great subject of their mission. But as the Convention had originated from Virginia and his colleagues supposed that some proposition was expected from them, they had imposed this task on him. He then commented on the difficulty of the crisis and the necessity of preventing the fulfilment of the prophecies of the American downfall.

He observed that in revising the federal system we ought to inquire (1) into the properties which such a government ought to possess; (2) the defects of the confederation; (3) the danger of our situation; and (4) the remedy.

The character of such a government ought to secure (1) against foreign invasion; (2) against dissensions between members of the Union or seditions in particular states; (3) to procure to the several states various blessings of which an isolated situation was incapable; (4) to be able to defend itself against encroachment; and (5) to be paramount to the state constitutions.

In speaking of the defects of the confederation he professed a high respect for its authors and considered them as having done all that patriots could do in the then-infancy of the science of constitutions and of confederacies. . . . He then proceeded to enumerate the [confederation's] defects:

(1) that the confederation produced no security against foreign invasion, Congress not being permitted to prevent a war nor to support it by their own authority. Of this, he cited many examples. . . .

(2) that the federal government could not check the quarrels between states nor a rebellion in any, not having constitutional power nor means to interpose according to the exigency.

(3) that there were many advantages which the United States might acquire, which were not attainable under the confederation—such as a productive impost [i.e., a tax on imports]—counteraction of the commercial regulations of other nations—pushing of commerce ad libitum [at pleasure]—etc., etc.

(4) that the federal government could not defend itself against the encroachments from the states.

(5) that it was not even paramount to the state constitutions ratified, as it was, in many of the states.

He next reviewed the danger of our situation, appealed to the sense of the best friends of the United States, the prospect of anarchy from the laxity of government everywhere, and to other considerations. He then proceeded to the remedy, the basis of which, he said, must be the republican principle. . . .

[After formally offering fifteen enumerated propositions or resolutions comprising the Virginia Plan,] he concluded with an exhortation not to suffer the present opportunity of establishing general peace, harmony, happiness, and liberty in the United States to pass away unimproved.*

———

It was then resolved "that the house will tomorrow resolve itself into a Committee of the Whole House to consider of the state of the Ameri-

———
*Another of the note takers at the Convention, Robert Yates, recorded that Randolph concluded his remarks by stating that he intended "a strong consolidated union, in which the idea of states should be nearly annihilated."

can Union," and that the propositions moved by Mr. Randolph be referred to the said committee.

. . .

WEDNESDAY, MAY 30.
[IN COMMITTEE OF THE WHOLE]

The delegates, when meeting in Convention, were bound to follow established rules of parliamentary procedure and decision-making much like those that still govern formal legislative assemblies in the United States. To facilitate their deliberations on the Virginia Plan, the delegates decided to sit initially as a committee composed of all the members (or "Committee of the Whole") rather than in Convention. Legislative committees typically utilize procedures that permit freer discussion and more flexible decision-making than those imposed on full legislative bodies, and this is true for committees of the whole as well as smaller committees. Like the recommendation of any committee, however, recommendations of a committee of the whole must still go before the formal legislative body for final consideration and approval. Utilizing this procedure for the proposed Constitution gave delegates the opportunity to consider each element of it at least twice— once in the Committee of the Whole and then in Convention—and allowed for them to experiment with new ideas, especially at the committee stage. Both in the Committee of the Whole and in Convention, state delegations voted by majority rule as a single unit either for or against a proposition, with one vote per state. If the delegates from a state split evenly on a proposition, that state's vote would be "divided."

On this day Gouverneur Morris explained the difference between a federal government, as the term was then understood, and the national government that he and his allies wished to create. The Convention proceeded to vote that the United States needed a national government, which the Articles of Confederation did not provide. With that decision, the Convention committed itself to plunging into the uncharted waters of designing a viable large-scale republic.

———

The propositions of Mr. RANDOLPH which had been referred to the committee being taken up. . . . It was agreed on motion of Mr. Butler, seconded by Mr. Randolph, to pass on to the third ["That a national government ought to be established consisting of a supreme legislative, executive, and judiciary"], which underwent a discussion, less however on its general merits than on the force and extent of the particular terms "national" and "supreme."

Mr. PINCKNEY wished to know of Mr. Randolph whether he meant to abolish the state governments altogether. Mr. Randolph replied that he meant by these general propositions merely to introduce the particular ones which explained the outlines of the system he had in view.

Mr. BUTLER said he had not made up his mind on the subject and was open to the light which discussion might throw on it. After some general observations, he concluded with saying that he had opposed the grant of powers to [the Confederation] Congress heretofore because the whole power was vested in one body. The proposed distribution of the powers into two different bodies changed the case and would induce him to go great lengths.

Gen. PINCKNEY expressed a doubt whether the act of [the Confederation] Congress recommending the Convention, or the commissions of the deputies to it, could authorize a discussion of a system founded on different principles from the federal constitution.

Mr. GERRY seemed to entertain the same doubt.

Mr. G. MORRIS explained the distinction between a federal and national, supreme government, the former being a mere compact resting on the good faith of the parties, the latter having a complete and compulsive operation. He contended that in all communities there must be one supreme power, and one only.

Mr. MASON observed that the present confederation was not only deficient in not providing for coercion and punishment against delinquent states, but argued very cogently that punishment could not in the nature of things be executed on the states collectively, and therefore that such a government was necessary as could directly operate on individuals and would punish those only whose guilt required it.

Mr. SHERMAN, who took his seat today, admitted that the confederation had not given sufficient power to Congress and that additional powers were necessary, particularly that of raising money, which, he said, would involve many other powers. He admitted also that the general and particular jurisdictions ought in no case to be concurrent. He seemed, however, not [to] be disposed to make too great inroads on the existing system, intimating as one reason that it would be wrong to lose every amendment by inserting such as would not be agreed to by the states.

...

On the question as moved by Mr. Butler ... it was resolved in Committee of the Whole that a national government ought to be established, consisting of a supreme legislative, executive, and judiciary: Mass., Pa., Del., Va., N.C., S.C., aye 6; Conn., no 1; N.Y., divided [meaning that the voting delegates from the state were evenly split so that the state's vote did not count].

...

THURSDAY, MAY 31.
[IN COMMITTEE OF THE WHOLE]

Following the vote on Wednesday, May 30, to draft a national government, delegates started discussing the details of the Virginia Plan. Another Georgia delegate arrived on this day, allowing the Georgia delegation to vote and bringing the total number of states represented to ten. The delegates easily agreed that the national legislature should have two branches. The first major controversial issue was deciding how to elect members to what the Virginia Plan termed "the first branch," which would become the House of Representatives. A number of delegates doubted that the people themselves could be trusted to elect members of Congress, while others insisted that it was critical that the people do so. More Americans were voting than had done so before. A number of states had lowered property requirements for the franchise, and only South Carolina still had a religious test. Up to 80 percent of adult white males could vote; similarly qualified free black males could vote in a few states; and women could vote in New Jersey.

—

Resolution 4, first clause, "that the members of the first branch of the national legislature ought to be elected by the people of the several states," being taken up.

Mr. SHERMAN opposed the election by the people, insisting that it ought to be by the state legislatures. The people, he said, immediately should have as little to do as may be about the government. They lack information and are constantly liable to be misled.

Mr. GERRY. The evils we experience flow from the excess of democracy. The people do not [lack] virtue, but are the dupes of pretended patriots. In Massachusetts, it had been fully confirmed by experience that they are daily misled into the most baneful measures and opinions by the false reports circulated by designing men, and which no one on the spot can refute. One principal evil arises from the want of due provision for those employed in the administration of government. It would seem to be a maxim of democracy to starve the public servants. He mentioned the popular clamor in Massachusetts for the reduction of salaries and the attack made on that of the governor, though secured by the spirit of the constitution itself. He had, he said, been too republican heretofore; he was still, however, republican, but had been taught by experience the danger of the leveling spirit.

Mr. MASON argued strongly for an election of the larger branch by the people. It was to be the grand depository of the democratic principle of the government. It was, so to speak, to be our House of Commons. It ought to know and sympathize with every part of the community; and ought therefore to be taken not only from different parts of the whole republic, but also from different districts of the larger members of it, which had in several instances, particularly in Virginia, different interests and views arising from difference of produce, of habits, etc., etc. He admitted that we had been too democratic but was afraid we should incautiously run into the opposite extreme....

Mr. WILSON contended strenuously for drawing the most numerous branch of the legislature immediately from the people.... No government could long subsist without the confidence of the people. In a republican government, this confidence was peculiarly essential. He also thought it wrong to increase the weight of the state legislatures by making them the electors of the national legislature.... On examination it would be found that the opposition of states to federal measures had proceeded much more from the officers of the states than from the people at large.

Mr. MADISON considered the popular election of one branch of the national legislature as essential to every plan of free government.... He thought, too, that the great fabric to be raised would be more stable

and durable if it should rest on the solid foundation of the people themselves than if it should stand merely on the pillars of the legislatures.

Mr. GERRY did not like the election by the people.... Experience,
he said, had shown that the state legislatures drawn immediately from
the people did not always possess their confidence. He had no objection, however, to an election by the people if it were so qualified that
men of honor and character might not be unwilling to be joined in the
appointments. He seemed to think the people might nominate a certain number out of which the state legislatures should be bound to
choose.

Mr. BUTLER thought an election by the people an impracticable
mode.

On the question for an election of the first branch of the national
legislature by the people: Mass., N.Y., Pa., Va., N.C., Ga., aye 6; N.J.,
S.C., no 2; Conn., Del., divided.

. . .

FRIDAY, JUNE 1.
[IN COMMITTEE OF THE WHOLE]

*On June 1, the delegates began considering the structure of the executive under
the Virginia Plan's proposed government. They were not yet sure what duties
would fall to the executive or even whether a single person would hold the position. The major issue they faced was one of balance: if the executive branch was
too strong and independent, many delegates feared, it might result in another
monarchy like the one against which they had recently revolted; but if the executive was too weak and dependent on the legislature, it might be ineffective. This
problem of balance bedeviled the Convention almost to its very end. The first
issue was, Should the executive be a single person?*

———

The Committee of the Whole proceeded to Resolution 7, "that a national executive be instituted, to be chosen by the national legislature
for the term of _____ years, etc., to be ineligible thereafter, to possess
the executive powers of Congress, etc."

. . .

Mr. WILSON moved that the executive consist of a single person.

Mr. PINCKNEY seconded the motion, so as to read "that a national executive, to consist of a single person, be instituted."

A considerable pause ensuing and the chairman asking if he should put the question [i.e., move to a vote], Dr. FRANKLIN observed that it was a point of great importance and wished that the gentlemen would deliver their sentiments on it before the question was put. [Some historians attribute the reluctance of the delegates to debate the question of a single executive at this point to embarrassment. Everyone in the room knew that Washington, the presiding officer at the Convention, would be the first president of the United States, and no one wanted to imply that they did not think him fit for the job by himself.]

Mr. RUTLEDGE animadverted on the shyness of gentlemen on this and other subjects. He said it looked as if they supposed themselves precluded by having frankly disclosed their opinions from afterwards changing them, which he did not take to be at all the case. He said he was for vesting the executive power in a single person, though he was not for giving him the power of war and peace. A single man would feel the greatest responsibility and administer the public affairs best.

Mr. SHERMAN said he considered the executive magistracy as nothing more than an institution for carrying the will of the legislature into effect, that the person or persons ought to be appointed by and accountable to the legislature only, which was the depositary of the supreme will of the society.... He wished the number might not be fixed but that the legislature should be at liberty to appoint one or more, as experience might dictate.

Mr. WILSON preferred a single magistrate, as giving most energy, dispatch, and responsibility to the office....

Mr. GERRY favored the policy of annexing a council to the executive in order to give weight and inspire confidence.

Mr. RANDOLPH strenuously opposed a unity in the executive magistracy. He regarded it as the fetus of monarchy.... He could not see why the great requisites for the executive department—vigor, dispatch, and responsibility—could not be found in three men as well as in one man. The executive ought to be independent. It ought, therefore, in order to support its independence, to consist of more than one.

Mr. WILSON said that unity in the executive instead of being the fetus of monarchy would be the best safeguard against tyranny....

Mr. Wilson's motion for a single magistrate was postponed by common consent, the committee seeming unprepared for any decision on it; and the first part of the clause agreed to, viz. [or "namely"], "that a national executive be instituted."

Although the delegates could not quickly agree how many people were to comprise the national executive, they quickly reached a preliminary agreement on the executive's tasks: "to carry into effect the national laws, to appoint to offices in cases not otherwise provided for, and to execute such other powers as may from time to time be delegated by the national legislature." Far more contentious were the questions of how the executive should be elected, how long the term should be, and whether it was safe to let the executive run for reelection.

The next clause in Resolution 7, relating to the mode of appointing and the duration of the executive being under consideration ["to be chosen by the national legislature for the term of _____ [years]"].

Mr. WILSON said he was almost unwilling to declare the mode which he wished to take place, being apprehensive that it might appear chimerical. He would say, however, at least that in theory he was for an election by the people. Experience, particularly in New York and Massachusetts, showed that an election of the first magistrate by the people at large was both a convenient and successful mode. The objects of choice in such cases must be persons whose merits have general notoriety [i.e., respect].

Mr. SHERMAN was for the appointment by the legislature and for making him absolutely dependent on that body, as it was the will of that which was to be executed. An independence of the executive on the supreme legislature was, in his opinion, the very essence of tyranny, if there was any such thing.

Mr. WILSON moves that the blank for the term of duration should be filled with three years, observing at the same time that he preferred this short period, on the supposition that a reeligibility [for office] would be provided for.

Mr. PINCKNEY moves for seven years.

Mr. SHERMAN was for three years and against the doctrine of rotation as throwing out of office the men best qualified to execute its duties.

Mr. MASON was for seven years at least and for prohibiting a re-eligibility as the best expedient both for preventing the effect of a false complaisance on the side of the legislature towards unfit characters and a temptation on the side of the executive to intrigue with the legislature for a reappointment.

Mr. BEDFORD was strongly opposed to so long a term as seven years. He begged the committee to consider what the situation of the country would be, in case the first magistrate should be saddled on it for such a period and it should be found on trial that he did not possess the qualifications ascribed to him or should lose them after his appointment. An impeachment, he said, would be no cure for this evil, as an impeachment would reach misfeasance only, not incapacity. He was for a triennial election and for an ineligibility after a period of nine years.

On the question for seven years: N.Y., N.J., Pa., Del., Va., aye 5; Conn., N.C., S.C., Ga., no 4; Mass., divided.

...

The mode of appointing the executive was the next question.

Mr. WILSON renewed his declarations in favor of an appointment by the people. He wished to derive not only both branches of the legislature from the people, without the intervention of the state legislatures, but the executive also, in order to make them as independent as possible of each other, as well as of the states.

Col. MASON favors the idea, but thinks it impracticable. He wishes however that Mr. Wilson might have time to digest it into his own form. The clause "to be chosen by the national legislature" was accordingly postponed.

Mr. RUTLEDGE suggests an election of the executive by the second branch [the future Senate] only of the national legislature.

The committee then rose and the house adjourned.

On Saturday, June 2, the Maryland delegation reached voting size, and eleven states were represented at the Convention. On that day, the Convention continued to refine its conception of the executive. The delegates could not agree whether the executive power would be held by a single person or a committee, but they did agree that the office's holder or holders would serve for single seven-year terms and could be removed from office after being impeached and convicted for "malpractice or neglect of duty."

MONDAY, JUNE 4.
IN COMMITTEE OF THE WHOLE

On June 4, the delegates voted that a single person would hold the executive power. They then tackled the question of whether the executive should have the power to block legislation through a veto, or "negative" as they called it, and if so, to what extent. The Virginia Plan called for a limited veto exercised by a Council of Revision composed of the executive and members of the federal judiciary. Elbridge Gerry opened this debate by noting that the judiciary would have the power to review the consistutionality of laws passed by the legislature—a power that delegates apparently took for granted throughout their deliberations.

———

First clause of Proposition 8 relating to a Council of Revision taken into consideration.

Mr. GERRY doubts whether the judiciary ought to form a part of it, as they will have a sufficient check against encroachments on their own department by their exposition of the laws, which involved a power of deciding on their constitutionality. In some states the judges had actually set aside laws as being against the constitution. This was done too with general approbation. It was quite foreign from the nature of their office to make them judges of the policy of public measures. He moves to postpone the clause in order to propose "that the national executive shall have a right to negative any legislative act which shall not be afterwards passed by _____ parts of each branch of the national legislature."

Mr. KING seconds the motion, observing that the judges ought to be able to expound the law as it should come before them, free from the bias of having participated in its formation.

Mr. WILSON thinks neither the original proposition nor the amendment go far enough. If the legislative, executive, and judiciary ought to be distinct and independent, the executive ought to have an absolute negative [i.e., one not subject to override by the legislature]. Without such a self-defense the legislature can at any moment sink it into nonexistence. He was for varying the proposition in such a manner as to give the executive and judiciary jointly an absolute negative.

On the question to postpone in order to take Mr. Gerry's proposition into consideration, it was agreed to: Mass., N.Y., Pa., N.C., S.C., Ga., aye 6; Conn., Del., Md., Va., no 4.

——

Mr. Gerry's proposition being now before committee, Mr. WILSON and Mr. HAMILTON move that the last part of it (viz., "which shall not be afterwards passed unless by _____ parts of each branch of the national legislature") be struck out, so as to give the executive an absolute negative on the laws. There was no danger, they thought, of such a power being too much exercised. It was mentioned by Col. HAMILTON that the king of Great Britain had not exerted his negative since the [English] Revolution [of 1688].

Mr. GERRY sees no necessity for so great a control over the legislature, as the best men in the community would be comprised in the two branches of it.

Dr. FRANKLIN said he was sorry to differ from his colleague, for whom he had a very great respect, on any occasion, but he could not help it on this. . . . It was true the king of Great Britain had not, as was said, exerted his negative since the Revolution, but that matter was easily explained. The bribes and emoluments now given to the members of Parliament rendered it unnecessary, everything being done according to the will of the ministers. He was afraid if a negative should be given as proposed, that more power and money would be demanded, till at last enough would be gotten to influence and bribe the legislature into a complete subjection to the will of the executive.

Mr. SHERMAN was against enabling any one man to stop the will of the whole. No one man could be found so far above all the rest in wisdom. He thought we ought to avail ourselves of his wisdom in revising the laws, but not permit him to overrule the decided and cool opinions of the legislature.

Mr. MADISON supposed that if a proper proportion of each branch should be required to overrule the objections of the executive, it would answer the same purpose as an absolute negative. It would rarely if ever happen that the executive constituted as ours is proposed to be would have firmness enough to resist the legislature, unless backed by a certain part of the body itself. The king of Great Britain, with all his splendid attributes, would not be able to withstand the unanimous and eager wishes of both houses of Parliament. To give such a prerogative would certainly be obnoxious to the temper of this country, its present temper at least.

Mr. WILSON believed as others did that this power would seldom be used. The legislature would know that such a power existed and would refrain from such laws as it would be sure to defeat. Its silent operation would therefore preserve harmony and prevent mischief.... It will not in this case, as in the one cited, be supported by the head of a great empire, actuated by a different and sometimes opposite interest....

The requiring a large proportion of each house to overrule the executive check might do in peaceable times; but there might be tempestuous moments in which animosities may run high between the executive and legislative branches and in which the former ought to be able to defend itself.

Mr. BUTLER had been in favor of a single executive magistrate, but could he have entertained an idea that a complete negative on the laws was to be given him, he certainly should have acted very differently. It had been observed that in all countries the executive power is in a constant course of increase. This was certainly the case in Great Britain. Gentlemen seemed to think that we had nothing to apprehend from an abuse of the executive power. But why might not a Cataline or a Cromwell [Roman and English dictators] arise in this country as well as in others?

Mr. BEDFORD was opposed to every check on the legislative.... The representatives of the people were the best judges of what was for their interest and ought to be under no external control whatever. The two branches would produce a sufficient control within the legislature itself.

Col. MASON observed that a vote had already passed, he found (he was out at the time), for vesting the executive powers in a single person. Among these powers was that of appointing to offices in certain cases. The probable abuses of a negative had been well explained by Dr. Franklin as proved by experience, the best of all tests. Will not the same door be opened here? The executive may refuse its assent to necessary measures till new appointments shall be referred to him; and having by degrees engrossed all these into his own hands, the American executive, like the British, will by bribery and influence save himself the trouble and odium of exerting his negative afterwards.

We are, Mr. Chairman, going very far in this business. We are not indeed constituting a British government, but a more dangerous monarchy, an elective one. We are introducing a new principle into our system, and not [a] necessary [one] as in the British government, where the executive has greater rights to defend. Do gentlemen mean to pave the way to hereditary monarchy? Do they flatter themselves that the people will ever consent to such an innovation? If they do, I venture to tell them they are mistaken. The people never will consent. And do gentlemen consider the danger of delay and the still greater danger of a rejection, not for a moment but forever, of the plan which shall be proposed to them? Notwithstanding the oppressions and injustice experienced among us from democracy, the genius of the people is in favor of it, and the genius of the people must be consulted. . . . He hoped that nothing like a monarchy would ever be attempted in this country. A hatred to its oppressions had carried the people through the late Revolution.

Will it not be enough to enable the executive to suspend offensive laws till they shall be coolly revised and the objections to them overruled by a greater majority than was required in the first instance? He never could agree to give up all the rights of the people to a single magistrate. If more than one had been fixed on, greater powers might have been entrusted to the executive. He hoped this attempt to give such powers would have its weight hereafter as an argument for increasing the number of the executive.

DR. FRANKLIN. . . . The first man put at the helm will be a good one. Nobody knows what sort may come afterwards. The executive will be always increasing here, as elsewhere, till it ends in a monarchy.

On the question for striking out so as to give executive an absolute negative: Mass., Conn., N.Y., Pa., Del., Md., Va., N.C., S.C., Ga., no 10.

With the absolute veto defeated, the Convention quickly agreed that the executive should have a conditional veto on legislation, subject to a two-thirds majority override in both houses. In line with the original Virginia Plan, James Wilson

*and James Madison then moved that this conditional veto be exercised jointly by
the executive and judiciary.*

[Mr. MADISON. The judiciary ought to be introduced in the business
of legislation. They will protect their department and, united with the
executive, make its negatives more strong. There is weight in the objections to this measure, but a check on the legislature is necessary. Experience proves it to be so and teaches us that what has been thought a
calumny on a republican government is nevertheless true. In all countries are diversity of interests, the rich and the poor, the debtors and
creditors, the followers of different demagogues, the diversity of religious sects. The effects of these divisions in ancient governments are
well known, and the like causes will now produce like effects. We must
therefore introduce in our system provisions against the measures of
an interested majority. A check is not only necessary to protect the executive power, but the minority in the legislature. The independence
of the executive, having the eyes of all upon him, will make him an
impartial judge. Add the judiciary, and you greatly increase his respectability.]*

*Upon Alexander Hamilton's objection that the motion of Wilson and Madison
was out of order, the Convention proceeded to consider the Virginia Plan's ninth
resolution, which related to a national judiciary. Without debate, the Convention
adopted the first clause of this resolution: "Resolved that a national judiciary be
established." It then agreed that there should be one supreme tribunal and one or
more inferior tribunals, an agreement that represented a slight modification from
the Virginia Plan.*

It was then moved and seconded to add these words to the first clause
of the ninth resolution, namely, "to consist of one supreme tribunal,
and of one or more inferior tribunals," which passed in the affirmative.
    The committee then rose and the house adjourned.

---

*From the notes of Robert Yates, replacing the passage from Madison's journal.

Tuesday, June 5.

IN COMMITTEE OF THE WHOLE

The judicial branch would serve as a major vehicle for enforcing the authority of the national government over the states. On this day, the delegates wrestled with the question of who could best be entrusted with choosing judges. As this debate unfolded, some delegates began to worry that a web of lower national courts spread across the country, with judges appointed from the national capital, might intrude excessively on the jurisdiction and sovereignty of the states. Only a deft compromise by Madison saved the lower court system.

———

The clause "that the national judiciary be chosen by the national legislature" being under consideration.

Mr. WILSON opposed the appointment of judges by the national legislature. Experience showed the impropriety of such appointments by numerous bodies. Intrigue, partiality, and concealment were the necessary consequences. A principal reason for unity in the executive was that officers might be appointed by a single responsible person.

Mr. RUTLEDGE was by no means disposed to grant so great a power to any single person. The people will think we are leaning too much towards monarchy. He was against establishing any national tribunal except a single supreme one. The state tribunals are most proper to decide in all cases in the first instance.

. . .

Mr. MADISON disliked the election of the judges by the legislature or any numerous body. Besides the danger of intrigue and partiality, many of the members were not judges of the requisite qualifications. The legislative talents, which were very different from those of a judge, commonly recommended men to the favor of legislative assemblies. It was known too that the accidental circumstances of presence and absence, of being a member or not a member, had a very undue influence on the appointment. On the other hand he was not satisfied with referring the appointment to the executive. He rather inclined to give it to the senatorial branch, as numerous enough to be confided in—as not so numerous as to be governed by the motives of the other branch, and as being sufficiently stable and independent to follow their deliberate judgments. He hinted this only and moved that the appointment by the legislature might be struck out, and a blank left to be hereafter filled on maturer reflection.

Mr. WILSON seconds it.

On the question for striking out: Mass., N.Y., N.J., Pa., Del., Md., Va., N.C., Ga., aye 9; Conn., S.C., no 2.

. . .

Mr. RUTLEDGE, having obtained a rule for reconsideration of the clause for establishing inferior tribunals under the national authority, now moved that that part of the clause in Proposition 9 should be expunged, arguing that the state tribunals might and ought to be left in all cases to decide in the first instance the right of appeal to the supreme national tribunal being sufficient to secure the national rights and uniformity of judgments; that it was making an unnecessary encroachment on the jurisdiction of the states and creating unnecessary obstacles to their adoption of the new system.

Mr. SHERMAN seconded the motion.

Mr. MADISON observed that unless inferior tribunals were dispersed throughout the republic with final jurisdiction in many cases, appeals would be multiplied to a most oppressive degree; that besides, an appeal would not in many cases be a remedy. What was to be done after improper verdicts in state tribunals, obtained under the biased directions of a dependent judge or the local prejudices of an undirected jury? To remand the cause for a new trial would answer no purpose. To order a new trial at the supreme bar would oblige the parties to bring up their witnesses, though ever so distant from the seat of the court. An effective judiciary establishment commensurate to the legislative authority was essential. A government without a proper executive and judiciary would be the mere trunk of a body, without arms or legs to act or move.

. . .

Mr. SHERMAN was in favor of the motion. He dwelt chiefly on the supposed expensiveness of having a new set of courts, when the existing state courts would answer the same purpose.

Mr. DICKINSON contended strongly that if there was to be a national legislature, there ought to be a national judiciary, and that the former ought to have authority to institute the latter.

On the question for Mr. Rutledge's motion to strike out "inferior tribunals": Conn., N.J., N.C., S.C., Ga., aye 5; Pa., Del., Md., Va., no 4; Mass., N.Y., divided.

———

Mr. WILSON and Mr. MADISON then moved, in pursuance of the idea expressed above by Mr. Dickinson, to add to Resolution 9 the words following, "that the national legislature be empowered to institute inferior tribunals." They observed that there was a distinction between establishing such tribunals absolutely and giving a discretion to the legislature to establish or not establish them. They repeated the necessity of some such provision.

Mr. BUTLER. The people will not bear such innovations. The states will revolt at such encroachments. Supposing such an establishment to be useful, we must not venture on it. We must follow the example of Solon, who gave the Athenians not the best government he could devise, but the best they would receive.

Mr. KING remarked as to the comparative expense that the establishment of inferior tribunals would cost infinitely less than the appeals that would be prevented by them.

On this question as moved by Mr. Wilson and Mr. Madison: Mass., N.J., Pa., Del., Md., Va., N.C., Ga., aye 8; Conn., S.C., no 2; N.Y., divided.

———

The committee then rose and the house adjourned to eleven o'clock tomorrow.

WEDNESDAY, JUNE 6.
IN COMMITTEE OF THE WHOLE

Having finessed the structure of the judiciary by deferring the issue of lower federal courts for resolution by Congress, the delegates returned to the unavoidable issue of the structure of the national legislature. Under the Virginia Plan this was to consist of a "first branch" (the future House of Representatives) and a "second branch" (the future Senate). The South Carolina delegation wished to revisit the decision that the people would elect the first branch. The debate raised

*the contentious issue of the relationship between the existing state governments
and the proposed national one.*

—

Mr. PINCKNEY, according to previous notice and rule obtained, moved
"that the first branch of the national legislature be elected by the state
legislatures, and not by the people," contending that the people were
less fit judges in such a case, and that the legislatures would be less
likely to promote the adoption of the new government if they were to
be excluded from all share in it.

Mr. RUTLEDGE seconded the motion.

. . .

Mr. WILSON. He wished for vigor in the government, but he wished
that vigorous authority to flow immediately from the legitimate source
of all authority. The government ought to possess not only, first, the
force, but, second, the mind or sense of the people at large. The legislature ought to be the most exact transcript of the whole society. Representation is made necessary only because it is impossible for the
people to act collectively. The opposition was to be expected, he said,
from the [state] governments, not from the citizens of the states. . . .

Mr. SHERMAN. If it were in view to abolish the state governments,
the elections ought to be by the people. If the state governments are to
be continued, it is necessary in order to preserve harmony between the
national and state governments that the elections to the former should
be made by the latter. The right of participating in the national government would be sufficiently secured to the people by their election of
the state legislatures. The objects of the Union, he thought, were few:
(1) defense against foreign danger; (2) against internal disputes and a
resort to force; (3) treaties with foreign nations; (4) regulating foreign
commerce and drawing revenue from it. These and perhaps a few lesser
objects alone rendered a confederation of the states necessary. All other
matters civil and criminal would be much better in the hands of the
states. The people are more happy in small than large states. States may
indeed be too small, as Rhode Island, and thereby be too subject to faction. Some others were perhaps too large, the powers of government
not being able to pervade them. He was for giving the general government power to legislate and execute within a defined province.

Col. MASON. Under the existing confederacy, Congress represents the states, not the people of the states. Their acts operate on the states, not the individuals. The case will be changed in the new plan of government. The people will be represented; they ought therefore to choose the representatives. . . .

Mr. MADISON considered an election of one branch at least of the legislature by the people immediately as a clear principle of free government and that this mode under proper regulations had the additional advantage of securing better representatives, as well as of avoiding too great an agency of the state governments in the general one. He differed from the member from Connecticut (Mr. Sherman) in thinking the objects mentioned to be all the principal ones that required a national government. Those were certainly important and necessary objects; but he combined with them the necessity of providing more effectually for the security of private rights and the steady dispensation of justice. Interferences with these were evils which had, more perhaps than anything else, produced this Convention.

Was it to be supposed that republican liberty could long exist under the abuses of it practiced in some of the states? The gentleman (Mr. Sherman) had admitted that in a very small state, faction and oppression would prevail. It was to be inferred then that wherever these prevailed, the state was too small. Had they not prevailed in the largest as well as the smallest, though less than in the smallest, and were we not thence admonished to enlarge the sphere as far as the nature of the government would admit? This was the only defense against the inconveniencies of democracy consistent with the democratic form of government.

All civilized societies would be divided into different sects, factions, and interests as they happened to consist of rich and poor, debtors and creditors, the landed, the manufacturing, the commercial interests, the inhabitants of this district or that district, the followers of this political leader or that political leader, the disciples of this religious sect or that religious sect. In all cases where a majority are united by a common interest or passion, the rights of the minority are in danger. . . . We have seen the mere distinction of color made in the most enlightened period of time, a ground of the most oppressive dominion ever exercised by man over man. . . . In a republican government, the majority, if united, have always an opportunity. The only remedy is to enlarge the sphere, and thereby divide the community into so great a number of interests and parties that in the first place, a majority will not be likely at the same moment to have a common interest separate from that of the whole or of the minority, and in the second place, that in case they should have such an interest, they may not be apt to unite in the pursuit of it.

. . .

Mr. READ. Too much attachment is betrayed to the state governments. We must look beyond their continuance. A national government must soon of necessity swallow all of them up. They will soon be reduced to the mere office of electing the national Senate.

. . .

Mr. WILSON would not have spoken again but for what had fallen from Mr. Read; namely, that the idea of preserving the state governments ought to be abandoned. He saw no incompatibility between the national and state governments, provided the latter were restrained to certain local purposes. . . .

On the question for electing the first branch by the state legislatures as moved by Mr. Pinckney, it was negatived: Conn., N.J., S.C., aye 3; Mass., N.Y., Pa., Del., Md., Va., N.C., Ga., no 8.

. . .

THURSDAY, JUNE 7.
IN COMMITTEE OF THE WHOLE

Having confirmed that the people would choose the first branch of the national legislature, the Convention moved on to the method of choosing members of the legislature's second branch, the future Senate. While members of the first branch were supposed to represent and speak for the people, the second branch was expected to be a more elite body. This expectation complicated the question of how to choose its members. That question itself raised once again the issue of the relationship of the states to the new national government.

———

Mr. DICKINSON now moved "that the members of the second branch ought to be chosen by the individual [state] legislatures."

Mr. SHERMAN seconded the motion, observing that the particular states would thus become interested in supporting the national government and that a due harmony between the two governments would be maintained. He admitted that the two ought to have separate and distinct jurisdictions, but that they ought to have a mutual interest in supporting each other.

. . .

Mr. DICKINSON had two reasons for his motion: (1) because the sense of the states would be better collected through their governments than immediately from the people at large; (2) because he wished the Senate to consist of the most distinguished characters, distinguished for their rank in life and their weight of property, and bearing as strong a likeness to the British House of Lords as possible; and he thought such characters more likely to be selected by the state legislatures than in any other mode. The greatness of the number was no objection with him. He hoped there would be eighty and twice eighty of them. If their number should be small, the popular branch could not be balanced by them. The legislature of a numerous people ought to be a numerous body.

Mr. WILLIAMSON preferred a small number of senators, but wished that each state should have at least one. He suggested twenty-five as a convenient number. The different modes of representation in the different branches will serve as a mutual check.

. . .

Mr. WILSON. If we are to establish a national government, that government ought to flow from the people at large. If one branch of it should be chosen by the legislatures and the other by the people, the two branches will rest on different foundations, and dissensions will naturally arise between them. He wished the Senate to be elected by the people as well as the other branch, and the people might be divided into proper districts for the purpose, and moved to postpone the motion of Mr. Dickinson in order to take up one of that import.

Mr. MORRIS seconded him.

Mr. READ proposed "that the Senate should be appointed by the executive magistrate out of a proper number of persons to be nominated by the individual legislatures." . . . His proposition was not seconded nor supported.

Mr. MADISON. If the motion of Mr. Dickinson should be agreed to, we must either depart from the doctrine of proportional representation or admit into the Senate a very large number of members. The first is inadmissible, being evidently unjust. The second is inexpedient.

The use of the Senate is to consist in its proceeding with more coolness, with more system, and with more wisdom than the popular branch. Enlarge their number and you communicate to them the vices which they are meant to correct.

He differed from Mr. Dickinson, who thought that the additional number would give additional weight to the body. On the contrary, it appeared to him that their weight would be in an inverse ratio to their number. . . . The more the representatives of the people, therefore, were multiplied, the more they partook of the infirmities of their constituents, the more liable they became to be divided among themselves, either from their own indiscretions or the artifices of the opposite faction, and, of course, the less capable of fulfilling their trust. When the weight of a set of men depends merely on their personal characters, the greater the number, the greater the weight. When it depends on the degree of political authority lodged in them, the smaller the number, the greater the weight. These considerations might perhaps be combined in the intended Senate; but the latter was the material one.

Mr. GERRY. Four modes of appointing the Senate have been mentioned:

(1) by the first branch of the national legislature. This would create a dependence contrary to the end proposed.

(2) by the national executive. This is a stride towards monarchy that few will think of.

(3) by the people. The people have two great interests, the landed interest [or farmers] and the commercial, including the stockholders. To draw both branches from the people will leave no security to the latter interest, the people being chiefly composed of the landed interest and erroneously supposing that the other interests are adverse to it.

(4) by the individual legislatures. The elections being carried through this refinement will be most likely to provide some check in favor of the commercial interest against the landed, without which oppression will take place, and no free government can last long where that is the case. He was therefore in favor of this last.

Mr. DICKINSON. The preservation of the states in a certain degree of agency is indispensable. It will produce that collision between the different authorities which should be wished for in order to check each other. To attempt to abolish the states altogether would degrade the councils of our country, would be impracticable, would be ruinous. He compared the proposed national system to the solar system, in which the states were the planets and ought to be left to move freely in their proper orbits. . . .

Mr. WILSON . . . was for an election by the people in large districts, which would be most likely to obtain men of intelligence and uprightness, subdividing the districts only for the accommodation of voters.

Mr. MADISON. . . . The true question was in what mode the best choice would be made. If an election by the people . . . promised as uncorrupt and impartial a preference of merit, there could surely be no necessity for an appointment by those legislatures. The great evils complained of were that the state legislatures run into schemes of paper money, etc., whenever solicited by the people and sometimes without even the sanction of the people. Their influence then, instead of checking a like propensity in the national legislature, may be expected to promote it. . . .

Mr. SHERMAN opposed elections by the people in districts as not likely to produce such fit men as elections by the state legislatures.

Mr. GERRY insisted that the commercial and monied interest would be more secure in the hands of the state legislatures than of the people at large. The former have more sense of character, and will be restrained by that from injustice. The people are for paper money when the legislatures are against it. . . .

Mr. PINCKNEY thought the second branch ought to be permanent and independent, and that the members of it would be rendered more so by receiving their appointment from the state legislatures. This mode would avoid the rivalships and discontents incident to the election by districts. . . .

Col. MASON. Whatever power may be necessary for the national government, a certain portion must necessarily be left in the states. It is impossible for one power to pervade the extreme parts of the United States so as to carry equal justice to them. The state legislatures also ought to have some means of defending themselves against encroachments of the national government. In every other department we have studiously endeavored to provide for its self-defense. Shall we leave the states alone unprovided with the means for this purpose? And what better means can we provide than the giving them some share in, or rather to make them a constituent part of, the national establishment? . . .

On Mr. Dickinson's motion for an appointment of the Senate by the state legislatures: Mass., Conn., N.Y., Pa., Del., Md., Va., N.C., S.C., Ga., aye 10.

. . .

On Friday, June 8, the delegates debated whether the national legislature should have the power to veto state laws. Madison strongly supported the proposal, but this effort to radically curtail the power of the states was decisively rejected, just as his effort to prevent the state legislatures from electing senators was defeated the day before.

SATURDAY, JUNE 9.
IN COMMITTEE OF THE WHOLE

On Saturday, the delegates turned for the first time to the explosive issue of how to proportion representation in the legislature among the states. Under the Articles of Confederation, each state had one vote. Should this arrangement continue under the new Constitution, or should the amount of representation each state had in the national government be based on population or taxable wealth? Delegates from small states without much total wealth, whose states would lose out if the basis of representation were changed, tended to argue for state representation on the grounds that the United States was a confederation of states. Delegates from large, wealthy states tended to favor some formula using population and wealth, claiming that the new national government was to represent the people, not the states. The special circumstances of each state complicated this split, however. Georgia, with the second smallest population, almost always voted with the large states, perhaps because, with its large size, its delegates anticipated that it would gain population. Further, some delegates from small states supported the principle of a strong national government (as long as the Constitution contained some protections for their states), while some delegates from large states steadfastly opposed such a government. New York was the fifth largest state, for example, but two of its three delegates resisted any major changes in the Articles of Confederation and eventually left the Convention.

———

Mr. PATERSON moves that the committee resume the clause relating to the rule of suffrage in the national legislature.

Mr. BREARLY seconds him. He was sorry, he said, that any question on this point was brought into view. It had been much agitated in [the Continental] Congress at the time of forming the confederation and was then rightly settled by allowing to each sovereign state an equal vote. Otherwise, the smaller states must have been destroyed instead of being saved.

The substitution of a ratio, he admitted, carried fairness on the face of it, but on a deeper examination was unfair and unjust. Judging of the disparity of the states by the quota of [the Confederation] Congress, Virginia would have sixteen votes and Georgia but one. A like proportion to the others will make the whole number ninety. There will be three large states and ten small ones. The large states, by which he meant Massachusetts, Pennsylvania, and Virginia, will carry everything before them. . . .

He had come to the Convention with a view of being as useful as he could in giving energy and stability to the federal government. When the proposition for destroying the equality of votes came forward, he was astonished, he was alarmed. Is it fair then, it will be asked, that Georgia should have an equal vote with Virginia? He would not say it was.

What remedy then? One only, that a map of the United States be spread out, that all the existing boundaries be erased, and that a new partition of the whole be made into thirteen equal parts.

Mr. PATERSON considered the proposition for a proportional representation as striking at the existence of the lesser states. He would premise, however, to an investigation of this question some remarks on the nature, structure, and powers of the Convention.

[Let us consider with what powers are we sent here? (Moved to have the credentials of Massachusetts [which gave its delegates the authority to revise the Articles of Confederation, not discard them] read, which was done.) By this and the other credentials, we see that the basis of our present authority is founded on a revision of the articles of the present confederation and to alter or amend them in such parts where they may appear defective. Can we on this ground form a national government? I fancy not. Our commissions give a complexion to the business, and can we suppose that when we exceed the bounds of our duty, the people will approve our proceedings?

We are met here as the deputies of thirteen independent, sovereign states for federal purposes. Can we consolidate their sovereignty and form one nation and annihilate the sovereignties of our states, who have sent us here for other purposes?]*

The idea of a national government, as contradistinguished from a federal one, never entered into the mind of any of them, and to the public mind we must accommodate ourselves. We have no power to go beyond the federal scheme, and if we had, the people are not ripe for any other. We must follow the people; the people will not follow us. . . .

If we are to be considered as a nation, all state distinctions must be abolished, the whole must be thrown into hotchpot, and when an equal division is made, then there may be fairly an equality of representation. . . . He said there was no more reason that a great individual state contributing much should have more votes than a small one contributing little than that a rich individual citizen should have more votes than an indigent one.

Give the large states an influence in proportion to their magnitude, and what will be the consequence? Their ambition will be proportionally increased, and the small states will have everything to fear. . . . New Jersey will never confederate on the plan before the committee. She would be swallowed up. He had rather submit to a monarch, to a despot, than to such a fate. He would not only oppose the plan here but on his return home do everything in his power to defeat it there.

Mr. WILSON hoped if the confederacy should be dissolved that a majority [of the population], that a minority of the states, would unite for their safety. He entered elaborately into the defense of a proportional representation, stating for his first position that, as all authority was derived from the people, equal numbers of people ought to have an equal number of representatives, and different numbers of people different numbers of representatives. This principle had been improperly violated in the confederation, owing to the urgent circumstances of the time. . . . If the small states will not confederate on this plan, Pennsylvania and, he presumed, some other states would not confederate on any other. . . . A new partition of the states is desirable, but evidently and totally impracticable.

. . .

The question being about to be put, Mr. PATERSON hoped that

---

*From the notes of Robert Yates, replacing the passage from Madison's journal.

as so much depended on it, it might be thought best to postpone the decision till tomorrow, which was done nem. con. [i.e., without dissent].

The committee rose and the house adjourned.

MONDAY, JUNE 11.
IN COMMITTEE OF THE WHOLE

On this day Roger Sherman from Connecticut, echoing a point made by John Dickinson on June 6, suggested what would later become the basis of the so-called Great (or Connecticut) Compromise on representation in the national legislature. His suggestion: use population in the first branch (the future House of Representatives) and use states in the second branch (the future Senate). Although Sherman warned that the Convention's success hinged on the acceptance of this arrangement, the Committee of the Whole opted by one vote for proportional representation in the second branch as well as in the first branch. As for the first branch, the Committee of the Whole agreed on this general basis for representation: total free population of a state plus three-fifths of its slave population (the formula proposed for determining state financial contributions to the federal government under a 1783 amendment to the Articles of Confederation that was never ratified). There would be much heated discussion and maneuvering about this formula by both northern and southern delegates in the months to come, but it survived all challenges.

———

The clause concerning the rule of suffrage in the national legislature postponed on Saturday was resumed.

Mr. SHERMAN proposed that the proportion of suffrage in the first branch should be according to the respective numbers of free inhabitants, and that in the second branch, or Senate, each state should have one vote and no more. He said as the states would remain possessed of certain individual rights, each state ought to be able to protect itself; otherwise, a few large states will rule the rest.

. . .

Mr. KING and Mr. WILSON, in order to bring the question to a point, moved "that the right of suffrage in the first branch of the national legislature ought not to be according [to] the rule established in the Articles of Confederation [one state, one vote], but according to some equitable ratio of representation."

...

On the question for agreeing to Mr. King's and Mr. Wilson's motion, it passed in the affirmative: Mass., Conn., Pa., Va., N.C., S.C., Ga., aye 7; N.Y., N.J., Del., no 3; Md., divided.

———

It was then moved by Mr. RUTLEDGE, seconded by Mr. BUTLER, to add to the words "equitable ratio of representation," at the end of the motion just agreed to, the words "according to the quotas of contribution." On motion of Mr. WILSON, seconded by Mr. PINCKNEY, this was postponed in order to add, after the words "equitable ratio of representation," the words following, "in proportion to the whole number of white and other free citizens and inhabitants of every age, sex, and condition, including those bound to servitude for a term of years, and three-fifths of all other persons not comprehended in the foregoing description, except Indians not paying taxes, in each state," this being the rule in the act of [the Confederation] Congress agreed to by eleven states for apportioning quotas of revenue on the states, and requiring a census only every five to seven, or ten, years.

Mr. GERRY. [The idea of property ought not to be the rule of representation. Blacks are property, and are used to the southward as horses and cattle to the northward, and why should their representation be increased to the southward on account of the number of slaves [more] than horses or oxen to the north?]*

On the question: Mass., Conn., N.Y., Pa., Md., Va., N.C., S.C., Ga., aye 9; N.J., Del., no 2.

———

Mr. SHERMAN moved that a question be taken whether each state shall have one vote in the second branch. Everything, he said, depended on this. The smaller states would never agree to the plan on any other principle than an equality of suffrage in this branch. Mr. ELLSWORTH seconded the motion.

On the question for allowing each state one vote in the second branch: Conn., N.Y., N.J., Del., Md., aye 5; Mass., Pa., Va., N.C., S.C., Ga., no 6.

*From the notes of Robert Yates, replacing the passage from Madison's journal.

Mr. WILSON and Mr. HAMILTON moved that the right of suffrage in the second branch ought to be according to the same rule as in the first branch.

On this question for making the ratio of representation in the second as in the first branch, it passed in the affirmative: Mass., Pa., Va., N.C., S.C., Ga., aye 6; Conn., N.Y., N.J., Del., Md., no 5.

...

TUESDAY, JUNE 12.
IN COMMITTEE OF [THE] WHOLE

On this day, after deciding (temporarily, as it turned out) that members of the legislature's first branch would serve for three-year terms, the delegates moved on to another contentious issue: how long should the terms be for members of the legislature's more elite second branch? If the terms were too short, the members would not have the independence to make disinterested decisions; if too long, they might forget that they were servants of the people and turn into self-serving aristocrats.

Mr. SPAIGHT moved to fill the blank for the duration of the appointments to the second branch of the national legislature with the words "seven years."

Mr. SHERMAN thought seven years too long. He grounded his opposition, he said, on the principle that if they did their duty well, they would be reelected. And if they acted amiss, an earlier opportunity should be allowed for getting rid of them. He preferred five years....

Mr. PIERCE proposed three years. Seven years would raise an alarm....

Mr. RANDOLPH was for the term of seven years. The democratic licentiousness of the state legislatures proved the necessity of a firm Senate. The object of this second branch is to control the democratic branch of the national legislature. If it be not a firm body, the other branch, being more numerous and coming immediately from the people, will overwhelm it. The senate of Maryland, constituted on like principles, had been scarcely able to stem the popular torrent. No mischief can be apprehended, as the concurrence of the other branch and, in some measure, of the executive will in all cases be necessary. A firmness and independence may be the more necessary also in this branch, as it ought to guard the Constitution against encroachments of the executive, who will be apt to form combinations with the demagogues of the popular branch.

Mr. MADISON considered seven years as a term by no means too long. What we wished was to give to the government that stability which was everywhere called for, and which the enemies of the republican form alleged to be inconsistent with its nature. He was not afraid of giving too much stability by the term of seven years. His fear was that the popular branch would still be too great an overmatch for it. . . . It was to be much lamented that we had so little direct experience to guide us. In the states where the senates were chosen in the same manner as the other branches of the legislature, and held their seats for four years, the institution was found to be no check whatever against the instabilities of the other branches. . . .

On the question for "seven years" as the term for the second branch: N.J., Pa., Del., Md., Va., N.C., S.C., Ga., aye 8; Conn., no 1; Mass., N.Y., divided.

The delegates, sitting as a Committee of the Whole, concluded their deliberations of the Virginia Plan on Wednesday, June 13, and reported the amended resolutions to the Convention, which then adjourned until the next day. On June 14 came the first consequence of the Committee of the Whole's rejection of Roger Sherman's compromise proposal on representation: William Paterson of New Jersey requested a further adjournment for an additional day so that "several deputations, particularly that of New Jersey," could complete work on an alternative plan for a new government that would be only slightly more centralized than the confederation. The issue, Paterson suggested, was whether the United States should be a confederation of states or a single nation-state. On June 15, Paterson submitted the so-called New Jersey Plan (see Appendix B) to the Convention, which then submitted both the New Jersey Plan and the amended Virginia Plan to the Committee of the Whole for consideration. The committee began considering those plans on Saturday, June 16.

Saturday, June 16.
IN COMMITTEE OF THE WHOLE ON RESOLUTIONS PROPOSED
BY MR. PATERSON AND MR. RANDOLPH

Mr. Lansing called for the reading of the first resolution of each plan, which he considered as involving principles directly in contrast; that of Mr. Paterson, says he, sustains the sovereignty of the respective states, that of Mr. Randolph destroys it. The latter requires a negative on all the laws of the particular states; the former, only certain general powers for the general good. The plan of Mr. Randolph, in short, absorbs all power except what may be exercised in the little local matters of the states which are not objects worthy of the supreme cognizance. He grounded his preference of Mr. Paterson's plan chiefly on two objections against that of Mr. Randolph: (1) want of power in the Convention to discuss and propose it; (2) the improbability of its being adopted.

(1) He was decidedly of opinion that the power of the Convention was restrained to amendments of a federal nature and having for their basis the confederacy in being. . . . New York would never have concurred in sending deputies to the Convention if she had supposed the deliberations were to turn on a consolidation of the states and a national government.

(2) Was it probable that the states would adopt and ratify a scheme which they had never authorized us to propose and which so far exceeded what they regarded as sufficient? . . . The states will never feel a sufficient confidence in a general government to give it a negative on their laws. The scheme is itself totally novel. There is no parallel to it to be found. The authority of [the Confederation] Congress is familiar to the people, and an augmentation of the powers of Congress will be readily approved by them.

Mr. Paterson said as he had on a former occasion given his sentiments on the plan proposed by Mr. Randolph, he would now, avoiding repetition as much as possible, give his reasons in favor of that proposed by himself. He preferred it because it accorded (1) with the powers of the Convention, (2) with the sentiments of the people. If the confederacy was radically wrong, let us return to our states and obtain larger powers, not assume them of ourselves. I came here not to speak my own sentiments, but the sentiments of those who sent me. Our object is not such a government as may be best in itself, but such a one as our constituents have authorized us to prepare and as they will approve. . . .

If we argue on the fact that a federal compact actually exists and consult the articles of it, we still find an equal sovereignty to be the basis of it. He reads the fifth article of confederation, giving each state a vote—and the thirteenth, declaring that no alteration shall be made without unanimous consent. This is the nature of all treaties. What is unanimously done must be unanimously undone. . . .*

Mr. WILSON [first stated the difference between the two plans. Virginia plan proposes two branches in the legislature; Jersey a single legislative body. Virginia, the legislative powers derived from the people; Jersey, from the states. Virginia, a single executive; Jersey, more than one. Virginia, a majority of the legislature can act; Jersey, a small minority can control. Virginia, the legislature can legislate on all national concerns; Jersey, only on limited objects. Virginia, legislature to negative all state laws; Jersey, giving power to the executive to compel obedience by force. Virginia, to remove the executive by impeachment; Jersey, on application of a majority of the states. Virginia, for the establishment of inferior judiciary tribunals; Jersey, no provision.]**

With regard to the power of the Convention, he conceived himself authorized to conclude nothing, but to be at liberty to propose anything. In this particular, he felt himself perfectly indifferent to the two plans.

With regard to the sentiments of the people, he conceived it difficult to know precisely what they are. Those of the particular circle in which one moved were commonly mistaken for the general voice. He

---

*As recorded in his journal of the Convention, Madison responded to this point on June 19 as follows: "It had been alleged (by Mr. Paterson) that the confederation, having been formed by unanimous consent, could be dissolved by unanimous consent only. Does this doctrine result from the nature of compacts? Does it arise from any particular stipulation in the Articles of Confederation? If we consider the federal union as analogous to the fundamental compact by which individuals compose one society, and which must, in its theoretic origin at least, have been the unanimous act of the component members, it cannot be said that no dissolution of the compact can be effected without unanimous consent. A breach of the fundamental principles of the compact by a part of the society would certainly absolve the other part from their obligations to it."

**From the notes of Robert Yates, replacing the passage from Madison's journal.

could not persuade himself that the state governments and sovereignties were so much the idols of the people, nor a national government so obnoxious to them, as some supposed. Why should a national government be unpopular? Has it less dignity? Will each citizen enjoy under it less liberty or protection? Will a citizen of Delaware be degraded by becoming a citizen of the United States?

Where do the people look at present for relief from the evils of which they complain? Is it from an internal reform of their governments? No, sir, it is from the national councils that relief is expected. For these reasons, he did not fear that the people would not follow us into a national government, and it will be a further recommendation of Mr. Randolph's plan that it is to be submitted to them, and not to the legislatures, for ratification.

Proceeding now to the first point on which he had contrasted the two plans, he observed that, anxious as he was for some augmentation of the federal powers, it would be with extreme reluctance indeed that he could ever consent to give powers to [the Confederation] Congress. He had two reasons, either of which was sufficient: (1) Congress as a legislative body does not stand on the people; (2) it is a single body. He would not repeat the remarks he had formerly made on the principles of representation. . . . Despotism comes on mankind in different shapes, sometimes in an executive, sometimes in a military one. Is there no danger of a legislative despotism? Theory and practice both proclaim it. If the legislative authority be not restrained, there can be neither liberty nor stability; and it can only be restrained by dividing it within itself into distinct and independent branches. In a single house there is no check but the inadequate one of the virtue and good sense of those who compose it. . . .

Mr. PINCKNEY. The whole comes to this, as he conceived. Give New Jersey an equal vote, and she will dismiss her scruples and concur in the national system. He thought the Convention authorized to go any length in recommending which they found necessary to remedy the evils which produced this Convention.

. . .

Mr. RANDOLPH was not scrupulous on the point of power. When the salvation of the republic was at stake, it would be treason to our trust not to propose what we found necessary. He painted in strong colors the imbecility of the existing confederacy and the danger of delaying a substantial reform.... The present moment is favorable and is probably the last that will offer.

The true question is whether we shall adhere to the federal plan or introduce the national plan. The insufficiency of the former has been fully displayed by the trial already made.... A provision for harmony among the states, as in trade, naturalization, etc., for crushing rebellion whenever it may rear its crest, and for certain other general benefits must be made. The powers for these purposes can never be given to a body inadequate as [the Confederation] Congress is in point of representation, elected in the mode in which they are and possessing no more confidence than they do: for notwithstanding what has been said to the contrary, his own experience satisfied him that a rooted distrust of Congress pretty generally prevailed.

A national government alone, properly constituted, will answer the purpose, and he begged it to be considered that the present is the last moment for establishing one. After this select experiment, the people will yield to despair.

The committee rose and the house adjourned.

MONDAY, JUNE 18.
IN COMMITTEE OF THE WHOLE ON THE PROPOSITIONS
OF MR. PATERSON AND MR. RANDOLPH

The brilliant New York delegate Alexander Hamilton said little at the Convention. In a dramatic exception, on June 18, he interjected himself in the middle of the debate over the respective merits of the Virginia and New Jersey Plans, explained why they were both inadequate, and offered his own astonishing proposal, calling for both an executive serving for life who could veto all laws and for lifetime tenure for members of the legislature's upper house. The Convention took no action on the proposal, but the strong sympathy for monarchy and hostility towards the states that Hamilton expressed in his speech help to explain why he would soon inspire deep distrust when he became the most powerful member of Washington's cabinet. Historians have speculated that Hamilton presented his plan partly for tactical reasons: it made the Virginia Plan look moderate by comparison and thus more palatable.

———

Mr. HAMILTON. . . . The great question is, What provision shall we make for the happiness of our country? He would first make a comparative examination of the two plans—prove that there were essential defects in both—and point out such changes as might render a national one efficacious. The great and essential principles necessary for the support of government are:

(1) an active and constant interest in supporting it. This principle does not exist in the states in favor of the federal government. . . . They constantly pursue internal interests adverse to those of the whole. They have their particular debts, their particular plans of finance, etc. All these, when opposed to, invariably prevail over the requisitions and plans of [the Confederation] Congress.

(2) the love of power. Men love power.* The same remarks are applicable to this principle. The states have constantly shown a disposition rather to regain the powers delegated by them than to part with more, or to give effect to what they had parted with. . . . Consider what such a state as Virginia will be in a few years, a few compared with the life of nations. How strongly will it feel its importance and self-sufficiency?

(3) an habitual attachment of the people. The whole force of this tie is on the side of the state government. Its sovereignty is immediately before the eyes of the people; its protection is immediately enjoyed by them. From its hand, distributive justice and all those acts which familiarize and endear government to a people are dispensed to them.

(4) force, by which may be understood a coercion of laws or coercion of arms. Congress have not the former except in few cases. . . .

(5) influence. He did not mean corruption, but a dispensation of those regular honors and emoluments which produce an attachment to the government. Almost all the weight of these is on the side of the states and must continue so as long as the states continue to exist.

All the passions then we see, of avarice, ambition, interest, which

———

*In his notes from the Convention for June 22, Yates records Hamilton adding, "One great error is that we suppose mankind more honest than they are. Our prevailing passions are ambition and interest; and it will ever be the duty of a wise government to avail itself of those passions, in order to make them subservient to the public good—for these ever induce us to action."

govern most individuals and all public bodies, fall into the current of the states and do not flow in the stream of the general government. The former, therefore, will generally be an overmatch for the general government and render any confederacy in its very nature precarious. . . .

How then are all these evils to be avoided? Only by such a complete sovereignty in the general government as will turn all the strong principles and passions above mentioned on its side. . . . The general power, whatever be its form, if it preserves itself, must swallow up the state powers. Otherwise it will be swallowed up by them. Two sovereignties cannot coexist within the same limits. The plan of New Jersey therefore will not do. What then is to be done?

Here he was embarrassed. The extent of the country to be governed discouraged him. The expense of a general government was also formidable, unless there were such a diminution of expense on the side of the state governments as the case would admit. If they were extinguished, he was persuaded that great economy might be obtained by substituting a general government. He did not mean, however, to shock the public opinion by proposing such a measure. On the other hand he saw no other necessity for declining it. They [the states] are not necessary for any of the great purposes of commerce, revenue, or agriculture. Subordinate authorities, he was aware, would be necessary. There must be district tribunals; corporations for local purposes. . . .

In his private opinion he had no scruple in declaring, supported as he was by the opinions of so many of the wise and good, that the British government was the best in the world and that he doubted much whether anything short of it would do in America. He hoped gentlemen of different opinions would bear with him in this, and begged them to recollect the change of opinion on this subject which had taken place and was still going on. It was once thought that the power of Congress was amply sufficient to secure the end of their institution. The error was now seen by everyone. The members most tenacious of republicanism, he observed, were as loud as any in declaiming against the vices of democracy. This progress of the public mind led him to anticipate the time when others as well as himself would join in the praise bestowed by Mr. Neckar on the British Constitution, namely, that it is the only government in the world "which unites public strength with individual security."

In every community where industry is encouraged, there will be a division of it into the few and the many. Hence, separate interests will arise. There will be debtors and creditors, etc. Give all power to the many, they will oppress the few. [The voice of the people has been said to be the voice of God, and however generally this maxim has been quoted and believed, it is not true in fact. The people are turbulent and changing; they seldom judge or determine right. Give therefore to the first [or upper] class a distinct, permanent share in the government. They will check the unsteadiness of the second [or lower classes], and as they cannot receive any advantage by a change, they therefore will ever maintain good government. Can a democratic assembly, who annually revolve in the mass of the people, be supposed steadily to pursue the public good? Nothing but a permanent body can check the imprudence of democracy.]*

Gentlemen differ in their opinions concerning the necessary checks from the different estimates they form of the human passions. They suppose seven years a sufficient period to give the Senate an adequate firmness, from not duly considering the amazing violence and turbulence of the democratic spirit. When a great object of government is pursued which seizes the popular passions, they spread like wildfire and become irresistible. He appealed to the gentlemen from the New England states whether experience had not there verified the remark. [This is an allusion to Shays's Rebellion.]

As to the executive, it seemed to be admitted that no good one could be established on republican principles. Was not this giving up the merits of the question, for can there be a good government without a good executive? The English model was the only good one on this subject. The hereditary interest of the king was so interwoven with that of the nation, and his personal emoluments so great, that he was placed above the danger of being corrupted from abroad—and at the same time was both sufficiently independent and sufficiently controlled to answer the purpose of the institution at home. One of the weak sides of republics was their being liable to foreign influence and corruption. Men of little character acquiring great power become easily the tools of intermeddling neighbors. . . .

What is the inference from all these observations? That we ought to

---

*From the notes of Robert Yates, replacing the passage from Madison's journal.

go as far in order to attain stability and permanency as republican principles will admit. [Let one body of the legislature be constituted during good behavior or life. Let one executive be appointed [for life] who dares execute his powers. It may be asked, Is this a republican system? It is strictly so, as long as they remain elective. And let me observe that an executive is less dangerous to the liberties of the people when in office during life than for seven years. It may be said this constitutes an elective monarchy! Pray, what is a monarchy? May not the governors of the respective states be considered in that light? But by making the executive subject to impeachment, the term "monarchy" cannot apply. . . .

I confess that this plan and that from Virginia are very remote from the idea of the people. Perhaps the Jersey Plan is nearest their expectation. But the people are gradually ripening in their opinions of government—they begin to be tired of an excess of democracy—and what even is the Virginia Plan, but pork still, with a little change of the sauce?]*

Committee rose and the house adjourned.

TUESDAY, JUNE 19.
IN COMMITTEE OF [THE] WHOLE ON THE PROPOSITIONS
OF MR. PATERSON AND MR. RANDOLPH

After rejecting the New Jersey Plan by a vote of seven to reject, three to accept (Delaware, New Jersey, and New York), and one divided (Maryland), the Committee of the Whole resubmitted its amended version of the Virginia Plan to the Convention and dissolved. The first sentence of the committee draft proposed establishing "a national government." The Convention began its deliberations on this draft by debating whether or not the United States was already intrinsically a nation as well as a confederation of states. Variations of this debate continued through, and beyond, the Civil War.

———

The Convention then proceeded to take the first plan into consideration.

---

*From the notes of Robert Yates, replacing the passage from Madison's journal.

The first resolve was read [stating in part "that a national government ought to be established consisting of a supreme legislative, judiciary, and executive"].

Mr. WILSON. [I am (to borrow a sea phrase) for taking a new departure, and I wish to consider in what direction we sail, and what may be the end of our voyage. I am for a national government, though the idea of federal is, in my view, the same. With me it is not a desirable object to annihilate the state governments, and here I differ from the honorable gentleman from New York. In all extensive empires a subdivision of power is necessary. Persia, Turkey, and Rome under its emperors are examples in point. These, although despots, found it necessary. A general government over a great extent of territory must, in a few years, make subordinate jurisdictions.... With this explanation, I shall be for the first resolve.]*

Col. HAMILTON coincided with the proposition as it stood in the report. He had not been understood yesterday. By an abolition of the states, he meant that no boundary could be drawn between the national and state legislatures; that the former must therefore have indefinite authority. If it were limited at all, the rivalry of the states would gradually subvert it. Even as corporations, the extent of some of them, as Virginia, Massachusetts, etc., would be formidable. As states, he thought they ought to be abolished. But he admitted the necessity of leaving in them subordinate jurisdictions. The examples of Persia and the Roman Empire cited by [Mr. Wilson] were, he thought, in favor of his doctrine: the great powers delegated to the satraps and proconsuls having frequently produced revolts and schemes of independence.

Mr. KING. ... The states were not "sovereigns" in the sense contended for by some. They did not possess the peculiar features of sovereignty; they could not make war, nor peace, nor alliances, nor treaties.... If the states ... retained some portion of their sovereignty, they had certainly divested themselves of essential portions of it. If they formed a confederacy in some respects, they formed a nation in others.... He doubted much the practicability of annihilating the states but thought that much of their power ought to be taken from them.

Mr. MARTIN said he considered that the separation from Great

*From the notes of Robert Yates, replacing the passage from Madison's journal.

Britain placed the thirteen states in a state of nature towards each other [i.e., they were independent of each other]; that they would have remained in that state till this time but for the confederation; that they entered into the confederation on the footing of equality; that they met now to amend it on the same footing; and that he could never accede to a plan that would introduce an inequality and lay ten states at the mercy of Virginia, Massachusetts, and Pennsylvania.

Mr. WILSON could not admit the doctrine that when the colonies became independent of Great Britain, they became independent also of each other. He read the Declaration of Independence, observing thereon that the united colonies were declared to be free and independent states and inferring that they were independent not individually, but unitedly. . . .

Col. HAMILTON assented to the doctrine of Mr. Wilson. He denied the doctrine that the states were thrown into a state of nature. . . . He admitted that the states met now on an equal footing but could see no inference from that against concerting a change of the system in this particular. . . .

On June 20, Oliver Ellsworth of Connecticut proposed that the term "a national government" in the first resolution of the committee draft be replaced by "the government of the United States." This amendment was adopted without opposition. This was only a concession of language to the small states, however, and a last-ditch effort by the small states to vest legislative power in the existing Confederation Congress was subsequently defeated. Roger Sherman warned again that some compromise over state representation in the legislature had to be reached.

On June 21, after further inconclusive discussion of the first resolution of the committee draft, the Convention approved the committee's second resolution, stating "that the legislature ought to consist of two branches," and began working through the committee's third resolution, relating to the first branch, or future House of Representatives. With New Jersey dissenting and Maryland divided, the Convention agreed to the key phrase of the second resolution, stating "that the members of the first branch of the legislature ought to be elected by the people."

The Convention continued debating provisions of the third resolution on June 22 and 23. Also on June 22, the Philadelphia street commissioners responded to the Convention's complaints of excessive traffic noise by agreeing to spread gravel over cobblestoned Chestnut Street.

MONDAY, JUNE 25.
IN CONVENTION

On Monday, June 25, the Convention began considering the committee's fourth resolution, relating to the second branch of the legislature, or future Senate. The resolution stated, in part, "that the members of the second branch of the legislature ought to be chosen by the individual legislatures, to be of the age of thirty years at least, to hold their offices for a term sufficient to ensure their independency, namely seven years." The high point of the proceedings on this day was a rhapsodic speech by the young South Carolina delegate and militant slaveholder Charles Pinckney on the United States as the land of equality.

———

Resolution 4 being taken up.

Mr. PINCKNEY spoke as follows: the efficacy of the system will depend on this article. In order to form a right judgment in the case, it will be proper to examine the situation of this country more accurately than it has yet been done. The people of the United States are perhaps the most singular of any we are acquainted with. Among them there are fewer distinctions of fortune and less of rank than among the inhabitants of any other nation. Every freeman has a right to the same protection and security, and a very moderate share of property entitles them to the possession of all the honors and privileges the public can bestow: hence arises a greater equality than is to be found among the people of any other country, and an equality which is more likely to continue. I say this equality is likely to continue, because in a new country, possessing immense tracts of uncultivated lands, where every temptation is offered to emigration and where industry must be rewarded with competency, there will be few poor, and few dependent. Every member of the society, almost, will enjoy an equal power of arriving at the supreme offices and consequently of directing the strength and sentiments of the whole community. None will be excluded by birth, and few by fortune, from voting for proper persons to fill the offices of government. The whole community will enjoy in the fullest sense that kind of political liberty which consists in the power the members of the state reserve to themselves, of arriving at the public offices, or at least of having votes in the nomination of those who fill them. . . .

If equality is, as I contend, the leading feature of the United States, where then are the riches and wealth whose representation and protection is the peculiar province of this permanent body? Are they in the hands of the few who may be called rich, in the possession of less than a hundred citizens? Certainly not. They are in the great body of the people, among whom there are no men of wealth and very few of real poverty. . . .

Our true situation appears to me to be this: a new extensive country containing within itself the materials for forming a government capable of extending to its citizens all the blessings of civil and religious liberty—capable of making them happy at home. This is the great end of republican establishments. We mistake the object of our government if we hope or wish that it is to make us respectable abroad. Conquest or superiority among other powers is not or ought not ever to be the object of republican systems. If they are sufficiently active and energetic to rescue us from contempt and preserve our domestic happiness and security, it is all we can expect from them. It is more than almost any other government ensures to its citizens. . . .

We must, as has been observed, suit our government to the people it is to direct. These are, I believe, as active, intelligent, and susceptible of good government as any people in the world. The confusion which has produced the present relaxed state is not owing to them. It is owing to the weakness and defects of a government incapable of combining the various interests it is intended to unite and destitute of energy. All that we have to do then is to distribute the powers of government in such a manner, and for such limited periods, as, while it gives a proper degree of permanency to the magistrate, will reserve to the people the right of election they will not or ought not frequently to part with. I am of opinion that this may be easily done; and that with some amendments the propositions before the committee will fully answer this end.

After Pinckney had finished, an intense debate erupted over the resolution's statement that state legislatures, not the people, would elect members of the future Senate. Madison and his allies objected that this would strengthen the authority of state legislatures, and thus states. Other delegates supported it for the very same reason, and it passed with only Virginia and Pennsylvania voting no. The Constitution would not require the direct popular election of senators until the Seventeenth Amendment was ratified in 1913.

Tuesday, June 26.

IN CONVENTION

The Convention continued to debate various provisions of the committee's fourth draft resolution on this day, relating to the future Senate. After agreeing on June 25 to strike the number seven from the length of a senator's term in office, the delegates disagreed over what number to put in its place. If the terms were too long, some argued, the Senate might become a body of self-serving aristocrats. If the terms were too short, others countered, it might become too responsive to popular pressure, including the pressure for a more equal distribution of wealth.

———

The duration of the second branch being under consideration.

Mr. GORHAM moved to fill the blank with "six years," one-third of the members to go out every second year.

Mr. WILSON seconded the motion.

. . .

Mr. MADISON. In order to judge of the form to be given to this institution, it will be proper to take a view of the ends to be served by it. These were: first, to protect the people against their rulers; secondly, to protect the people against the transient impressions into which they themselves might be led. A people deliberating in a temperate moment, and with the experience of other nations before them, on the plan of government most likely to secure their happiness, would first be aware that those charged with the public happiness might betray their trust. An obvious precaution against this danger would be to divide the trust between different bodies of men, who might watch and check each other. . . .

It would next occur to such a people that they themselves were liable to temporary errors through want of information as to their true interest, and that men chosen for a short term, and employed but a small portion of that in public affairs [like those in the legislature's first branch], might err from the same cause.

This reflection would naturally suggest that the government be so constituted as that one of its branches might have an opportunity of acquiring a competent knowledge of the public interests. Another reflection equally becoming a people on such an occasion would be that they themselves, as well as a numerous body of representatives, were liable to err also from fickleness and passion. A necessary fence against this danger would be to select a portion of enlightened citizens whose limited number and firmness might seasonably interpose against impetuous councils.

It ought finally to occur to a people deliberating on a government for themselves that as different interests necessarily result from the liberty meant to be secured, the major interest might under sudden impulses be tempted to commit injustice on the minority. In all civilized countries the people fall into different classes having a real or supposed difference of interests. There will be creditors and debtors, farmers, merchants, and manufacturers. There will be particularly the distinction of rich and poor. . . .

In framing a system which we wish to last for ages, we should not lose sight of the changes which ages will produce. An increase of population will of necessity increase the proportion of those who will labor under all the hardships of life and secretly sigh for a more equal distribution of its blessings. . . . How is this danger [of an attack of the poor upon the wealthy] to be guarded against on republican principles? How is the danger in all cases of interested coalitions to oppress the minority to be guarded against? Among other means, by the establishment of a body in the government sufficiently respectable for its wisdom and virtue to aid on such emergences the preponderance of justice by throwing its weight into that scale.

Such being the objects of the second branch in the proposed government, he thought a considerable duration ought to be given to it. . . . He observed that as it was more than probable we were now digesting a plan which in its operation would decide forever the fate of republican government, we ought not only to provide every guard to liberty that its preservation could require, but be equally careful to supply the defects which our own experience had particularly pointed out.

Mr. SHERMAN. Government is instituted for those who live under it. It ought therefore to be so constituted as not to be dangerous to their liberties. The more permanency it has, the worse if it be a bad government. Frequent elections are necessary to preserve the good behavior of rulers. They also tend to give permanency to the government by preserving that good behavior because it ensures their reelection. . . . He wished to have provision made for steadiness and wisdom in the system to be adopted, but he thought six or four years would be sufficient. He should be content with either.

. . .

Mr. HAMILTON. He did not mean to enter particularly into the subject. He concurred with Mr. Madison in thinking we were now to decide forever the fate of republican government; and that if we did not give to that form due stability and wisdom, it would be disgraced and lost among ourselves, disgraced and lost to mankind forever.

He acknowledged himself not to think favorably of republican government, but addressed his remarks to those who did think favorably of it, in order to prevail on them to tone their government as high as possible. He professed himself to be as zealous an advocate for liberty as any man whatever and trusted he should be as willing a martyr to it, though he differed as to the form in which it was most eligible.

He concurred also in the general observations of Mr. Madison on the subject. . . . It was certainly true that nothing like an equality of property existed; that an inequality would exist as long as liberty existed; and that it would unavoidably result from that very liberty itself. This inequality of property constituted the great and fundamental distinction in society. . . .

Mr. GERRY. . . . There were not 1/1,000 part of our fellow citizens who were not against every approach towards monarchy. Will they ever agree to a plan [like long Senate terms] which seems to make such an approach? The Convention ought to be extremely cautious in what they hold out to the people. . . . He did not deny the position of Mr. Madison that the majority will generally violate justice when they have an interest in so doing, but did not think there was any such temptation in this country. Our situation was different from that of Great Britain, and the great body of lands yet to be parceled out and settled would very much prolong the difference. . . . He admitted the evils arising from a frequency of elections and would agree to give the Senate a duration of four or five years. A longer term would defeat itself. It never would be adopted by the people.

Mr. WILSON did not mean to repeat what had fallen from others but would add an observation or two which he believed had not yet been suggested. Every nation may be regarded in two relations: (1) to its own citizens; (2) to foreign nations. It is therefore not only liable to anarchy and tyranny within, but has wars to avoid and treaties to obtain from abroad. The Senate will probably be the depositary of the powers concerning the latter objects. It ought therefore to be made respectable in the eyes of foreign nations. The true reason why Great Britain has not yet listened to a commercial treaty with us has been because she had no confidence in the stability or efficacy of our government. Nine years with a rotation will provide these desirable qualities and give our government an advantage in this respect over monarchy itself. In a monarchy, much must always depend on the temper of the man. In such a body, the personal character will be lost in the political.

He would add another observation. The popular objection against appointing any public body for a long term was that it might by gradual encroachments prolong itself first into a body for life and finally become a hereditary one. It would be a satisfactory answer to this objection that as one-third would go out triennially, there would be always three divisions holding their places for unequal terms and consequently acting under the influence of different views and different impulses.

On the question for nine years, one-third to go out triennially: Pa., Del., Va., aye 3; Mass., Conn., N.Y., N.J., Md., N.C., S.C., Ga., no 8.

On the question for six years, one-third to go out biennially: Mass., Conn., Pa., Del., Md., Va., N.C., aye 7; N.Y., N.J., S.C., Ga., no 4.

After concluding its deliberation on the Committee of the Whole's fourth resolution, relating to the future Senate, the Convention quickly approved the committee's fifth resolution, stating "that each branch ought to possess the right of originating acts," and adjourned for the day.

WEDNESDAY, JUNE 27.
IN CONVENTION

The Convention postponed considering the committee's sixth resolution, defining the powers of the legislature, and moved on to the seventh resolution. This resolution established representation in the first branch on the basis of a state's free population and three-fifths of its slaves. It had passed the committee without much difficulty on June 11, but that was before the committee approved a similar arrangement for the future Senate and thereby put the small states at a great disadvantage in both branches of the legislature. At this point the patience of the small-state delegates was at an end. Luther Martin of Maryland opened this debate with a long, fiery speech denouncing the large states and defending the principle of the United States as a federation of equal states.

—

Mr. MARTIN contended at great length and with great eagerness that the general government was meant merely to preserve the state governments, not to govern individuals; that its powers ought to be kept within narrow limits; that if too little power was given to it, more might be added, but that if too much, it could never be resumed; . . . that an equal vote in each state was essential to the federal idea and was founded in justice and freedom, not merely in policy; that though the states may give up this right of sovereignty, yet they had not, and ought not; . . . that the propositions on the table were a system of slavery for ten states; that as Virginia, Massachusetts, and Pennsylvania have 42/90 of the votes, they can do as they please without a miraculous union of the other ten; that they will have nothing to do but to gain over one of the ten to make them complete masters of the rest; that they can then appoint an executive and judiciary and legislate for them as they please; . . . that instead of a junction of the small states as a remedy, he thought a division of the large states would be more eligible.

This was the substance of a speech which was continued more than three hours. He was too much exhausted, he said, to finish his remarks and reminded the house that he should tomorrow resume them.

Adjourned.

THURSDAY, JUNE 28.
IN CONVENTION

On this day, after Martin finished his speech, Jonathan Dayton of New Jersey and John Lansing of New York launched a counterattack from the small states by introducing an amendment to the seventh resolution that would make representation in the first house equal for all states. Benjamin Franklin then tried to cool tempers with a proposal.

—

Mr. MARTIN resumed his discourse, contending that . . . the large states were weak at present in proportion to their extent and could only be made formidable to the small ones by the weight of their votes; that in case a dissolution of the Union should take place, the small states would have nothing to fear from their power; that if in such a case the three great states should league themselves together, the other ten could do so too; and that he had rather see partial confederacies take place than the plan on the table. . . .

Mr. LANSING and Mr. DAYTON moved to strike out "not" so that the seventh article might read that the rights of suffrage in the first branch ought to be according to the rule established by the confederation [for voting by states, not by population].

. . .

Mr. MADISON said . . . he could neither be convinced that the rule contended for was just nor necessary for the safety of the small states against the large states. . . . Why are counties of the same states represented in proportion to their numbers? Is it because the representatives are chosen by the people themselves? So will be the representatives in the national legislature. Is it because the larger have more at stake than the smaller? The case will be the same with the larger and smaller states. Is it because the laws are to operate immediately on their persons and properties? . . . The same will be the case. . . .

That it is not necessary to secure the small states against the large ones he conceived to be equally obvious. Was a combination of the large ones dreaded? This must arise either from some interest common to Virginia, Massachusetts, and Pennsylvania and distinguishing them from the other states or from the mere circumstance of similarity of size. Did any such common interest exist?

In point of situation they could not have been more effectually separated from each other by the most jealous citizen of the most jealous state. In point of manners, religion, and the other circumstances which sometimes beget affection between different communities, they were not more assimilated than the other states. In point of the staple productions, they were as dissimilar as any three other states in the Union. The staple of Massachusetts was fish, of Pennsylvania, flour, of Virginia, tobacco.

Was a combination to be apprehended from the mere circumstance of equality of size? Experience suggested no such danger. It had never been seen that different counties in the same state, conformable in extent but disagreeing in other circumstances, betrayed a propensity to such combinations. Experience rather taught a contrary lesson. Among individuals of superior eminence and weight in society, rivalships were much more frequent than coalitions. Among independent nations, preeminent over their neighbors, the same remark was verified. Carthage and Rome tore one another to pieces instead of uniting their forces to devour the weaker nations of the Earth. The houses of Austria and France were hostile as long as they remained the greatest powers of Europe. England and France have succeeded to the preeminence and to the enmity. To their mutual hostility we owe, perhaps, our liberty. A coalition between those powers would have been fatal to us....

. . .

Mr. SHERMAN. [In society, the poor are equal to the rich in voting, although one pays more than the other. This arises from an equal distribution of liberty among all ranks; and it is, on the same grounds, secured to the states in the confederation. . . . The plan now before us gives the power to four states to govern nine states. As they will have the purse, they may raise troops, and can also make a king when they please.]*

The determination of the question from striking out the word "not" was put off till tomorrow at the request of the deputies of New York....

Dr. FRANKLIN. Mr. President, the small progress we have made after four or five weeks' close attendance and continual reasonings with each other—our different sentiments on almost every question, several of the last producing as many noes as ayes—is, methinks, a melancholy proof of the imperfection of the human understanding. We indeed seem to feel our own want of political wisdom, since we have been running about in search of it....

In this situation of this assembly, groping, as it were, in the dark to find political truth and scarce able to distinguish it when presented to us, how has it happened, sir, that we have not hitherto once thought of humbly applying to the Father of Lights to illuminate our understandings? In the beginning of the contest with Great Britain, when we

---

*From the notes of Robert Yates, replacing the passage from Madison's journal.

were sensible of danger we had daily prayer in this room for the divine protection. Our prayers, sir, were heard, and they were graciously answered. . . .

And have we now forgotten that powerful friend? Or do we imagine that we no longer need his assistance? . . . I believe that without his concurring aid we shall succeed in this political building no better than the builders of Babel. We shall be divided by our little partial local interests; our projects will be confounded; and we ourselves shall become a reproach and byword down to future ages. And what is worse, mankind may hereafter from this unfortunate instance despair of establishing governments by human wisdom and leave it to chance, war, and conquest.

I therefore beg leave to move that henceforth prayers imploring the assistance of Heaven and its blessings on our deliberations be held in this assembly every morning before we proceed to business, and that one or more of the clergy of this city be requested to officiate in that service.

Mr. SHERMAN seconded the motion.

Mr. HAMILTON and several others expressed their apprehensions that however proper such a resolution might have been at the beginning of the Convention, it might at this late day (1) bring on it some disagreeable animadversions, and (2) lead the public to believe that the embarrassments and dissensions within the Convention had suggested this measure. [Tradition has Hamilton dismissing Franklin's motion on the ground that the Convention did not need "foreign aid."]

It was answered by Dr. FRANKLIN, Mr. SHERMAN, and others that the past omission of a duty could not justify a further omission; that the rejection of such a proposition would expose the Convention to more unpleasant animadversions than the adoption of it; and that the alarm out-of-doors that might be excited for the state of things within would at least be as likely to do good as ill.

Mr. WILLIAMSON observed that the true cause of the omission of a clergyman could not be mistaken. The Convention had no funds.

Mr. RANDOLPH proposed, in order to give a favorable aspect to the measure, that a sermon be preached at the request of the Convention on 4th of July, the anniversary of independence, and thenceforward prayers be used in the Convention every morning.

Dr. FRANKLIN seconded this motion. After several unsuccessful attempts for silently postponing the matter by adjourning, the adjournment was at length carried, without any vote on the motion.

FRIDAY, JUNE 29.
IN CONVENTION

Lansing's amendment to the seventh resolution that would make the states equally represented in the future House of Representatives remained under debate and continued to anger the large-state delegates. William Samuel Johnson of Connecticut again proposed the compromise that voting in one branch of the legislature be based on population and in the other on states, only to have representatives from the large states vehemently dismiss him.

———

Dr. JOHNSON. The controversy must be endless while gentlemen differ in the grounds of their arguments, those on one side considering the states as districts of people composing one political society, those on the other considering them as so many political societies. The fact is that the states do exist as political societies, and a government is to be formed for them in their political capacity as well as for the individuals composing them. Does it not seem to follow that if the states as such are to exist, they must be armed with some power of self-defense? This is the idea of Colonel Mason, who appears to have looked to the bottom of this matter. . . .

On the whole, he thought that as in some respects the states are to be considered in their political capacity and in others as districts of individual citizens, the two ideas, embraced on different sides, instead of being opposed to each other ought to be combined; that in one branch, the people ought to be represented, in the other, the states.

Mr. GORHAM. The states as now confederated have, no doubt, a right to refuse to be consolidated or to be formed into any new system. But he wished the small states, which seemed most ready to object, to consider which are to give up most, they or the larger ones. He conceived that a rupture of the Union would be an event unhappy for all, but surely the large states would be least unable to take care of themselves and to make connections with one another. The weak, therefore, were most interested in establishing some general system for maintaining order. If among individuals, composed partly of weak and partly of strong, the former most need the protection of law and government, the case is exactly the same with weak and powerful states. What would be the situation of Delaware (for these things he found must be spoken out, and it might as well be done first as last) . . . in case of a separation of the states? Would she not lie at the mercy of Pennsylvania? . . .

Mr. ELLSWORTH did not despair. He still trusted that some good plan of government would be devised and adopted.

. . .

Mr. MADISON . . . entreated the gentlemen representing the small states to renounce a principle which was confessedly unjust, which could never be admitted, and if admitted must infuse mortality into a Constitution which we wished to last forever.

He prayed them to ponder well the consequences of suffering the confederacy to go to pieces. . . . The same causes which have rendered the Old World the theater of incessant wars and have banished liberty from the face of it would soon produce the same effects here. The weakness and jealousy of the small states would quickly introduce some regular military force against sudden danger from their powerful neighbors. The example would be followed by others, and would soon become universal. . . . The means of defense against foreign danger have been always the instruments of tyranny at home. Throughout all Europe, the armies kept up under the pretext of defending have enslaved the people. . . . These consequences, he conceived, ought to be apprehended, whether the states should run into a total separation from each other or should enter into partial confederacies. Either event would be truly deplorable, and those who might be accessory to either could never be forgiven by their country nor by themselves.

Mr. HAMILTON. . . . As states are a collection of individual men, which ought we to respect most, the rights of the people composing them or of the artificial beings resulting from the composition? Nothing could be more preposterous or absurd than to sacrifice the former to the latter. It has been said that if the smaller states renounce their equality, they renounce at the same time their liberty. The truth is, it is a contest for power, not for liberty. . . .

Some of the consequences of a dissolution of the Union and the establishment of partial confederacies had been pointed out. He would add another of a most serious nature. Alliances will immediately be formed with different rival and hostile nations of Europe, who will foment disturbances among ourselves and make us parties to all their own quarrels. Foreign nations having American dominions are and must be jealous of us. Their representatives betray the utmost anxiety for our fate and for the result of this meeting, which must have an essential influence on it.

It had been said that respectability in the eyes of foreign nations was not the object at which we aimed; that the proper object of republican government was domestic tranquility and happiness. This was an ideal distinction. No government could give us tranquility and happiness at home which did not possess sufficient stability and strength to make us respectable abroad. This was the critical moment for forming such a government....

Mr. PIERCE. [The great difficulty in [the Confederation] Congress arose from the mode of voting. Members spoke on the floor as state advocates and were biased by local advantages. What is federal? No more than a compact between states, and the one heretofore formed is insufficient. We are now met to remedy its defects, and our difficulties are great, but not, I hope, insurmountable. State distinctions must be sacrificed so far as the general government shall render it necessary—without, however, destroying them altogether. Although I am here as a representative from a small state, I consider myself as a citizen of the United States, whose general interest I will always support.]*

Mr. GERRY urged that we never were independent states, were not such now, and never could be, even on the principles of the confederation. The states and the advocates for them were intoxicated with the idea of their sovereignty. He was a member of [the Continental] Congress at the time the federal articles were formed. The injustice of allowing each state an equal vote was long insisted on. He voted for it, but it was against his judgment, and under the pressure of public danger and the obstinacy of the lesser states.

The present confederation he considered as dissolving. The fate of the Union will be decided by the Convention. If they do not agree on something, few delegates will probably be appointed to [the Confederation] Congress. If they do, Congress will probably be kept up till

---

*From the notes of Robert Yates, replacing the passage from Madison's journal.

the new system should be adopted. He lamented that instead of coming here like a band of brothers belonging to the same family, we seemed to have brought with us the spirit of political negotiators.

Mr. MARTIN remarked that the language of the states being sovereign and independent was once familiar and understood, though it seemed now so strange and obscure. He read those passages in the Articles of Confederation which describe them in that language.

Lansing's amendment was defeated, with only four states (Connecticut, New York, New Jersey, and Delaware) voting for it, and the original clause was passed.

On the motion to agree to the clause as reported, "that the rule of suffrage in the first branch ought not to be according to that established by the Articles of Confederation": Mass., Pa., Va., N.C., S.C., Ga., aye 6; Conn., N.Y., N.J., Del., no 4; Md., divided.

The Convention's narrow vote reaffirmed that the legislature's first branch (the future House of Representatives) would not be apportioned with equal votes for each state. Now the Convention moved to consider the committee's eighth draft resolution, stating "that the right of suffrage in the second branch of the legislature ought to be according to the rule established for the first"—i.e., by population, not by states. Oliver Ellsworth of Connecticut proposed in response that representation in the second branch be by states, not population, and was blunt about what was at stake.

Mr. ELLSWORTH moved that the rule of suffrage in the second branch be the same with that established by the Articles of Confederation. He was not sorry on the whole, he said, that the vote just passed had determined against this rule in the first branch. He hoped it would become a ground of compromise with regard to the second branch. We were partly national, partly federal. The proportional representation in the first branch was conformable to the national principle and would secure the large states against the small. An equality of voices was conformable to the federal principle and was necessary to secure the small states against the large. He trusted that on this middle ground a compromise would take place. He did not see that it could on any other.

And if no compromise should take place, our meeting would not only be in vain but worse than in vain. In New England, he was sure Massachusetts was the only state that would listen to a proposition for excluding the states as equal political societies from an equal voice in both branches. The others would risk every consequence rather than part with so dear a right. An attempt to deprive them of it was at once cutting the body of America in two. . . . He could never admit that there was no danger of combinations among the large states. . . . Let a strong executive, a judiciary, and legislative power be created, but let not too much be attempted, by which all may be lost. He was not in general a halfway man, yet he preferred doing half the good we could rather than do nothing at all. The other half may be added when the necessity shall be more fully experienced.

Mr. BALDWIN . . . thought the second branch ought to be the representation of property, and that in forming it, therefore, some reference ought to be had to the relative wealth of their constituents and to the principles on which the senate of Massachusetts was constituted. . . .

Adjourned.

SATURDAY, JUNE 30.
IN CONVENTION

The debate over Ellsworth's motion grew increasingly heated. Madison unsuccessfully tried to divert the Convention from the quarrel between larger and smaller states to what he saw as a more serious division between northern and southern states, while Franklin gave a pithy, if somewhat cynical, summary of the differences.

———

The motion of Mr. Ellsworth resumed for allowing each state an equal vote in the second branch.

Mr. WILSON did not expect such a motion after the establishment of the contrary principle in the first branch and considering the reasons which would oppose it even if an equal vote had been allowed in the house. The gentleman from Connecticut (Mr. Ellsworth) had pronounced that if the motion should not be acceded to, of all the states north of Pennsylvania, one only would agree to any general government. He hoped the alarms exceeded their cause and that they would not abandon a country to which they were bound by so many strong and endearing ties. But should the deplored event happen, it would neither stagger his sentiments nor his duty. If the minority of the people of America refuse to coalesce with the majority on just and proper principles, if a separation must take place, it could never happen on better grounds. . . .

The gentlemen from Connecticut, in supposing that the preponderancy secured to the majority in the first branch had removed the objections to an equality of votes in the second branch for the security of the minority, narrowed the case extremely. Such an equality will enable the minority to control, in all cases whatsoever, the sentiments and interests of the majority. Seven states will control six: seven states, according to the estimates that had been used, composed 24/90 of the whole people. It would be in the power then of less than one-third to overrule two-thirds whenever a question should happen to divide the states in that manner. Can we forget for whom we are forming a government? Is it for men or for the imaginary beings called states? Will our honest constituents be satisfied with metaphysical distinctions? Will they, ought they, to be satisfied with being told that the one-third compose the greater number of states? The rule of suffrage ought on every principle to be the same in the second as in the first branch. . . . We talk of states till we forget what they are composed of. . . .

Mr. ELLSWORTH. The capital objection of Mr. Wilson "that the minority will rule the majority" is not true. The power is given to the few to save them from being destroyed by the many. . . .

Mr. MADISON . . . contended that the states were divided into different interests not by their difference of size but by other circumstances, the most material of which resulted partly from climate but principally from the effects of their having or not having slaves. These two causes concurred in forming the great division of interests in the United States. It did not lie between the large and small states, it lay between the northern and southern, and if any defensive power were necessary, it ought to be mutually given to these two interests. He was so strongly impressed with this important truth that he had been casting about in his mind for some expedient that would answer the purpose. The one which had occurred was that instead of proportioning the votes of the states in both branches to their respective numbers of inhabitants, computing the slaves in the ratio of five to three, they should be represented in one branch according to the number of free inhabitants only and in the other according to the whole number, counting the slaves as if free. By this arrangement the southern scale would have the advantage in one house and the northern in the other.... We were partly federal, partly national in our Union, and he did not see why the government might not in some respects operate on the states, in others on the people.

. . .

Dr. FRANKLIN. The diversity of opinions turns on two points. If a proportional representation takes place, the small states contend that their liberties will be in danger. If an equality of votes is to be put in its place, the large states say their money will be in danger....

. . .

Mr. KING ... could not but repeat his amazement that when a just government founded on a fair representation of the people of America was within our reach, we should renounce the blessing from an attachment to the ideal freedom and importance of states; that should this wonderful illusion continue to prevail, his mind was prepared for every event rather than to sit down under a government founded in a vicious principle of representation and which must be as short-lived as it would be unjust....

. . .

Mr. MARTIN would never confederate if it could not be done on just principles.

. . .

Mr. BEDFORD contended that there was no middle way between a perfect consolidation and a mere confederacy of the states. The first is out of the question, and in the latter they must continue if not perfectly, yet equally, sovereign.... We must, like Solon, make such a government as the people will approve. Will the smaller states ever agree to the proposed degradation of them? It is not true that the people will not agree to enlarge the powers of the present Congress.

[What have the people already said? "We find the confederation defective—go, and give additional powers to the confederation; give to it the imposts, regulation of trade, power to collect taxes, and the means to discharge our foreign and domestic debts." Can we not then, as their delegates, agree upon these points? As their ambassadors, can we not clearly grant those powers? Why then, when we are met, must entire, distinct, and new grounds be taken, and a government, of which the people had no idea, be instituted?]* The little states are willing to observe their engagements but will meet the large ones on no ground but that of the confederation.

We have been told with a dictatorial air that this is the last moment for a fair trial in favor of a good government. . . . The large states dare not dissolve the confederation. If they do, the small ones will find some foreign ally of more honor and good faith who will take them by the hand and do them justice. He did not mean by this to intimidate or alarm. It was a natural consequence which ought to be avoided by enlarging the federal powers, not annihilating the federal system. This is what the people expect. All agree in the necessity of a more efficient government, and why not make such a one as they desire?

Mr. ELLSWORTH. Under a national government he should participate in the national security, as remarked by (Mr. King), but that was all. What he wanted was domestic happiness. The national government could not descend to the local objects on which this depended. It could only embrace objects of a general nature. He turned his eyes, therefore, for the preservation of his rights to the state governments. From these alone he could derive the greatest happiness he expects in this life. His happiness depends on their existence as much as a newborn infant on its mother for nourishment. . . .

Mr. KING . . . could not sit down without taking some notice of the language of the honorable gentleman from Delaware (Mr. Bedford). It was not he that had uttered a dictatorial language. This intemperance had marked the honorable gentleman himself. It was not he who, with a vehemence unprecedented in that house, had declared himself ready to turn his hopes from our common country and court the protection of some foreign hand. This too was the language of the honorable member himself. He was grieved that such a thought had entered into his heart. He was more grieved that such an expression had dropped from his lips. The gentleman could only excuse it to himself on the score of passion. For himself, whatever might be his distress, he would never court relief from a foreign power.

Adjourned.

*From the notes of Robert Yates, replacing the passage from Madison's journal.

MONDAY, JULY 2.
IN CONVENTION

On this day, the Convention voted on Ellsworth's motion for equal representation by states in the legislature's second branch. The resulting tie meant that the Convention was now formally deadlocked on its most divisive issue. After being absent for all of June, Pennsylvania delegate Gouverneur Morris resumed his seat at the Convention, and thereafter played a major role in its deliberations.

———

On the question for allowing each state one vote in the second branch as moved by Mr. Ellsworth: Conn., N.Y., N.J., Del., Md., aye 5; Mass., Pa., Va., N.C., S.C., no 5; Ga., divided.

Georgia's critical split vote, which took it out of the large-state voting block, resulted from two of its four delegates leaving the Convention to attend the Confederation Congress, then meeting in New York. One of Georgia's two remaining delegates, who hailed from Connecticut, now supported the small-state position.

Mr. SHERMAN. We are now at a full stop, and nobody, he supposed, meant that we should break up without doing something. A committee he thought most likely to hit on some expedient.

Mr. G. MORRIS thought a committee advisable, as the Convention had been equally divided. He had a stronger reason also.

The mode of appointing the second branch tended, he was sure, to defeat the object of it. What is this object? To check the precipitation, changeableness, and excesses of the first branch. Every man of observation had seen in the democratic branches of the state legislatures precipitation; in [the Confederation] Congress, changeableness; in every department, excesses against personal liberty, private property, and personal safety. What qualities are necessary to constitute a check in this case? Abilities and virtue are equally necessary in both branches. Something more then is now wanted. (1) The checking branch must have a personal interest in checking the other branch; one interest must be opposed to another interest. Vices, as they exist, must be turned against each other. (2) It must have great personal property; it must have the aristocratic spirit; it must love to lord it through pride. Pride is indeed the great principle that actuates both the poor and the rich.

It is this principle which in the former resists, in the latter abuses authority. (3) It should be independent. In religion, the creature is apt to forget its creator. That it is otherwise in political affairs, the late debates here are an unhappy proof. The aristocratic body should be as independent and as firm as the democratic. If the members of it are to revert to a dependence on the democratic choice, the democratic scale will preponderate. All the guards contrived by America have not restrained the senatorial branches of the [state] legislatures from a servile complaisance to the democratic. If the second branch is to be dependent, we are better without it.

To make it independent, it should be for life. It will then do wrong, it will be said. He believed so. He hoped so. The rich will strive to establish their dominion and enslave the rest. They always did. They always will. The proper security against them is to form them into a separate interest. The two forces will then control each other. Let the rich mix with the poor, and in a commercial country they will establish an oligarchy. Take away commerce, and the democracy will triumph. Thus it has been all the world over. So it will be among us. Reason tells us we are but men, and we are not to expect any particular interference of Heaven in our favor. By thus combining and setting apart the aristocratic interest, the popular interest will be combined against it. There will be a mutual check and mutual security....

. . .

Mr. MADISON opposed the commitment. He had rarely seen any other effect than delay from such committees in [the Confederation] Congress....

Mr. GERRY was for the commitment. Something must be done, or we shall disappoint not only America but the whole world. He suggested a consideration of the state we should be thrown into by the failure of the Union. We should be without an umpire to decide controversies and must be at the mercy of events. What, too, is to become of our treaties; what of our foreign debts, what of our domestic? We must make concessions on both sides. Without these, the constitutions of the several states would never have been formed.

On the question "for committing [the matter of representation in the legislature's second branch to committee for consideration]" generally: Mass., Conn., N.Y., Pa., Md., Va., N.C., S.C., Ga., aye 9; N.J., Del., no 2.

On the question for committing "to a member from each state": Mass., Conn., N.Y., N.J., Del., Md., Va., N.C., S.C., Ga., aye 10; Pa., no 1.

———

The committee elected by ballot were Mr. Gerry, Mr. Ellsworth, Mr. Yates, Mr. Paterson, Dr. Franklin, Mr. Bedford, Mr. Martin, Mr. Mason, Mr. Davie, Mr. Rutledge, Mr. Baldwin. [The Convention had not chosen the most determined large-state nationalists, like Madison, Wilson, and Gouverneur Morris, to be on this committee, a sign that it was seriously interested in finding a compromise.]

That time might be given to the committee, and to such as chose to attend to the celebrations on the anniversary of independence, the Convention adjourned till Thursday.

THURSDAY, JULY 5.
IN CONVENTION

Having met on July 3 to consider the matter of representation in the legislature's second branch (the future Senate) and to resolve outstanding issues relating to the legislature's first branch (the future House of Representatives), the so-called Grand Committee reported to the Convention on July 5. The committee recommended that each state have one member in the second branch, as the Connecticut delegates had long been suggesting. Moreover, all money bills would originate in the first branch and could not be altered or amended in the second branch. This arrangement was intended to relax the fear of the large states that if the small states could outvote them in the second branch, they would plunder their wealth. The committee also proposed that representation in the first branch be allocated at a ratio of one representative for every 40,000 people, with no specific reference to slaves in its proposal. All these recommendations provoked controversy.

———

Mr. MADISON could not regard the exclusive privilege of originating money bills as any concession on the side of the small states. Experience proved that it had no effect. If seven states in the upper branch wished a bill to be originated, they might surely find some member from some of the same states in the lower branch who would originate it. The restriction as to amendments was of as little consequence.

Amendments could be handed privately by the Senate to members in the other house. . . .

He conceived that the Convention was reduced to the alternative of either departing from justice in order to conciliate the smaller states and the minority of the people of the United States or of displeasing these by justly gratifying the larger states and the majority of the people. . . .

Mr. BUTLER said he could not let down his idea of the people of America so far as to believe they would from mere respect to the Convention adopt a plan evidently unjust. He did not consider the privilege concerning money bills as of any consequence. He urged that the second branch ought to represent the states according to their property.

Mr. G. MORRIS. . . . This country must be united. If persuasion does not unite it, the sword will. He begged that this consideration might have its due weight. The scenes of horror attending civil commotion cannot be described, and the conclusion of them will be worse than the term of their continuance. The stronger party will then make traitors of the weaker, and the gallows and halter will finish the work of the sword. How far foreign powers would be ready to take part in the confusions he would not say. . . .

. . .

Mr. GERRY. Though he had assented to the report in the committee, he had very material objections to it. We were, however, in a peculiar situation. We were neither the same nation nor different nations. We ought not, therefore, to pursue the one or the other of these ideas too closely. If no compromise should take place, what will be the consequence? A secession, he foresaw, would take place, for some gentlemen seem decided on it. Two different plans will be proposed, and the result no man could foresee. If we do not come to some agreement among ourselves, some foreign sword will probably do the work for us.

Mr. MASON. . . . There must be some accommodation on this point, or we shall make little further progress in the work. And however liable the report might be to objections, he thought it preferable to an appeal to the world by the different sides, as had been talked of by some gentlemen. It could not be more inconvenient to any gentleman to remain absent from his private affairs than it was for him, but he would bury his bones in this city rather than expose his country to the consequences of a dissolution of the Convention without anything being done.

As the debate moved to the issue of allocating representation in the first branch on the basis of one representative for every 40,000 people, Gouverneur Morris expressed concern.

Mr. G. MORRIS objected to that scale of apportionment. He thought property ought to be taken into the estimate as well as the number of inhabitants. Life and liberty were generally said to be of more value than property. An accurate view of the matter would nevertheless prove that property was the main object of society. The savage state was more favorable to liberty than the civilized, and sufficiently so to life. It was preferred by all men who had not acquired a taste for property; it was only renounced for the sake of property, which could only be secured by the restraints of regular government. If property then was the main object of government, certainly it ought to be one measure of the influence due to those who were to be affected by the government.

He looked forward also to that range of new states which would soon be formed in the West. He thought the rule of representation ought to be so fixed as to secure to the Atlantic states a prevalence in the national councils. The new states will know less of the public interest than these, will have an interest in many respects different, in particular will be little scrupulous of involving the community in wars, the burdens and operations of which would fall chiefly on the maritime states. Provision ought therefore to be made to prevent the maritime states from being hereafter outvoted by them. He thought this might be easily done by irrevocably fixing the number of representatives which the Atlantic states should respectively have and the number which each new state will have. This would not be unjust, as the western settlers would previously know the conditions on which they were to possess their lands. It would be politic, as it would recommend the plan to the present as well as future interest of the states which must decide the fate of it.

Mr. RUTLEDGE. The gentleman last up had spoken some of his sentiments precisely. Property was certainly the principal object of society. If numbers should be made the rule of representation, the Atlantic states will be subjected to the western. . . .

Col. MASON said the case of new states was not unnoticed in the committee, but it was thought and he was himself decidedly of opinion that if they [were] made a part of the Union, they ought to be subject to no unfavorable discriminations. Obvious considerations required it.
. . .

FRIDAY, JULY 6.
IN CONVENTION

Failing to reach agreement on how to allocate representation in the first branch, the Convention on this day referred the issue to a special five-member committee, the so-called Committee of Five, composed of Gouverneur Morris, Nathaniel Gorham, Edmund Randolph, John Rutledge, and Rufus King. The Convention then returned to the provision in the Grand Committee's report for originating money bills in the first branch. Many large-state delegates were not impressed with this concession.

————

Mr. WILSON could see nothing like a concession here on the part of the smaller states. If both branches were to say yes or no, it was of little consequence which should say yes or no first, which last. . . . He hoped if there was any advantage in the privilege [of originating money bills] that it would be pointed out.

Mr. WILLIAMSON thought that if the privilege were not common to both branches, it ought rather to be confined to the second, as the bills in that case would be more narrowly watched than if they originated with the branch having most of the popular confidence.

Mr. MASON. The consideration which weighed with the committee was that the first branch would be the immediate representatives of the people, the second would not. Should the latter have the power of giving away the people's money, they might soon forget the source from whence they received it. We might soon have an aristocracy. He was a friend to proportional representation in both branches but supposed that some points must be yielded for the sake of accommodation.

Mr. WILSON. If he had proposed that the second branch should have an independent disposal of public money, the observations of (Col. Mason) would have been a satisfactory answer. But nothing could be farther from what he had said. His question was, How is the power of the first branch increased or that of the second diminished by giving the proposed privilege to the former? Where is the difference in which branch it begins if both must concur in the end?

Mr. GERRY would not say that the concession was a sufficient one on the part of the small states. But he could not but regard it in the light of a concession. It would make it a constitutional principle that the second branch were not possessed of the confidence of the people in money matters, which would lessen their weight and influence....

Mr. PINCKNEY thought it evident that the concession was wholly on one side, that of the large states, the privilege of originating money bills being of no account.

Mr. G. MORRIS had waited to hear the good effects of the restriction. As to the alarm sounded of an aristocracy, his creed was that there never was, nor ever will be, a civilized society without an aristocracy. His endeavor was to keep it as much as possible from doing mischief. The restriction, if it has any real operation, will deprive us of the services of the second branch in digesting and proposing money bills, of which it will be more capable than the first branch. It will take away the responsibility of the second branch, the great security for good behavior. It will always leave a plea as to an obnoxious money bill that it was disliked but could not be constitutionally amended nor safely rejected. It will be a dangerous source of disputes between the two houses....

Again, what use may be made of such a privilege in case of great emergency? Suppose an enemy at the door and money instantly and absolutely necessary for repelling him; may not the popular branch avail itself of this duress to extort concessions from the Senate destructive of the Constitution itself?...

Dr. FRANKLIN did not mean to go into a justification of the report, but as it had been asked what would be the use of restraining the second branch from meddling with money bills, he could not but remark that it was always of importance that the people should know who had disposed of their money and how it had been disposed of. It was a maxim that those who feel can best judge. This end would, he thought, be best attained if money affairs were to be confined to the immediate representatives of the people. This was his inducement to concur in the report. . . .

. . .

Gen. PINCKNEY was astonished that this point should have been considered as a concession. . . .

On the question whether the clause relating to money bills in the report of the committee consisting of a member from each state should stand as part of the report: Conn., N.J., Del., Md., N.C., aye 5; Pa., Va., S.C., no 3; Mass., N.Y., Ga., divided.

The North Carolina delegation, previously voting with the large states, sided with the small states on this vote due to the concession on money bills, and a number of large-state delegations were now split. Interest in a compromise was clearly growing. Despite the lack of an absolute majority in favor (only five of eleven states voted in favor of the clause), the Convention accepted this vote as carried in the affirmative by a vote of nine to two.

On July 7, the Convention turned to the Grand Committee's recommendation "that in the second branch of the legislature each state shall have an equal vote." After brief but intense debate, the Convention voted (by a margin of six to three, with two states divided) to retain this recommendation as part of the Grand Committee's report, but then voted (by a margin of six to five) to postpone any decision on whether to adopt the Grand Committee's full report until after the Committee of Five made its recommendation on the allocation of representation in the first branch.

MONDAY, JULY 9.
IN CONVENTION

Reporting on July 9, the Committee of Five made two recommendations regarding representation in the first branch. First, removing the one representative for every 40,000 inhabitants ratio, it proposed that the first branch begin with fifty-six seats, with each state allocated a particular number of those seats, ranging from nine for Virginia to one each for Delaware and Rhode Island. This allocation gave the northern states, with a substantial majority of the population, a substantial majority of the seats. Second, as the country developed and new states joined the Union, it recommended that the legislature itself reallocate seats in the first branch "upon the principles of their wealth and number of inhabitants." It did not require that the legislature do this, however, nor did it require that any reallocation treat new states equally. The recommendation made no mention of slaves.

———

Mr. SHERMAN wished to know on what principles or calculations the report [of the Committee of Five] was founded. It did not appear to correspond with any rule of numbers or of any requisition hitherto adopted by Congress.

Mr. GORHAM. Some provision of this sort was necessary in the outset. The number of blacks and whites with some regard to supposed wealth was the general guide. Two objections prevailed against the rate of one member for every 40,000 inhabitants. The first was that the representation would soon be too numerous; the second that the western states, who may have a different interest, might, if admitted on that principle, by degrees outvote the Atlantic. Both these objections are removed. . . .

. . .

Mr. G. MORRIS and Mr. RUTLEDGE moved to postpone the first paragraph, relating to the number of members to be allowed each state in the first instance, and to take up the second paragraph, authorizing the legislature to alter the number from time to time according to wealth and inhabitants. The motion was agreed to nem. con.

On the question on the second paragraph, taken without any debate: Mass., Conn., Pa., Del., Md., Va., N.C., S.C., Ga., aye 9; N.Y., N.J., no 2.

———

Mr. SHERMAN moved to refer the first part, apportioning the representatives, to a committee of a member from each state.

Mr. G. MORRIS seconded the motion. . . . The report is little more than a guess. . . . The committee meant little more than to bring the matter to a point for the consideration of the house.

. . .

Mr. RANDOLPH disliked the report of the committee [of which he had been a member] but had been unwilling to object to it. He was apprehensive that as the number was not to be changed till the national legislature should please, a pretext would never be wanting to postpone alterations and keep the power in the hands of those possessed of it. He was in favor of the commitment to a member from each state.

Mr. PATERSON considered the proposed estimate for the future according to the combined rule of numbers and wealth as too vague. For this reason, New Jersey was against it. He could regard Negro slaves in no light but as property. They are no free agents, have no personal liberty, no faculty of acquiring property, but, on the contrary, are themselves property, and like other property, entirely at the will of the master. Has a man in Virginia a number of votes in proportion to the number of his slaves? And if Negroes are not represented in the states to which they belong, why should they be represented in the general government? What is the true principle of representation? It is an expedient by which an assembly of certain individuals chosen by the people is substituted in place of the inconvenient meeting of the people themselves. If such a meeting of the people was actually to take place, would the slaves vote? They would not. Why then should they be represented? . . .

. . .

Mr. KING had always expected that as the southern states are the richest, they would not league themselves with the northern unless some respect were paid to their superior wealth. If the northern states expect those preferential distinctions in commerce and other advantages which they will derive from the new government, they must not expect to receive them without allowing some advantages in return. Eleven out of thirteen of the states had agreed to consider slaves in the apportionment of taxation; and taxation and representation ought to go together.

On the question for committing the first paragraph of the report to [a committee composed of] a member from each state: Mass., Conn., N.J., Pa., Del., Md., Va., N.C., Ga., aye 9; N.Y., S.C., no 2.

———

The committee [members] appointed were Mr. King, Mr. Sherman, Mr. Yates, Mr. Brearly, Mr. Govr. Morris, Mr. Read, Mr. Carroll, Mr. Madison, Mr. Williamson, Mr. Rutledge, Mr. Houston.

Adjourned.

Tuesday, July 10.
IN CONVENTION

The committee that was appointed on July 9 to recommend how many seats each state should have in the legislature's first branch reported on July 10. It proposed that the first branch begin with sixty-five seats, ranging from ten for Virginia to one each for Delaware and Rhode Island. The North retained its substantial majority. The Convention then returned to the second part of the recommendation of the Committee of Five, dealing with subsequent reallocations of seats in the first branch. To understand much of what follows, it is helpful to know that at this time, the probable initial "western" states were also southern (Kentucky and Tennessee), and that it was widely assumed, erroneously, that the southern and new southwestern states would soon have a majority of the population in the Union. It was in part to protect their own future interests that southern delegates proved keen to compel the legislature to periodically adjust representation through a census.

——

Gen. PINCKNEY. The report before it was committed was more favorable to the southern states than as it now stands. . . . He did not expect the southern states to be raised to a majority of representatives but wished them to have something like an equality. . . .

Mr. WILLIAMSON. . . . The southern interest must be extremely endangered by the present arrangement. The northern states are to have a majority in the first instance and the means of perpetuating it.

. . .

Mr. RANDOLPH moved as an amendment to the report of the Committee of Five "that in order to ascertain the alterations in the population and wealth of the several states, the legislature should be required to cause a census, an estimate to be taken within one year after its first meeting, and every _____ years thereafter—and that the legislature arrange the representation accordingly."

Mr. G. MORRIS opposed it as fettering the legislature too much. Advantage may be taken of it in time of war or the apprehension of it by new states to extort particular favors. If the mode was to be fixed for taking a census, it might certainly be extremely inconvenient; if unfixed, the legislature may use such a mode as will defeat the object and perpetuate the inequality. He was always against such shackles on the legislature. They had been found very pernicious in most of the state constitutions. He dwelt much on the danger of throwing such a preponderancy into the western scale, suggesting that in time the western people would outnumber the Atlantic states. He wished therefore to put it in the power of the latter to keep a majority of votes in their own hands.

Delegates regularly came and went from the Convention. Between thirty and forty delegates probably attended on a typical day. This day John Lansing and Robert Yates, two of the three delegates from New York, left and never returned. They would fight against the Constitution's ratification. Along with Madison, Yates had served as the Convention's most faithful note taker. Alexander Hamilton from New York would still periodically attend, but as New York required the presence of two delegates in order to vote, Hamilton could not vote alone. Ten states were now represented at the Convention.

WEDNESDAY, JULY 11.
IN CONVENTION

Debate continued on details for periodic reallocations of seats in the legislature's lower branch. As northern delegates dragged their feet about requiring the legislature to periodically reapportion its numbers, suspicious southerners grew more insistent, even extremist, not only about a census but about specifically ensuring that slaves were counted.

———

Mr. RANDOLPH's motion requiring the legislature to take a periodical census for the purpose of redressing inequalities in the representation was resumed.

Mr. SHERMAN was against shackling the legislature too much. We ought to choose wise and good men and then confide in them.

Mr. MASON. The greater the difficulty we find in fixing a proper rule of representation, the more unwilling ought we to be to throw the task from ourselves on the general legislature. . . . According to the present population of America, the northern part of it had a right to preponderate, and he could not deny it. But he wished it not to preponderate hereafter when the reason no longer continued. From the nature of man we may be sure that those who have power in their hands will not give it up while they can retain it. . . . He must declare he could neither vote for the system here, nor support it in his state.

Strong objections had been drawn from the danger to the Atlantic interests from new western states. Ought we to sacrifice what we know to be right in itself, lest it should prove favorable to states which are not yet in existence? If the western states are to be admitted into the Union, as they arise, they must, he would repeat, be treated as equals. . . . It has been said they will be poor and unable to make equal contributions to the general treasury. He did not know but that in time they would be both more numerous and more wealthy than their Atlantic brethren. The extent and fertility of their soil made this probable. . . . He urged that numbers of inhabitants, though not always a precise standard of wealth, was sufficiently so for every substantial purpose.

Mr. WILLIAMSON was for making it the duty of the legislature to do what was right and not leaving it at liberty to do or not do it. He moved that Mr. Randolph's proposition be postponed in order to consider the following, "that in order to ascertain the alterations that may happen in the population and wealth of the several states, a census shall be taken of the free white inhabitants and three-fifths of those of other descriptions on the first year after this government shall have been adopted and every year thereafter; and that the representation be regulated accordingly."

Mr. RANDOLPH agreed that Mr. Williamson's proposition should stand in the place of his.

. . .

Mr. BUTLER and Gen. PINCKNEY insisted that blacks be included in the rule of representation equally with the whites, and for that purpose moved that the words "three-fifths" be struck out.

Mr. GERRY thought that three-fifths of them was, to say the least, the full proportion that could be admitted.

Mr. GORHAM. This ratio was fixed by [the Confederation] Congress as a rule of taxation. Then, it was urged by the delegates representing the states having slaves that the blacks were still more inferior to freemen. At present, when the ratio of representation is to be established, we are assured that they are equal to freemen. The arguments on the former occasion had convinced him that three-fifths was pretty near the just proportion, and he should vote according to the same opinion now.

Mr. BUTLER insisted that the labor of a slave in South Carolina was as productive and valuable as that of a freeman in Massachusetts; that as wealth was the great means of defense and utility to the nation they were equally valuable to it with freemen; and that consequently an equal representation ought to be allowed for them in a government which was instituted principally for the protection of property and was itself to be supported by property.

Mr. MASON could not agree to the motion, notwithstanding it was favorable to Virginia, because he thought it unjust. It was certain that the slaves were valuable, as they raised the value of land, increased the exports and imports (and, of course, the revenue would supply the means of feeding and supporting an army) and might in cases of emergency become themselves soldiers. As in these important respects they were useful to the community at large, they ought not to be excluded from the estimate of representation. He could not, however, regard them as equal to freemen and could not vote for them as such. He added as worthy of remark that the southern states have this peculiar species of property over and above the other species of property common to all the states.

Mr. WILLIAMSON reminded Mr. Gorham that if the southern states contended for the inferiority of blacks to whites when taxation was in view, the eastern states on the same occasion contended for their equality. He did not, however, either then or now, concur in either extreme, but approved of the ratio of three-fifths.

On Mr. Butler's motion for considering blacks as equal to whites in the apportionment of representation: Del., S.C., Ga., aye 3; Mass., Conn., N.J., Pa., Md., Va., N.C., no 7.

Delegates then resumed debating Mr. Williamson's motion for a periodic census counting "free white inhabitants and three-fifths of those of other descriptions" for purposes of determining representation in the first branch.

Mr. GORHAM. If the Convention, who are comparatively so little biased by local views, are so much perplexed, how can it be expected that the legislature hereafter under the full bias of those views will be able to settle a standard? He was convinced by the arguments of others and his own reflections that the Convention ought to fix some standard or other.

Mr. G. MORRIS. The arguments of others and his own reflections had led him to a very different conclusion. If we can't agree on a rule that will be just at this time, how can we expect to find one that will be just in all times to come? Surely those who come after us will judge better of things present than we can of things future. He could not persuade himself that numbers would be a just rule at any time.... Another objection with him against admitting the blacks into the census was that the people of Pennsylvania would revolt at the idea of being put on a footing with slaves. They would reject any plan that was to have such an effect.... The best course that could be taken would be to leave the interests of the people to the representatives of the people.

Mr. MADISON was not a little surprised to hear this implicit confidence urged by a member who on all occasions had inculcated so strongly the political depravity of men and the necessity of checking one vice and interest by opposing to them another vice and interest.... The truth was that all men having power ought to be distrusted to a certain degree....

. . .

On the question on the first clause of Mr. Williamson's motion as to taking a census of the free inhabitants, it passed in the affirmative: Mass., Conn., N.J., Pa., Va., N.C., aye 6; Del., Md., S.C., Ga., no 4.

———

The next clause as to three-fifths of the Negroes considered.

Mr. KING, being much opposed to fixing numbers as the rule of representation, was particularly so on account of the blacks. He thought the admission of them along with whites at all would excite great discontents among the states having no slaves.

. . .

Mr. WILSON did not well see on what principle the admission of blacks in the proportion of three-fifths could be explained. Are they admitted as citizens? Then why are they not admitted on an equality with white citizens? Are they admitted as property? Then why is not other property admitted into the computation? These were difficulties, however, which he thought must be overruled by the necessity of compromise. . . .

Mr. G. MORRIS was compelled to declare himself reduced to the dilemma of doing injustice to the southern states or to human nature, and he must therefore do it to the former. For he could never agree to give such encouragement to the slave trade as would be given by allowing them a representation for their Negroes, and he did not believe those states would ever confederate on terms that would deprive them of that trade.

On question for agreeing to include three-fifths of the blacks: Conn., Va., N.C., Ga., aye 4; Mass., N.J., Pa., Del., Md., S.C., no 6.

Having rejected this key part of Williamson's amendment, the Convention then voted unanimously to reject the entire amendment and adjourned for the day.

THURSDAY, JULY 12.
IN CONVENTION

Upon reconvening on July 12, the deeply divided Convention immediately returned to Randolph's proposed census. The bottom line for most northern delegates was basically a cosmetic one: the census had to be worded in such a way that it did not appear that slaves were being directly counted simply to determine representation. The bottom line for the southern delegates was insurance that slavery would remain a factor in representation.

———

Mr. G. MORRIS moved to add to the clause empowering the legislature to vary the representation according to the principles of wealth and number of inhabitants a "proviso that taxation shall be in proportion to representation."

. . .

Mr. WILSON approved the principle, but could not see how it could be carried into execution unless restrained to direct taxation.

Mr. G. MORRIS having so varied his motion by inserting the word "direct," it passed nem. con. as follows, "provided . . . always that direct taxation ought to be proportioned to representation."

Mr. DAVIE said it was high time now to speak out. He saw that it was meant by some gentlemen to deprive the southern states of any share of representation for their blacks. He was sure that North Carolina would never confederate on any terms that did not rate them at least as three-fifths. If the eastern states meant therefore to exclude them altogether, the business was at an end.

Dr. JOHNSON thought that wealth and population were the true, equitable rule of representation, but he conceived that these two principles resolved themselves into one, population being the best measure of wealth. . . .

Mr. G. MORRIS. It has been said that it is high time to speak out; as one member, he would candidly do so. He came here to form a compact for the good of America. He was ready to do so with all the states. He hoped and believed that all would enter into such a compact. If they would not, he was ready to join with any states that would. But as the compact was to be voluntary, it is in vain for the eastern states to insist on what the southern states will never agree to. It is equally vain for the latter to require what the other states can never admit, and he verily believed the people of Pennsylvania will never agree to a representation of Negroes. What can be desired by these states more than has been already proposed: that the legislature shall from time to time regulate representation according to population and wealth?

Gen. PINCKNEY desired that the rule of wealth should be ascertained and not left to the pleasure of the legislature and that property in slaves should not be exposed to danger under a government instituted for the protection of property.

. . .

Mr. ELLSWORTH, in order to carry into effect the principle established, moved to add to the last clause adopted by the house the words following, "and that the rule of contribution by direct taxation for the support of the government of the United States shall be the number of white inhabitants, and three-fifths of every other description in the several states, until some other rule that shall more accurately ascertain the wealth of the several states can be devised and adopted by the legislature."

Mr. BUTLER seconded the motion in order that it might be committed.

Mr. RANDOLPH was not satisfied with the motion. The danger will be revived that the ingenuity of the legislature may evade or pervert the rule so as to perpetuate the power where it shall be lodged in the first instance. He proposed in lieu of Mr. Ellsworth's motion "that in order to ascertain the alterations in representation that may be required from time to time by changes in the relative circumstances of the states, a census shall be taken within two years from the first meeting of the general legislature of the United States, and once within the term of every _____ years afterwards, of all the inhabitants in the manner and according to the ratio recommended by [the Confederation] Congress in their resolution of the 18th day of April, 1783 (rating the blacks at three-fifths of their number), and that the legislature of the United States shall arrange the representation accordingly." He urged strenuously that express security ought to be provided for including slaves in the ratio of representation. He lamented that such a species of property existed. But as it did exist, the holders of it would require this security. It was perceived that the design was entertained by some of excluding slaves altogether; the legislature therefore ought not to be left at liberty.

Mr. ELLSWORTH withdraws his motion and seconds that of Mr. Randolph.

After debating a series of amendments making minor changes in the language of Randolph's amendment and setting ten years as the interval between censuses, the Convention voted on the revised amendment before adjourning for the day.

On the question on the whole proposition, as proportioning representation to direct taxation and both to the white and three-fifths of black inhabitants, and requiring a census within six years and within every ten years afterwards: Conn., Pa., Md., Va., N.C., Ga., aye 6; N.J., Del., no 2; Mass., S.C., divided.

FRIDAY, JULY 13.
IN CONVENTION

Having agreed to the proposition that representation in the legislature's first branch should be based on a state's free population and three-fifths of its slave population, the Convention revisited its earlier (now inapplicable) vote to base such

representation on population and wealth. Although this was little more than a pro-
cedural formality whose outcome was preordained, it gave individual delegates
who opposed the three-fifths rule another opportunity to speak out against it.

———

On the motion of Mr. Randolph, the vote . . . authorizing the legislature to adjust from time to time the representation upon the principles
of wealth and numbers of inhabitants was reconsidered by common
consent in order to strike out "wealth" and adjust the resolution to that
requiring periodical revisions according to the number of whites and
three-fifths of the blacks.

. . .

Mr. G. MORRIS opposed the alteration as leaving still an incoher-
ence. If Negroes were to be viewed as inhabitants and the revision was
to proceed on the principle of numbers of inhabitants, they ought to
be added in their entire number and not in the proportion of three-
fifths. If as property, the word "wealth" was right, and striking it out
would produce the very inconsistency which it was meant to get rid
of. . . . He sees, however, that it is persisted in, and that the southern
gentlemen will not be satisfied unless they see the way open to their
gaining a majority in the public councils. . . .

Mr. BUTLER. The security the southern states want is that their
Negroes may not be taken from them, which some gentlemen within
or without doors have a very good mind to do.

Mr. WILSON. . . . Again he could not agree that property was the
sole or the primary object of government and society. The cultivation
and improvement of the human mind was the most noble object. With
respect to this object, as well as to other personal rights, numbers were
surely the natural and precise measure of representation. And with
respect to property, they could not vary much from the precise measure. . . .

On the question to strike out wealth and to make the change as
moved by Mr. Randolph, it passed in the affirmative: Mass., Conn., N.J.,
Pa., Md., Va., N.C., S.C., Ga., aye 9; Del., divided.

After two weeks of intense debate over the most difficult issues facing the dele-
gates, on Monday, July 16, the Convention adopted the much amended report of

the Grand Committee. As amended by the Convention, the report incorporated both the so-called Great Compromise, providing for representation in the legislature's first branch by population, in its second branch by state, and for the origination of money bills in the first branch with no amending power in the second branch; and the so-called Three-fifths Compromise, providing for a national census every ten years counting free inhabitants and three-fifths of others for purposes of allocating seats in the first branch. The report passed by the narrowest of margins, with five states (Connecticut, New Jersey, Delaware, Maryland, and North Carolina) voting for it, four states (Pennsylvania, Virginia, South Carolina, and Georgia) voting against it, and Massachusetts divided.

For Madison and other nationalists, admitting the principle of state representation into the Constitution was a bitter defeat. There were angry exchanges on the Convention floor, and some large-state delegates talked of drawing up their own plan of government. By Tuesday, July 17, emotions had calmed and the delegates were ready to proceed in forging a government with a novel Congress split between the old confederation principle of an assembly of states and the Virginia Plan principle of a national assembly based on population.

With the issue of representation in Congress resolved, the Convention moved through a number of issues quickly. Most of the debate was technical, and only a sample of the high points appears below.

TUESDAY, JULY 17.
IN CONVENTION

On this day, the Convention gave Congress broad discretionary legislative powers, but Madison's proposal that it have the power to review and veto state laws went down again in crashing defeat, with only three states (Massachusetts, Virginia, and North Carolina) voting for it. In its place, Luther Martin proposed what would eventually become the Constitution's supremacy clause. Martin's resolution, taken from the New Jersey Plan, affirmed that all laws and treaties passed by Congress would be the "supreme law of the several states" and that state courts would be obliged to follow them in their rulings, regardless of state laws. It passed without any dissent.

The Convention then turned its attention to the question of how to elect the executive, or future president. The revised Virginia Plan envisioned the executive as a single person chosen by the legislature for one seven-year term. Many delegates had their doubts about this arrangement. Some feared that having the legislature choose the executive would make the executive too dependent on the legislature. Others worried that not allowing the executive to run for a second term would deter qualified candidates from seeking the position. On this day the delegates debated the relative merits of having the people or the national legislature elect the executive.

———

Ninth resolution: "that national executive consist of a single person." Agreed to nem. con.

"To be chosen by the national legislature":

Mr. G. MORRIS was pointedly against his being so chosen. He will be the mere creature of the legislature if appointed, and impeachable by that body. He ought to be elected by the people at large, by the freeholders of the country. That difficulties attend this mode, he admits. But they have been found superable in New York and in Connecticut and would, he believed, be found so in the case of an executive for the United States. If the people should elect, they will never fail to prefer some man of distinguished character or services, some man, if he might so speak, of continental reputation. If the legislature elect, it will be the work of intrigue, of cabal, and of faction; it will be like the election of a pope by a conclave of cardinals; real merit will rarely be the title to the appointment. He moved to strike out "national legislature" and insert "citizens of the United States."

Mr. SHERMAN thought that the sense of the nation would be better expressed by the legislature than by the people at large. The latter will never be sufficiently informed of characters and, besides, will never give a majority of votes to any one man. They will generally vote for some man in their own state, and the largest state will have the best chance for the appointment. If the choice be made by the legislature, a majority of voices may be made necessary to constitute an election.

. . .

Mr. PINCKNEY did not expect this question would again have been brought forward, an election by the people being liable to the most obvious and striking objections. They will be led by a few active and designing men. The most populous states, by combining in favor of the same individual, will be able to carry their points. The national legislature, being most immediately interested in the laws made by themselves, will be most attentive to the choice of a fit man to carry them properly into execution.

Mr. G. MORRIS. It is said that in case of an election by the people, the populous states will combine and elect whom they please. Just the reverse. The people of such states cannot combine. If there be any combination, it must be among their representatives in the legislature. It is said the people will be led by a few designing men. This might happen in a small district. It can never happen throughout the continent. In the election of a governor of New York, it sometimes is the case in particular spots that the activity and intrigues of little partisans are successful, but the general voice of the state is never influenced by such artifices. It is said the multitude will be uninformed. It is true they would be uninformed of what passed in the legislative conclave if the election were to be made there, but they will not be uninformed of those great and illustrious characters which have merited their esteem and confidence. If the executive be chosen by the national legislature, he will not be independent of it, and if not independent, usurpation and tyranny on the part of the legislature will be the consequence....

Col. MASON.... He conceived it would be as unnatural to refer the choice of a proper character for chief magistrate to the people as it would to refer a trial of colors to a blind man. The extent of the country renders it impossible that the people can have the requisite capacity to judge of the respective pretensions of the candidates.

...

Mr. WILLIAMSON conceived that there was the same difference between an election in this case by the people and by the legislature as between an appointment by lot and by choice. There are at present distinguished characters who are known perhaps to almost every man. This will not always be the case. The people will be sure to vote for some man in their own state, and the largest state will be sure to succeed.... As the salary of the executive will be fixed and he will not be eligible a second time, there will not be such a dependence on the legislature as has been imagined.

Question on an election by the people instead of the legislature, which passed in the negative: Pa., aye 1; Mass., Conn., N.J., Del., Md., Va., N.C., S.C., no 8.

...

On the question on the words "to be chosen by the national legislature," it passed unanimously in the affirmative.

Having reaffirmed that the legislature would choose the executive, the Convention then voted to allow a sitting executive to run for reelection.

Wednesday, July 18.
IN CONVENTION

After postponing further consideration of the executive, the Convention took up the Committee on the Whole's draft resolution dealing with the national judiciary. The delegates agreed to exclude the judiciary from any role in the lawmaking process. As before, they agreed on the need for a single supreme court but differed over how to appoint judges and the need for inferior courts.

———

Resolution 11, "that a national judiciary be established to consist of one supreme tribunal," agreed to nem. con. "The judges of which to be appointed by the second branch of the national legislature."

Mr. Gorham would prefer an appointment by the second branch to an appointment by the whole legislature but he thought even that branch too numerous and too little personally responsible to ensure a good choice. He suggested that the judges be appointed by the executive with the advice and consent of the second branch in the mode prescribed by the constitution of Massachusetts. This mode had been long practiced in that country and was found to answer perfectly well.

...

Mr. Martin was strenuous for an appointment by the second branch. Being taken from all the states, it would be best informed of characters and most capable of making a fit choice.

...

Mr. Gorham. As the executive will be responsible, in point of character at least, for a judicious and faithful discharge of his trust, he will be careful to look through all the states for proper characters. The senators will be as likely to form their attachments at the seat of government where they reside as the executive. If they cannot get the man of the particular state to which they may respectively belong, they will be indifferent to the rest. Public bodies feel no personal responsibility and give full play to intrigue and cabal.

. . .

Mr. SHERMAN was clearly for an election by the Senate. It would be composed of men nearly equal to the executive and would, of course, have on the whole more wisdom. They would bring into their deliberations a more diffusive knowledge of characters. It would be less easy for candidates to intrigue with them than with the executive magistrate. For these reasons he thought there would be a better security for a proper choice in the Senate than in the executive.

. . .

Mr. GORHAM moved "that the judges be nominated and appointed by the executive by and with the advice and consent of the second branch, and every such nomination shall be made at least _____ days prior to such appointment." This mode, he said, had been ratified by the experience of 140 years in Massachusetts. If the appointment should be left to either branch of the legislature, it will be a mere piece of jobbing.

Mr. G. MORRIS seconded and supported the motion.

Mr. SHERMAN thought it less objectionable than an absolute appointment by the executive but disliked it as too much fettering the Senate.

Question on Mr. Gorham's motion: Mass., Pa., Md., Va., aye 4; Conn., Del., N.C., S.C., no 4; Ga., absent.

Having deadlocked, the Convention postponed further consideration of the manner of appointing federal judges until July 21, when it tentatively voted "for agreeing to the clause as it stands by which the judges are to be appointed by the second branch." Meanwhile, on July 18, the delegates took up the issue of inferior national courts. Although this issue had proved contentious earlier and divisions over it remained, the Convention quickly accepted the compromise fashioned by the Committee of the Whole to authorize (rather than mandate) the creation of such courts.

Twelfth resolution, "that national legislature be empowered to appoint inferior tribunals."

Mr. BUTLER could see no necessity for such tribunals. The state tribunals might do the business.

Mr. MARTIN concurred. They will create jealousies and opposi-tions in the state tribunals with the jurisdiction of which they will interfere.

Mr. GORHAM. . . . Inferior tribunals are essential to render the au-thority of the national legislature effectual.

Mr. RANDOLPH observed that the courts of the states cannot be trusted with the administration of the national laws. The objects of ju-risdiction are such as will often place the general and local policy at variance.

Mr. G. MORRIS urged also the necessity of such a provision.

Mr. SHERMAN was willing to give the power to the legislature but wished them to make use of the state tribunals whenever it could be done with safety to the general interest.

Col. MASON thought many circumstances might arise not now to be foreseen which might render such a power absolutely necessary.

On question for agreeing to twelfth resolution, empowering the na-tional legislature to appoint "inferior tribunals": agreed to nem. con.

. . .

THURSDAY, JULY 19.

IN CONVENTION

On this day, the Convention revisited its decision to let the executive, who would be elected by the national legislature, run for reelection. Many delegates feared that this arrangement would make the executive too deferential to the legislature. Most of them did not trust the people to elect the executive, however. After much debate, the Convention decided to have electors chosen by state legislatures choose the executive. The electors would presumably be better informed than the people, yet since the electoral college would be a temporary body, the executive could nei-ther come under its influence nor seek its favor.

———

On reconsideration of the vote rendering the executive reeligible a second time, Mr. MARTIN moved to reinstate the words "to be ineligi-ble a second time."

Mr. G. MORRIS. It is necessary to take into one view all that relates to the establishment of the executive, on the due formation of which must depend the efficacy and utility of the Union among the present and future states. It has been a maxim in political science that republican government is not adapted to a large extent of country because the energy of the executive magistracy cannot reach the extreme parts of it. Our country is an extensive one. We must either then renounce the blessings of the Union or provide an executive with sufficient vigor to pervade every part of it.

This subject was of so much importance that he hoped to be indulged in an extensive view of it. One great object of the executive is to control the legislature. The legislature will continually seek to aggrandize and perpetuate themselves and will seize those critical moments produced by war, invasion, or convulsion for that purpose. It is necessary then that the executive magistrate should be the guardian of the people, even of the lower classes, against legislative tyranny, against the great and the wealthy who, in the course of things, will necessarily compose the legislative body. Wealth tends to corrupt the mind and to nourish its love of power and to stimulate it to oppression. History proves this to be the spirit of the opulent. The people at large, who will know, will see, will feel, the effects of them. Again, who can judge so well of the discharge of military duties for the protection and security of the people as the people themselves who are to be protected and secured?

He finds too that the executive is not to be reeligible. What effect will this have?

(1) It will destroy the great incitement to merit public esteem by taking away the hope of being rewarded with a reappointment. It may give a dangerous turn to one of the strongest passions in the human breast. The love of fame is the great spring to noble and illustrious actions. Shut the civil road to glory, and he may be compelled to seek it by the sword.

(2) It will tempt him to make the most of the short space of time allotted him to accumulate wealth and provide for his friends.

(3) It will produce violations of the very Constitution it is meant to secure. In moments of pressing danger, the tried abilities and established character of a favorite magistrate will prevail over respect for the forms of the Constitution.

The executive is also to be impeachable. This is a dangerous part of the plan. It will hold him in such dependence that he will be no check on the legislature, will not be a firm guardian of the people and of the public interest. He will be the tool of a faction, of some leading demagogue in the legislature.

These, then, are the faults of the executive establishment as now proposed. Can no better establishment be devised? If he is to be the guardian of the people, let him be appointed by the people. If he is to be a check on the legislature, let him not be impeachable. Let him be of short duration, that he may with propriety be reeligible.

It has been said that the candidates for this office will not be known to the people. If they be known to the legislature, they must have such a notoriety and eminence of character that they cannot possibly be unknown to the people at large. It cannot be possible that a man shall have sufficiently distinguished himself to merit this high trust without having his character proclaimed by fame throughout the empire.

As to the danger from an unimpeachable magistrate, he could not regard it as formidable. There must be certain great officers of state; a minister of finance, of war, of foreign affairs, etc. These, he presumes, will exercise their functions in subordination to the executive and will be amenable by impeachment to the public justice. Without these ministers, the executive can do nothing of consequence. These were the general ideas which occurred to him on the subject and which led him to wish and move that the whole constitution of the executive might undergo reconsideration.

Mr. RANDOLPH urged the motion of Mr. Luther Martin for restoring the words making the executive ineligible a second time. If he ought to be independent, he should not be left under a temptation to court a reappointment. . . .

Mr. KING did not like the ineligibility. He thought there was great force in the remark of Mr. Sherman, that he who has proved himself to be most fit for an office ought not to be excluded by the Constitution from holding it. He would therefore prefer any other reasonable plan that could be substituted. He was much disposed to think that in such cases the people at large would choose wisely. There was indeed some difficulty arising from the improbability of a general concurrence of the people in favor of any one man. On the whole, he was of opinion that an appointment by electors chosen by the people for the purpose would be liable to fewest objections.

Mr. Paterson's ideas nearly coincided, he said, with those of Mr.

King. He proposed that the executive should be appointed by electors to be chosen by the states in a ratio that would allow one elector to the smallest and three to the largest states.

Mr. WILSON. It seems to be the unanimous sense that the executive should not be appointed by the legislature unless he be rendered ineligible a second time. He perceived with pleasure that the idea was gaining ground of an election mediately or immediately by the people.

Mr. MADISON. If it be a fundamental principle of free government that the legislative, executive, and judiciary powers should be separately exercised, it is equally so that they be independently exercised. There is the same and perhaps greater reason why the executive should be independent of the legislature than why the judiciary should: a coalition of the two former powers would be more immediately and certainly dangerous to public liberty. It is essential then that the appointment of the executive should either be drawn from some source or held by some tenure that will give him a free agency with regard to the legislature. This could not be if he was to be appointable from time to time by the legislature. . . .

He was disposed for these reasons to refer the appointment to some other source. The people at large was, in his opinion, the fittest in itself. It would be as likely as any that could be devised to produce an executive magistrate of distinguished character. The people generally could only know and vote for some citizen whose merits had rendered him an object of general attention and esteem.

There was one difficulty, however, of a serious nature attending an immediate choice by the people. The right of suffrage was much more diffusive in the northern than the southern states, and the latter could have no influence in the election on the score of the Negroes. The substitution of electors obviated this difficulty and seemed on the whole to be liable to fewest objections.

Mr. GERRY. If the executive is to be elected by the legislature, he certainly ought not to be reeligible. This would make him absolutely dependent. He was against a popular election. The people are uninformed and would be misled by a few designing men. He urged the expediency of an appointment of the executive by electors to be chosen by the state executives. The people of the states will then choose the first branch; the legislatures of the states, the second branch of the national legislature; and the executives of the states, the national executive. This, he thought, would form a strong attachment in the states to the national system. The popular mode of electing the chief magistrate would certainly be the worst of all. If he should be so elected and should do his duty, he will be turned out for it like Governor Bowdoin in Massachusetts and President Sullivan in New Hampshire.

On the question on Mr. Gouverneur Morris's motion to reconsider generally the constitution of the executive: all aye.

———

Mr. ELLSWORTH moved to strike out the appointment by the national legislature and insert "to be chosen by electors appointed by the legislatures of the states in the following ratio: to wit, one for each state not exceeding 200,000 inhabitants, two for each above that number and not exceeding 300,000, and three for each state exceeding 300,000."

Mr. BROOM seconded the motion.

Mr. RUTLEDGE was opposed to all the modes except the appointment by the national legislature. He will be sufficiently independent if he be not reeligible.

Mr. GERRY preferred the motion of Mr. Ellsworth to an appointment by the national legislature or by the people, though not to an appointment by the state executives. . . .

The question as moved by Mr. Ellsworth being divided, on the first part, Shall the national executive be appointed by electors? Conn., N.J., Pa., Del., Md., Va., aye 6; N.C., S.C., Ga., no 3; Mass., divided.

On second part, Shall the electors be chosen by state legislatures? Mass., Conn., N.J., Pa., Del., Md., N.C., Ga., aye 8; Va., S.C., no 2.

The part relating to the ratio in which the states should choose electors was postponed nem. con.

———

Mr. MARTIN moved that the executive be ineligible a second time.

Mr. WILLIAMSON seconded the motion. He had no great confidence in the electors to be chosen for the special purpose. They would not be the most respectable citizens but persons not occupied in the high offices of government. They would be liable to undue influence, which might the more readily be practiced as some of them will probably be in appointment six or eight months before the object of it comes on.

Mr. ELLSWORTH supposed any persons might be appointed electors, excepting solely members of the national legislature.

On the question, Shall he be ineligible a second time? N.C., S.C., aye 2; Mass., Conn., N.J., Pa., Del., Md., Va., Ga., no 8.

The delegates would soon begin to question the decisions about the executive made on this day. By July 26, they reluctantly returned to the position of election of the executive by the national legislature for a single term.

SATURDAY, JULY 21.
IN CONVENTION

Having reached tentative agreement on the basic outlines of the executive and the judiciary, the Convention considered whether these two branches of the government should share in the veto power over legislation.

———

Mr. WILSON moved as an amendment to Resolution 10 "that the supreme national judiciary should be associated with the executive in the revisionary power." This proposition had been before made and failed, but he was so confirmed by reflection in the opinion of its utility that he thought it incumbent on him to make another effort. The judiciary ought to have an opportunity of remonstrating against projected encroachments on the people as well as on themselves. It had been said that the judges, as expositors of the laws, would have an opportunity of defending their constitutional rights. There was weight in this observation, but this power of the judges did not go far enough. Laws may be unjust, may be unwise, may be dangerous, may be destructive; and yet may not be so unconstitutional as to justify the judges in refusing to give them effect. Let them have a share in the revisionary power, and they will have an opportunity of taking notice of these two characters of a law and of counteracting, by the weight of their opinions, the improper views of the legislature.

Mr. MADISON seconded the motion.

. . .

Mr. GERRY did not expect to see this point, which had undergone full discussion, again revived. The object, he conceived, of the revisionary power was merely to secure the executive department against legislative encroachment. The executive, therefore, who will best know and be ready to defend his rights ought alone to have the defense of them.

. . .

Mr. MARTIN considered the association of the judges with the executive as a dangerous innovation, as well as one which could not produce the particular advantage expected from it. A knowledge of mankind and of legislative affairs cannot be presumed to belong in a higher degree to the judges than to the legislature. And as to the constitutionality of laws, that point will come before the judges in their proper official character. In this character they have a negative on the laws. Join them with the executive in the revision and they will have a double negative.

. . .

Col. MASON observed that the defense of the executive was not the sole object of the revisionary power. He expected even greater advantages from it. . . . It had been said (by Mr. L. Martin) that if the judges were joined in this check on the laws, they would have a double negative, since in their expository capacity of judges they would have one negative. He would reply that in this capacity they could impede in one case only, the operation of laws. They could declare an unconstitutional law void. But with regard to every law, however unjust, oppressive, or pernicious, which did not come plainly under this description, they would be under the necessity as judges to give it a free course. He wished the further use to be made of the judges, of giving aid in preventing every improper law. Their aid will be the more valuable as they are in the habit and practice of considering laws in their true principles and in all their consequences.

. . .

Mr. RUTLEDGE thought the judges, of all men, the most unfit to be concerned in the revisionary council. The judges ought never to give their opinion on a law till it comes before them. He thought it equally unnecessary. The executive could advise with the officers of state, as of war, finance, and etc., and avail himself of their information and opinions.

On question on Mr. Wilson's motion for joining the judiciary in the revision of laws, it passed in the negative: Conn., Md., Va., aye 3; Mass., Del., N.C., S.C., no 4; Pa., Ga., divided; N.J., not present.

Resolution 10, giving the executive a qualified veto, without the amendment, was then agreed to nem. con.

. . .

MONDAY, JULY 23.
IN CONVENTION

On June 23, the Convention considered the critical question of how the Constitution should be ratified: by state legislatures or by special state conventions whose members would be elected by the people for that purpose? If state legislatures ratified the Constitution, some might argue that the Constitution derived its authority from those legislatures and was thus inferior to state constitutions. If the people ratified the Constitution through special conventions, however, then the authority of the Constitution came from the American people. Supporters of ratifying conventions also believed that those conventions would be more likely than state legislatures to favor a strong national government that would necessarily diminish the powers of state legislatures. The Articles of Confederation, however, required that state legislatures consent to any alterations to it. On this day, delegates from New Hampshire took their seats for the first time, bringing the number of states officially represented at the Convention back to eleven.

———

Resolution 19, "referring the new Constitution to assemblies to be chosen by the people for the express purpose of ratifying it," was next taken into consideration.

Mr. ELLSWORTH moved that it be referred to the legislatures of the states for ratification. Mr. PATERSON seconded the motion.

Col. MASON considered a reference of the plan to the authority of the people as one of the most important and essential of the resolutions. The legislatures have no power to ratify it. They are the mere creatures of the state constitutions and cannot be greater than their creators. And he knew of no power in any of the constitutions, he knew there was no power in some of them, that could be competent to this object.

Whither then must we resort? To the people, with whom all power remains that has not been given up in the constitutions derived from them. It was of great moment, he observed, that this doctrine should be cherished as the basis of free government.

Another strong reason was that, admitting the legislatures to have a competent authority, it would be wrong to refer the plan to them, because succeeding legislatures having equal authority could undo the acts of their predecessors, and the national government would stand in each state on the weak and tottering foundation of an act of assembly.

There was a remaining consideration of some weight. In some of the states the governments were not derived from the clear and undisputed authority of the people. This was the case in Virginia. Some of the best and wisest citizens considered the constitution as established by an assumed authority. A national constitution derived from such a source would be exposed to the severest criticisms.

Mr. RANDOLPH. One idea has pervaded all our proceedings, to wit, that opposition as well from the states as from individuals will be made to the system to be proposed. Will it not then be highly imprudent to furnish any unnecessary pretext by the mode of ratifying it?

Whose opposition will be most likely to be excited against the system? That of the local demagogues who will be degraded by it from the importance they now hold. These will spare no efforts to impede that progress in the popular mind which will be necessary to the adoption of the plan, and which every member will find to have taken place in his own, if he will compare his present opinions with those brought with him into the Convention.

It is of great importance, therefore, that the consideration of this subject should be transferred from the legislatures, where this class of men have their full influence, to a field in which their efforts can be less mischievous. It is, moreover, worthy of consideration that some of the states are averse to any change in their constitution and will not take the requisite steps unless expressly called upon to refer the question to the people.

Mr. GERRY. . . . He considered the [Articles of] Confederation to be paramount to any state constitution. The last article of it, authorizing alterations, must consequently be so as well as the others, and everything done in pursuance of the article must have the same high authority with the article.

Great confusion, he was confident, would result from a recurrence to the people. They would never agree on anything. He could not see any ground to suppose that the people will do what their rulers will not. The rulers will either conform to or influence the sense of the people.

. . .

Mr. ELLSWORTH. . . . He observed that a new set of ideas seemed to have crept in since the Articles of Confederation were established. Conventions of the people, or with power derived expressly from the people, were not then thought of. The legislatures were considered as competent. Their ratification has been acquiesced in without complaint. To whom have [the Confederation] Congress applied on subsequent occasions for further powers? To the legislatures, not to the people. The fact is that we exist at present, and we need not enquire how, as a federal society united by a charter, one article of which is that alterations therein may be made by the legislative authority of the states. . . .

Mr. WILLIAMSON thought the resolution so expressed as that it might be submitted either to the legislatures or to conventions recommended by the legislatures. He observed that some legislatures were evidently unauthorized to ratify the system. He thought too that conventions were to be preferred as more likely to be composed of the ablest men in the states.

Mr. G. MORRIS. . . . Mr. Ellsworth erroneously supposes that we are proceeding on the basis of the confederation. This Convention is unknown to the confederation.

Mr. KING thought with Mr. Ellsworth that the legislatures had a competent authority, the acquiescence of the people of America in the confederation being equivalent to a formal ratification by the people. At the same time, he preferred a reference to the authority of the people expressly delegated to conventions as the most certain means of obviating all disputes and doubts concerning the legitimacy of the new Constitution, as well as the most likely means of drawing forth the best men in the states to decide on it. . . .

Mr. MADISON thought it clear that the legislatures were incompetent to the proposed changes. . . . There might indeed be some constitutions within the Union which had given a power to the legislature to concur in alterations of the federal compact. But there were certainly some which had not, and in the case of these, a ratification must of necessity be obtained from the people. . . . He considered the difference between a system founded on the legislatures only and one founded on the people to be the true difference between a league or treaty and a constitution. . . . Comparing the two modes in point of expediency, he thought all the considerations which recommended this Convention in preference to [the Confederation] Congress for proposing the reform were in favor of state conventions in preference to the legislatures for examining and adopting it.

On question on Mr. Ellsworth's motion to refer the plan to the legislatures of the states: Conn., Del., Md., aye 3; N.H., Mass., Pa., Va., N.C., S.C., Ga., no 7.

. . .

On question for agreeing to Resolution 19, touching the mode of ratification as reported from the Committee of the Whole, viz., to refer the Constitution after the approbation of [the Confederation] Congress to assemblies chosen by the people: N.H., Mass., Conn., Pa., Md., Va., N.C., S.C., Ga., aye 9; Del., no 1.

. . .

Gen. PINCKNEY reminded the Convention that if the committee should fail to insert some security to the southern states against an emancipation of slaves and taxes on exports, he should be bound by duty to his state to vote against their report.

On July 26, the Convention completed its work on the Virginia Plan as amended by the Committee of the Whole. It sent a total of twenty-two approved resolutions to a Committee of Detail to compose them into a single draft Constitution. The Convention then adjourned for ten days while the Committee of Detail (which included many of the delegates) did its work.

The Committee of Detail drew on many sources in fleshing out and sometimes modifying the Convention's resolutions: the Articles of Confederation, the New Jersey Plan, a plan submitted by South Carolina delegate Charles Pinckney, and various state constitutions. It presented its finished draft (see Appendix C) to the Convention on Monday, August 6. The draft embodied for the first time the basic structure of the United States Constitution, complete with a preamble and twenty-three numbered articles designated by roman numerals. This document

*introduced the term "President" for the executive, "Congress" for the national
legislature, "House of Representatives" for the legislature's first branch, and "Senate" for the legislature's second branch.*

*Beginning on Tuesday, August 7, the Convention began working its way
through the articles, taking them up in numerical order. As the Convention dealt
with the various provisions contained in each article, if an issue could not be resolved expeditiously, the delegates typically deferred it until later and often appointed a special committee to find a solution. Many delegates were keen to return
home, and a few left for good in August. Some sharp debates still occurred.*

TUESDAY, AUGUST 7.
IN CONVENTION

*On this day, among other sections, the delegates debated Article IV, Section 1:
". . . The qualifications of the electors [for the House of Representatives] shall be
the same . . . as those of the electors in the several states, of the most numerous
branch of their own legislatures." The potential problem with this clause was that
since the Revolution many states had lowered property requirements for voting.
Some delegates saw that trend as a threat to the long-term survival of republican
government. Gouverneur Morris proposed that only landowners (or "freeholders,"
as they were called) could vote for members of the future House of Representatives.*

———

Mr. G. MORRIS moved to strike out the last member of the section beginning with the words "qualifications of electors" in order that some
other provision might be substituted which would restrain the right of
suffrage to freeholders.

Mr. FITZSIMONS seconded the motion.

. . .

Mr. WILSON. This part of the report was well considered by the
committee, and he did not think it could be changed for the better. It
was difficult to form any uniform rule of qualifications for all the
states. Unnecessary innovations, he thought too, should be avoided. It
would be very hard and disagreeable for the same persons at the same
time to vote for representatives in the state legislature and to be excluded from a vote for those in the national legislature.

Mr. G. MORRIS. Such a hardship would be neither great nor novel.

The people are accustomed to it and not dissatisfied with it in several of the states. In some, the qualifications are different for the choice of the governor and representatives, in others, for different houses of the legislature. Another objection against the clause as it stands is that it makes the qualifications of the national legislature depend on the will of the states, which he thought not proper.

Mr. ELLSWORTH thought the qualifications of the electors stood on the most proper footing. The right of suffrage was a tender point and strongly guarded by most of the state constitutions. The people will not readily subscribe to the national constitution if it should subject them to be disfranchised. The states are the best judges of the circumstances and temper of their own people.

Col. MASON. The force of habit is certainly not attended to by those gentlemen who wish for innovations on this point. Eight or nine states have extended the right of suffrage beyond the freeholders. What will the people there say if they should be disfranchised? A power to alter the qualifications would be a dangerous power in the hands of the legislature.

Mr. BUTLER. There is no right of which the people are more jealous than that of suffrage....

Mr. DICKINSON had a very different idea of the tendency of vesting the right of suffrage in the freeholders of the country. He considered them as the best guardians of liberty and the restriction of the right to them as a necessary defense against the dangerous influence of those multitudes without property and without principle, with which our country, like all others, will in time abound. As to the unpopularity of the innovation, it was, in his opinion, chimerical. The great mass of our citizens is composed at this time of freeholders and will be pleased with it.

Mr. ELLSWORTH. How shall the freehold be defined? Ought not every man who pays a tax vote for the representative who is to levy and dispose of his money? Shall the wealthy merchants and manufacturers, who will bear a full share of the public burdens, be not allowed a voice in the imposition of them? Taxation and representation ought to go together.

Mr. G. MORRIS. He had long learned not to be the dupe of words. The sound of aristocracy therefore had no effect on him. It was the thing, not the name, to which he was opposed, and one of his principal objections to the Constitution as it is now before us is that it threatens this country with an aristocracy. The aristocracy will grow out of the House of Representatives. Give the votes to people who have no property and they will sell them to the rich who will be able to buy them. We should not confine our attention to the present moment. The time is not distant when this country will abound with mechanics and manufacturers [industrial workers], who will receive their bread from their employers. Will such men be the secure and faithful guardians of liberty? Will they be the impregnable barrier against aristocracy?

He was as little duped by the association of the words "taxation and representation." The man who does not give his vote freely is not represented. It is the man who dictates the vote. Children do not vote. Why? Because they want prudence, because they have no will of their own. The ignorant and the dependent can be as little trusted with the public interest. He did not conceive the difficulty of defining "freeholders" to be insuperable, still less that the restriction could be unpopular. Nine-tenths of the people are at present freeholders, and these will certainly be pleased with it. As to merchants, etc., if they have wealth and value the right, they can acquire it. If not, they don't deserve it.

Col. MASON. We all feel too strongly the remains of ancient prejudices, and view things too much through a British medium. A freehold is the qualification in England, and hence it is imagined to be the only proper one. The true idea, in his opinion, was that every man having evidence of attachment to and permanent common interest with the society ought to share in all its rights and privileges....

Mr. MADISON. The right of suffrage is certainly one of the fundamental articles of republican government and ought not to be left to be regulated by the legislature. A gradual abridgment of this right has been the mode in which aristocracies have been built on the ruins of popular forms. Whether the constitutional qualification ought to be a freehold would with him depend much on the probable reception such a change would meet with in states where the right was now exercised by every description of people.

In several of the states a freehold was now the qualification. Viewing the subject in its merits alone, the freeholders of the country would be the safest depositaries of republican liberty. In future times a great majority of the people will not only be without landed but any other sort of property. These will either combine under the influence of their common situation, in which case the rights of property and the public liberty will not be secure in their hands, or, which is more probable, they will become the tools of opulence and ambition, in which case there will be equal danger on another side. . . .

Dr. FRANKLIN. It is of great consequence that we should not depress the virtue and public spirit of our common people, of which they displayed a great deal during the war, and which contributed principally to the favorable issue of it. . . . He was persuaded also that such a restriction as was proposed would give great uneasiness in the populous states. The sons of a substantial farmer, not being themselves freeholders, would not be pleased at being disfranchised, and there are a great many persons of the description.

Mr. MERCER. The Constitution is objectionable in many points, but in none more than the present. He objected to the footing on which the qualification was put, but particularly to the mode of election by the people. The people cannot know and judge of the characters of candidates. The worst possible choice will be made. He quoted the case of the senate in Virginia as an example in point. The people in towns can unite their votes in favor of one favorite and by that means always prevail over the people of the country, who, being dispersed, will scatter their votes among a variety of candidates.

Mr. RUTLEDGE thought the idea of restraining the right of suffrage to the freeholders a very unadvised one. It would create division among the people and make enemies of all those who should be excluded.

On the question for striking out, as moved by Mr. Govr. Morris, from the word "qualifications" to the end of the fourth article: Del., aye 1; N.H., Mass., Conn., Pa., Va., N.C., S.C., no 7; Md., divided; Ga., not present.

Adjourned.

WEDNESDAY, AUGUST 8.
IN CONVENTION

On August 8, the Convention reached Article IV, Section 4. This section established the periodic reallocation of seats in the House of Representatives on the basis of the formula for determining the direct taxation of each state: free population and three-fifths of the slaves. The Committee of Detail had worded the arrangement in a way that was not clear enough for Hugh Williamson of North Carolina. His proposed clarification triggered another debate about slavery.

Article IV, Section 4, taken up. ["As the proportions of numbers in different states will alter from time to time . . . the legislature shall, in each of these cases, regulate the number of representatives by the number of inhabitants, according to the provisions herein after made, at the rate of one for every forty thousand."]

Mr. WILLIAMSON moved to strike out "according to the provisions herein after made" and to insert the words "according to the rule hereafter to be provided for direct taxation"—see Article VII, Section 3 [providing that states would be subject to direct taxation on the basis of "the whole number of white and other free citizens and inhabitants" and "three-fifths of all other persons not comprehended in the foregoing description," a euphemism for slaves].

On the question for agreeing to Mr. Williamson's amendment: N.H., Mass., Conn., Pa., Md., Va., N.C., S.C., Ga., aye 9; N.J., Del., no 2.

Mr. KING wished to know what influence the vote just passed was meant to have on the succeeding part of the report, concerning the admission of slaves into the rule of representation. He could not reconcile his mind to the article if it was to prevent objections to the latter part. The admission of slaves was a most grating circumstance to his mind and he believed would be so to a great part of the people of America. He had not made a strenuous opposition to it heretofore, because he had hoped that this concession would have produced a readiness, which had not been manifested, to strengthen the general government and to mark a full confidence in it. The report under consideration had, by the tenor of it, put an end to all those hopes.

In two great points the hands of the legislature were absolutely tied. The importation of slaves could not be prohibited—exports could not be taxed. [The second point was a prime demand from the southern states, whose wealth came from the export of their agricultural products.] Is this reasonable? What are the great objects of the general system? (1) Defense against foreign invasion; (2) against internal sedition. Shall all the states then be bound to defend each, and shall each be at liberty to introduce a weakness which will render defense more difficult? Shall one part of the United States be bound to defend another part, and that other part be at liberty not only to increase its own danger, but to withhold the compensation for the burden? If slaves are to be imported, shall not the exports produced by their labor supply a revenue the better to enable the general government to defend their masters?

There was so much inequality and unreasonableness in all this that the people of the northern states could never be reconciled to it. No candid man could undertake to justify it to them. He had hoped that some accommodation would have taken place on this subject; that at least a time would have been limited for the importation of slaves. He never could agree to let them be imported without limitation and then be represented in the national legislature. Indeed, he could so little persuade himself of the rectitude of such a practice that he was not sure he could assent to it under any circumstances. At all events, either slaves should not be represented or exports should be taxable.

Mr. SHERMAN regarded the slave trade as iniquitous. But the point of representation having been settled after much difficulty and deliberation, he did not think himself bound to make opposition, especially as the present article as amended did not preclude any arrangement whatever on that point [i.e., the slave trade] in another place of the report.

Mr. MADISON objected to one for every 40,000 inhabitants as a perpetual rule. The future increase of population, if the Union should be permanent, will render the number of representatives excessive.

Mr. GORHAM. It is not to be supposed that the government will last so long as to produce this effect. Can it be supposed that this vast country, including the western territory, will 150 years hence remain one nation?

Mr. ELLSWORTH. If the government should continue so long, alterations may be made in the Constitution in the manner proposed in a subsequent article.

Mr. SHERMAN and Mr. MADISON moved to insert the words "not exceeding" before the words "one for every forty thousand," which was agreed to nem. con.

Mr. G. MORRIS moved to insert "free" before the word "inhabitants." Much, he said, would depend on this point. He never would concur in upholding domestic slavery. It was a nefarious institution. It was the curse of heaven on the states where it prevailed. Compare the free regions of the middle states, where a rich and noble cultivation marks the prosperity and happiness of the people, with the misery and poverty which overspread the barren wastes of Virginia, Maryland, and the other states having slaves. Travel through the whole continent and you behold the prospect continually varying with the appearance and disappearance of slavery. The moment you leave the eastern states and enter New York, the effects of the institution become visible; passing through the Jerseys and entering Pennsylvania, every criterion of superior improvement witnesses the change. Proceed southwardly, and every step you take through the great region of slaves presents a desert increasing with the increasing proportion of these wretched beings.

Upon what principle is it that the slaves shall be computed in the representation? Are they men? Then make them citizens and let them vote. Are they property? Why then is no other property included? The houses in this city (Philadelphia) are worth more than all the wretched slaves which cover the rice swamps of South Carolina. The admission of slaves into the representation, when fairly explained, comes to this: that the inhabitant of Georgia and South Carolina who goes to the coast of Africa and, in defiance of the most sacred laws of humanity, tears away his fellow creatures from their dearest connections and damns them to the most cruel bondages shall have more votes in a government instituted for protection of the rights of mankind than the citizen of Pennsylvania or New Jersey, who views with a laudable horror so nefarious a practice.

He would add that domestic slavery is the most prominent feature in the aristocratic countenance of the proposed Constitution. The vassalage of the poor has ever been the favorite offspring of aristocracy.

And what is the proposed compensation to the northern states for a sacrifice of every principle of right, of every impulse of humanity? They are to bind themselves to march their militia for the defense of the southern states for their defense against those very slaves of whom they complain. They must supply vessels and seamen in case of foreign attack. The legislature will have indefinite power to tax them by excises and duties on imports, both of which will fall heavier on them than on the southern inhabitants, for the bohea tea used by a northern freeman will pay more tax than the whole consumption of the miserable slave, which consists of nothing more than his physical subsistence and the rag that covers his nakedness.

On the other side, the southern states are not to be restrained from importing fresh supplies of wretched Africans, at once to increase the danger of attack and the difficulty of defense; nay, they are to be encouraged to it by an assurance of having their votes in the national government increased in proportion, and are at the same time to have their exports and their slaves exempt from all contributions for the public service.

Let it not be said that direct taxation is to be proportioned to representation. It is idle to suppose that the general government can stretch its hand directly into the pockets of the people scattered over so vast a country. They can only do it through the medium of exports, imports, and excises. For what then are all these sacrifices to be made? He would sooner submit himself to a tax for paying for all the Negroes in the United States than saddle posterity with such a constitution.

Mr. DAYTON seconded the motion. He did it, he said, that his sentiments on the subject might appear, whatever might be the fate of the amendment.

Mr. SHERMAN did not regard the admission of the Negroes into the ratio of representation as liable to such insuperable objections. It was the freemen of the southern states who were, in fact, to be represented according to the taxes paid by them, and the Negroes are only included in the estimate of the taxes. This was his idea of the matter.

Mr. PINCKNEY considered the fisheries and the western frontier as more burdensome to the United States than the slaves. He thought this could be demonstrated if the occasion were a proper one.

Mr. WILSON thought the motion premature. An agreement to the clause would be no bar to the object of it.

Question on motion to insert "free" before "inhabitants": N.J., aye 1; N.H., Mass., Conn., Pa., Del., Md., Va., N.C., S.C., Ga., no 10.

. . .

MONDAY, AUGUST 13.
IN CONVENTION

On August 13, the delegates reached the section of the draft Constitution requiring that revenue bills originate in the House of Representatives, with no amendments in the Senate. This section was the vital element of the Great Compromise that convinced North Carolina to vote with the small states. Delegates from other large states, however, had regarded it as neither an important concession nor a good idea, and the provision came under anxious attack again today. At issue was whether it was wise to leave so much control over money bills to the representatives of the "people."

——

Article IV, Section 5, being reconsidered. ["All bills for raising or appropriating money . . . shall originate in the House of Representatives, and shall not be altered or amended by the Senate. . . ."]

Mr. RANDOLPH moved that the clause be altered so as to read, "bills for raising money for the purpose of revenue or for appropriating the same shall originate in the House of Representatives and shall not be so amended or altered by the Senate as to increase or diminish the sum to be raised, or change the mode of levying it, or the objects of its appropriation." He would not repeat his reasons, but barely remind the members from the smaller states of the compromise by which the larger states were entitled to this privilege.

Col. MASON. This amendment removes all the objections urged against the section as it stood at first. By specifying purposes of revenue, it obviated the objection that the section extended to all bills under which money might incidentally arise. By authorizing amendments in the Senate, it got rid of the objections that the Senate could not correct errors of any sort and that it would introduce into the House of Representatives the practice of tacking foreign matter to money bills.

These objections being removed, the arguments in favor of the proposed restraint on the Senate ought to have their full force. The Senate did not represent the people but the states in their political character. It was improper therefore that it should tax the people. . . .

Again, the Senate is not like the House of Representatives, chosen frequently and obliged to return frequently among the people. They are to be chosen by the states for six years, will probably settle themselves at the seat of government, will pursue schemes for their own aggrandizement—will be able, by wearying out the House of Representatives and taking advantage of their impatience at the close of a long session, to extort measures for that purpose. If they should be paid, as he expected would be yet determined and wished to be so, out of the national treasury, they will particularly extort an increase of their wages. A bare negative was a very different thing from that of originating bills. . . .

He did not mean by what he had said to oppose the permanency of the Senate. On the contrary, he had no repugnance to an increase of it—nor to allowing it a negative, though the Senate was not by its present constitution entitled to it. But in all events he would contend that the purse strings should be in the hands of the representatives of the people.

Mr. WILSON was himself directly opposed to the equality of votes granted to the Senate by its present constitution. At the same time, he wished not to multiply the vices of the system. . . . The House of Representatives will insert other things in money bills and by making them conditions of each other, destroy the deliberative liberty of the Senate. . . . War, commerce, and revenue were the great objects of the general government. All of them are connected with money. The restriction in favor of the House of Representatives would exclude the Senate from originating any important bills whatever.

Mr. GERRY considered this as a part of the plan that would be much scrutinized. Taxation and representation are strongly associated in the minds of the people, and they will not agree that any but their immediate representatives shall meddle with their purses. In short, the acceptance of the plan will inevitably fail if the Senate be not restrained from originating money bills.

Mr. G. MORRIS. . . . The effects commented on may be produced by a negative only in the Senate. They can tire out the other house and extort their concurrence in favorite measures as well by withholding their negative as by adhering to a bill introduced by themselves.

Mr. MADISON thought if the substitute offered by Mr. Randolph for the original section is to be adopted it would be proper to allow the Senate at least so to amend as to diminish the sum to be raised. Why should they be restrained from checking the extravagance of the other house?

One of the greatest evils incident to republican government was the spirit of contention and faction. The proposed substitute, which in some respects lessened the objections against the section, had a contrary effect with respect to this particular. It laid a foundation for new difficulties and disputes between the two houses. . . . [Madison went on to argue at length that the requirement that money bills originate in the House of Representatives was not reasonable.]

Mr. DICKINSON. Experience must be our only guide. Reason may mislead us. It was not reason that discovered ... or ever could have discovered the odd and, in the eye of those who are governed by reason, the absurd mode of trial by jury.... And has not experience verified the utility of restraining money bills to the immediate representatives of the people? ...

He observed that all the prejudices of the people would be offended by refusing this exclusive privilege to the House of Representatives, and these prejudices should never be disregarded by us when no essential purpose was to be served. When this plan goes forth it will be attacked by the popular leaders. Aristocracy will be the watchword, the shibboleth among its adversaries. Eight states have inserted in their constitutions the exclusive right of originating money bills in favor of the popular branch of the legislature. Most of them, however, allowed the other branch to amend. This, he thought, would be proper for us to do.

Mr. RANDOLPH regarded this point as of such consequence that as he valued the peace of this country, he would press the adoption of it. We had numerous and monstrous difficulties to combat. Surely we ought not to increase them. When the people behold in the Senate the countenance of an aristocracy, and in the president the form, at least, of a little monarch, will not their alarms be sufficiently raised without taking from their immediate representatives a right which has been so long appropriated to them?

The executive will have more influence over the Senate than over the House of Representatives. Allow the Senate to originate in this case, and that influence will be sure to mix itself in their deliberations and plans. ... The Senate will be more likely to be corrupt than the House of Representatives and should therefore have less to do with money matters. His principal object, however, was to prevent popular objections against the plan and to secure its adoption.

Mr. RUTLEDGE. ... Will not the people say that this restriction [that the Senate can amend revenue bills but not originate them] is but a mere tub to the whale? They cannot but see that it is of no real consequence and will be more likely to be displeased with it as an attempt to bubble them than to impute it to a watchfulness over their rights.

For his part, he would prefer giving the exclusive right to the Senate, if it was to be given exclusively at all. The Senate, being more conversant in business and having more leisure, will digest the bills much better, and as they are to have no effect till examined and approved by the House of Representatives, there can be no possible danger. . . .

Mr. CARROLL. The most ingenious men in Maryland are puzzled to define the case of money bills or explain the constitution on that point, though it seemed to be worded with all possible plainness and precision. It is a source of continual difficulty and squabble between the two houses.

The Convention put off any final decision, and on Saturday, September 8, it agreed that the Senate should have the power of amending revenue bills. Maryland and Delaware dissented.

TUESDAY, AUGUST 14.
IN CONVENTION

On this day, delegates dealt with the compensation and employment of national legislators. They rejected the Committee of Detail's provision that states (rather than the national government) would pay members of Congress. They then debated a provision in the draft Constitution putting restrictions on members of Congress holding other federal offices. This provision lay at the intersection of two deeply felt but conflicting concerns: (1) how to restrain the possibility of elected officials using their position to enrich themselves at the public expense, and (2) how to make sure that ambitious and talented people were not discouraged from taking public office by unnecessary restrictions. All the delegates knew how English monarchs manipulated Parliament through their ability to confer offices on members.

———

Article VI, Section 9, taken up. ["The members of each house shall be ineligible to . . . any office under the authority of the United States, during the time for which they shall respectively be elected; and the members of the Senate shall be ineligible to . . . any such office for one year afterwards."]

Mr. PINCKNEY argued that the making the members ineligible to offices was degrading to them and the more improper as their election into the legislature implied that they had the confidence of the people; that it was inconvenient, because the Senate might be supposed to contain the fittest men—he hoped to see that body become a school of public ministers, a nursery of statesmen; that it was impolitic, because the legislature would cease to be a magnet to the first talents and abilities. He moved to postpone the section in order to take up the following proposition, viz., "the members of each house shall be incapable of holding any office under the United States for which they or any others for their benefit receive any salary, fees, or emoluments of any kind, and the acceptance of such office shall vacate their seats respectively."

Gen. MIFFLIN seconded the motion.

Col. MASON ironically proposed to strike out the whole section as a more effectual expedient for encouraging that exotic corruption which might not otherwise thrive so well in the American soil; for completing that aristocracy which was probably in the contemplation of some among us; and for inviting into the legislative service those generous and benevolent characters who will do justice to each other's merit by carving out offices and rewards for it. In the present state of American morals and manners, few friends, it may be thought, will be lost to the plan by the opportunity of giving premiums to a mercenary and depraved ambition.

Mr. MERCER. It is a first principle in political science that wherever the rights of property are secured, an aristocracy will grow out of it. Elective governments also necessarily become aristocratic because the rulers, being few, can and will draw emoluments for themselves from the many. The governments of America will become aristocracies. They are so already. The public measures are calculated for the benefit of the governors, not of the people. The people are dissatisfied and complain. They change their rulers, and the public measures are changed, but it is only a change of one scheme of emolument to the rulers for another. The people gain nothing by it but an addition of instability and uncertainty to their other evils.

Governments can only be maintained by force or influence. The executive has not force; deprive him of influence by rendering the members of the legislature ineligible to executive offices, and he becomes a mere phantom of authority. The aristocratic part will not even let him in for a share of the plunder. The legislature must and will be composed of wealth and abilities, and the people will be governed by a junto.

The executive ought to have a council, being members of both houses. Without such an influence, the war will be between the aristocracy and the people. He wished it to be between the aristocracy and the executive. Nothing else can protect the people against those speculating legislatures which are now plundering them throughout the United States.

Mr. GERRY ... could not think with Mr. Pinckney that the disqualification was degrading. Confidence is the road to tyranny. As to ministers and ambassadors, few of them were necessary. It is the opinion of a great many that they ought to be discontinued on our part; that none may be sent among us, and that source of influence be shut up. If the Senate were to appoint ambassadors, as seemed to be intended, they will multiply embassies for their own sakes. He was not so fond of those productions as to wish to establish nurseries for them. If they are once appointed, the House of Representatives will be obliged to provide salaries for them, whether they approve of the measures or not. If men will not serve in the legislature without a prospect of such offices, our situation is deplorable indeed. If our best citizens are actuated by such mercenary views, we had better choose a single despot at once. It will be more easy to satisfy the rapacity of one than of many. According to the idea of one gentleman (Mr. Mercer), our government, it seems, is to be a government of plunder. In that case, it certainly would be prudent to have but one rather than many to be employed in it.

We cannot be too circumspect in the formation of this system. It will be examined on all sides and with a very suspicious eye. The people who have been so lately in arms against Great Britain for their liberties will not easily give them up. He lamented the evils existing at present under our governments but imputed them to the faults of those in office, not to the people. The misdeeds of the former will produce a critical attention to the opportunities afforded by the new system to like or greater abuses.

As it now stands, it is as complete an aristocracy as ever was framed. If great powers should be given to the Senate, we shall be governed in reality by a junto, as has been apprehended. He remarked that it would be very differently constituted from [the Confederation] Congress. (1) There will be but two deputies from each state [in the Senate]; in [the Confederation] Congress there may be seven and are generally five. (2) They are chosen for six years; those of [the Confederation] Congress, annually. (3) They are not subject to recall; those of [the Confederation] Congress are. (4) In [the Confederation] Congress, nine states are necessary for all great purposes; here eight will suffice.

Is it to be presumed that the people will ever agree to such a system? He moved to render the members of the House of Representatives, as well as of the Senate, ineligible not only during, but for one year after, the expiration of their terms. If it should be thought that this will injure the legislature by keeping out of it men of abilities who are willing to serve in other offices, it may be required as a qualification for other offices that the candidate shall have served a certain time in the legislature.

Mr. G. MORRIS. . . . He was against rendering the members of the legislature ineligible to offices. He was for rendering them eligible again after having vacated their seats by accepting office. Why should we not avail ourselves of their services if the people choose to give them their confidence? There can be little danger of corruption, either among the people or the legislatures who are to be the electors. If they say, "We see their merits, we honor the men, we choose to renew our confidence in them," have they not a right to give them a preference, and can they be properly abridged of it?

Mr. WILLIAMSON introduced his opposition to the motion by referring to the question concerning "money bills." That clause, he said, was dead [from the vote on August 13]. Its ghost, he was afraid, would, notwithstanding, haunt us. It had been a matter of conscience with him to insist upon it as long as there was hope of retaining it. He had swallowed the vote of rejection with reluctance. He could not digest it. All that was said on the other side was that the restriction was not convenient. We have now got a House of Lords which is to originate money bills. To avoid another inconveniency, we are to have a whole legislature at liberty to cut out offices for one another. He thought a self-denying ordinance for ourselves would be more proper. Bad as the Constitution has been made by expunging the restriction on the Senate concerning money bills, he did not wish to make it worse by expunging the present section. He had scarcely seen a single corrupt measure in the legislature of North Carolina which could not be traced up to office hunting.

Mr. SHERMAN. The Constitution should lay as few temptations as possible in the way of those in power. Men of abilities will increase as the country grows more populous and the means of education are more diffused.

Mr. PINCKNEY. No state has rendered the members of the legislature ineligible to offices. In South Carolina the judges are eligible into the legislature. It cannot be supposed then that the motion will be offensive to the people. If the state constitutions should be revised, he believed restrictions of this sort would be rather diminished than multiplied.

Mr. WILSON could not approve of the section as it stood.... Nothing seemed to be wanting to prostrate the national legislature but to render its members ineligible to national offices and, by that means, take away its power of attracting those talents which were necessary to give weight to the government and to render it useful to the people.

He was far from thinking the ambition which aspired to offices of dignity and trust an ignoble or culpable one. He was sure it was not politic to regard it in that light or to withhold from it the prospect of those rewards which might engage it in the career of public service. He observed that the state of Pennsylvania, which had gone as far as any state into the policy of fettering power, had not rendered the members of the legislature ineligible to offices of government.

Mr. ELLSWORTH did not think the mere postponement of the reward would be any material discouragement of merit. Ambitious minds will serve two years or seven years in the legislature for the sake of qualifying themselves for other offices. This he thought a sufficient security for obtaining the services of the ablest men in the legislature, although while members they should be ineligible to public offices. Besides, merit will be most encouraged when most impartially rewarded. If rewards are to circulate only within the legislature, merit out of it will be discouraged.

Mr. MERCER was extremely anxious on this point. What led to the appointment of this Convention? The corruption and mutability of the legislative councils of the states. If the plan does not remedy these, it will not recommend itself, and we shall not be able in our private capacities to support and enforce it; nor will the best part of our citizens exert themselves for the purpose....

...

Mr. G. MORRIS put the case of a war, and the citizen the most capable of conducting it happening to be a member of the legislature. What might have been the consequence of such a regulation at the commencement, or even in the course, of the late contest for our liberties?

On question for postponing in order to take up Mr. Pinckney's motion, it was lost: N.H., Pa., Del., Md., Va., aye 5; Mass., Conn., N.J., N.C., S.C., no 5; Ga., divided.

. . .

Mr. BUTLER and Mr. PINCKNEY urged a general postponement of Article VI, Section 9, till it should be seen what powers would be vested in the Senate, when it would be more easy to judge of the expediency of allowing the officers of state to be chosen out of that body. A general postponement was agreed to nem. con. [Article VI, Section 9, was debated, slightly modified, and approved on Tuesday, September 4.]

The Virginia Plan gave the new national legislature all of the power possessed by the old Confederation Congress plus the power to "legislate in all cases to which the separate states are incompetent." The Committee of Detail replaced this generalized grant with an enumerated list in its Article VII: among other powers, Congress had the authority to tax, coin money, establish post offices, make treaties, establish a uniform rule of naturalization, raise armies, call up the state militias, wage war, and regulate commerce. The list was mostly an amplification of powers widely recognized as needed under a revised and augmented Articles of Confederation. It passed through the Convention in August with little controversy.

The Committee of Detail draft also gave Congress the power to "make all laws that shall be necessary and proper for carrying into execution the foregoing powers, and all other powers vested by this Constitution in the government of the United States." The "necessary and proper" clause passed the Convention without vocal dissent, but the vast amount of undefined power that it potentially conferred on the new government was one reason why delegates Elbridge Gerry, George Mason, and Edmund Randolph later refused to sign the Constitution. The "necessary and proper" clause provided the argument that Congress had implied powers as well as specific ones, an argument soon used by Alexander Hamilton to defend Congress's power to create a national bank in 1791.

One item on the original list in Article VII failed to make it through the Convention: the power to issue paper money (or "bills of credit," as the Committee of Detail termed it). These men of property considered paper money, as it had been handled by the states, to be a fiscally irresponsible tool of debtors against creditors like themselves. As a result, the Constitution forbade the states to issue any kind of money. On August 16, Gouverneur Morris moved to deny the national government the power to issue paper money. A few farsighted delegates countered that the government might need to issue paper money at some point in the future, but other delegates leapt at the opportunity to "bar the door against paper money," as Oliver Ellsworth put it. Only New Jersey and Maryland voted in favor of keeping this power. The United States did need to issue paper money during the Civil War, and in 1871 the Supreme Court found the issuing of paper money constitutional under the "necessary and proper" clause, which surely would have astounded many of the delegates.

Friday, August 17.
IN CONVENTION

One by one, the Convention worked through the various provisions contained in the Constitution as drafted by the Committee of Detail—spending more time on some than others. On this day, the Convention altered one of the enumerated powers of Congress: "to make war" became "to declare war." The president, with the advice and consent of the Senate, would hold the power to make treaties, including treaties of peace.

———

"To make war."

Mr. PINCKNEY opposed the vesting [of] this power in the legislature. Its proceedings were too slow. It would meet but once a year. The House of Representatives would be too numerous for such deliberations. The Senate would be the best depositary, being more acquainted with foreign affairs and most capable of proper resolutions. If the states are equally represented in [the] Senate so as to give no advantage to large states, the power will, notwithstanding, be safe, as the small have their all at stake in such cases as well as the large states. It would be singular for one authority to make war and another peace.

Mr. BUTLER. The objections against the legislature lie in great degree against the Senate. He was for vesting the power in the president, who will have all the requisite qualities and will not make war but when the nation will support it.

Mr. MADISON and Mr. GERRY moved to insert "declare," striking out "make" war, leaving to the executive the power to repel sudden attacks.

Mr. SHERMAN thought it stood very well. The executive should be able to repel and not to commence war. "Make" better than "declare," the latter narrowing the power too much.

Mr. GERRY never expected to hear in a republic a motion to empower the executive alone to declare war.

Mr. ELLSWORTH. There is a material difference between the cases of making war and making peace. It should be more easy to get out of war than into it. War also is a simple and overt declaration. Peace attended with intricate and secret negotiations.

Mr. MASON was against giving the power of war to the executive, because not safely to be trusted with it, or to the Senate, because not so constructed as to be entitled to it. He was for clogging rather than facilitating war, but for facilitating peace. He preferred "declare" to "make."

On the motion to insert "declare" in place of "make," it was agreed to: Pa., Del., Md., Va., N.C., S.C., Ga., aye 7; N.H., Conn., no 2; Mass., abstain.

———

Mr. PINCKNEY's motion to strike out whole clause disagreed to without call of states.

Mr. BUTLER moved to give the legislature power of peace as they were to have that of war.

Mr. GERRY seconds him. Eight senators may possibly exercise the power if vested in that body, and fourteen if all should be present, and may consequently give up part of the United States. The Senate are more liable to be corrupted by an enemy than the whole legislature.

On the motion for adding "and peace" after "war": N.H., Mass., Conn., Pa., Del., Md., Va., N.C., S.C., Ga., no 10.

Adjourned.

TUESDAY, AUGUST 21.
IN CONVENTION

The five-person Committee of Detail included three southerners, which may explain why Article VII, Sections 4 and 6, were heavily tilted in favor of slavery

*and the South's economic interests: slaves were the only imports that the govern-
ment could not tax or regulate; there were no taxes on exports (the South's economy
depended almost entirely on its agricultural exports); and any acts regulating international shipping, or "navigation acts," would require a two-thirds vote of each
house (the South did not have its own shipping trade). These clauses proved controversial and reawakened tensions that were largely, but not entirely, sectional.*

———

Article VII, Section 4. [This section prohibited taxes on exports and
forbade the government from taxing or otherwise interfering with the
importation of slaves. The euphemism the committee used to describe
slaves was "such persons as the several states shall think proper to
admit."]

. . .

Mr. ELLSWORTH. There are solid reasons against Congress taxing
exports. (1) It will discourage industry, as taxes on imports discourage
luxury. (2) The produce of different states is such as to prevent uniformity in such taxes. There are indeed but a few articles that could be
taxed at all, as tobacco, rice, and indigo, and a tax on these alone would
be partial and unjust. (3) The taxing of exports would engender incur-
able jealousies.

Mr. WILLIAMSON. . . . He would never agree to this power. Should
it take place, it would destroy the last hope of an adoption of the plan.

Mr. G. MORRIS. If no tax can be laid on exports, an embargo cannot be laid, though in time of war such a measure may be of critical
importance. Tobacco, lumber, and livestock are three objects belonging to different states of which great advantage might be made by a
power to tax exports. To these may be added ginseng and masts for
ships, by which a tax might be thrown on other nations. The state of
the country also will change and render duties on exports, as skins,
beaver, and other peculiar raw materials, politic in the view of encouraging American manufactures.

Mr. BUTLER was strenuously opposed to a power over exports as
unjust and alarming to the staple states.

. . .

Mr. DICKINSON. The power of taxing exports may be inconvenient
at present, but it must be of dangerous consequence to prohibit it with

respect to all articles and forever. He thought it would be better to except particular articles from the power.

Mr. SHERMAN. It is best to prohibit the national legislature in all cases. The states will never give up all power over trade. An enumeration of particular articles would be difficult, invidious, and improper.

Mr. MADISON. As we ought to be governed by national and permanent views, it is a sufficient argument for giving the power over exports that a tax, though it may not be expedient at present, may be so hereafter. A proper regulation of exports may and probably will be necessary hereafter, and for the same purposes as the regulation of imports, viz., for revenue—domestic manufactures—and procuring equitable regulations from other nations. An embargo may be of absolute necessity and can alone be effectuated by the general authority. . . .

Mr. ELLSWORTH did not conceive an embargo by the Congress interdicted by this section.

Mr. McHENRY conceived that power to be included in the power of war.

Mr. WILSON. . . . To deny this power is to take from the common government half the regulation of trade. It was his opinion that a power over exports might be more effectual than that over imports in obtaining beneficial treaties of commerce.

Mr. GERRY was strenuously opposed to the power over exports. It might be made use of to compel the states to comply with the will of the general government and to grant it any new powers which might be demanded. We have given it more power already than we know how will be exercised. It will enable the general government to oppress the states as much as Ireland is oppressed by Great Britain.

Mr. FITZSIMONS would be against a tax on exports to be laid immediately but was for giving a power of laying the tax when a proper time may call for it. This would certainly be the case when America should become a manufacturing country. . . .

Col. MASON. If he were for reducing the states to mere corporations, as seemed to be the tendency of some arguments, he should be for subjecting their exports as well as imports to a power of general taxation. He went on a principle often advanced and in which he concurred, that "a majority when interested will oppress the minority." This maxim had been verified by our own legislature (of Virginia). If we compare the states in this point of view, the eight northern states have an interest different from the five southern states and have in one branch of the legislature thirty-six votes against twenty-nine, and in the other, in the proportion of eight against five. The southern states had, therefore, good ground for their suspicions. The case of exports was not the same with that of imports. The latter were the same throughout the states, the former very different.

Mr. CLYMER remarked that every state might reason with regard to its particular productions in the same manner as the southern states. The middle states may apprehend an oppression of their wheat, flour, provisions, etc., and with more reason, as these articles were exposed to a competition in foreign markets not incident to tobacco, rice, etc. They may apprehend also combinations against them between the eastern and southern states as much as the latter can apprehend them between the eastern and middle. . . .

. . .

Mr. MADISON, in order to require two-thirds of each house to tax exports—as a lesser evil than a total prohibition—moved to insert the words "unless by consent of two-thirds of the legislature."

Mr. WILSON seconds, and on this question, it passed in the negative: N.H., Mass., N.J., Pa., aye 4; Conn., Del., Md., Va., N.C., S.C., Ga., no 7.

Question on Section 4, Article VII, as far as to "no tax should be laid on exports," it passed in the affirmative: Conn., Del., Md., Va., N.C., S.C., Ga., aye 7; N.H., Mass., N.J., Pa., no 4.

———

Mr. MARTIN proposed to vary the Section 4, Article VII, so as to allow a prohibition or tax on the importation of slaves. (1) As five slaves are to be counted as three free men in the apportionment of representatives, such a clause would leave an encouragement to this traffic. (2) Slaves weakened one part of the Union which the other parts were bound to protect; the privilege of importing them was therefore unreasonable. (3) It was inconsistent with the principles of the revolution and dishonorable to the American character to have such a feature in the Constitution.

Mr. RUTLEDGE did not see how the importation of slaves could be encouraged by this section. He was not apprehensive of insurrections and would readily exempt the other states from the obligation to protect the southern against them. Religion and humanity had nothing to do with this question. Interest alone is the governing principle with nations. The true question at present is whether the southern states shall or shall not be parties to the Union. If the northern states consult their interest, they will not oppose the increase of slaves, which will increase the commodities of which they will become the carriers.

Mr. ELLSWORTH was for leaving the clause as it stands. Let every state import what it pleases. The morality or wisdom of slavery are considerations belonging to the states themselves. What enriches a part enriches the whole, and the states are the best judges of their particular interest. The old confederation had not meddled with this point, and he did not see any greater necessity for bringing it within the policy of the new one.

Mr. PINCKNEY. South Carolina can never receive the plan if it prohibits the slave trade. In every proposed extension of the powers of the Congress, that state has expressly and watchfully excepted that of meddling with the importation of Negroes. If the states be all left at liberty on this subject, South Carolina may perhaps by degrees do of herself what is wished, as Virginia and Maryland have already done.

Adjourned.

WEDNESDAY, AUGUST 22.
IN CONVENTION

The debate over regulation of the importation of slaves continued.

—

Article VII, Section 4, resumed.

Mr. SHERMAN was for leaving the clause as it stands. He disapproved of the slave trade, yet as the states were now possessed of the right to import slaves, as the public good did not require it to be taken from them, and as it was expedient to have as few objections as possible to the proposed scheme of government, he thought it best to leave the matter as we find it. He observed that the abolition of slavery seemed to be going on in the United States and that the good sense of the several states would probably by degrees complete it. He urged on the Convention the necessity of dispatching its business.

Col. MASON. This infernal traffic originated in the avarice of British merchants. The British government constantly checked the attempts of Virginia to put a stop to it. The present question concerns not the importing states alone but the whole Union. The evil of having slaves was experienced during the late war. Had slaves been treated as they might have been by the enemy, they would have proved dangerous instruments in their hands. But their folly dealt by the slaves as it did by the Tories. He mentioned the dangerous insurrections of the slaves in Greece and Sicily and the instructions given by Cromwell to the commissioners sent to Virginia to arm the servants and slaves in case other means of obtaining its submission should fail.

Maryland and Virginia, he said, had already prohibited the importation of slaves expressly. North Carolina had done the same in substance. All this would be in vain if South Carolina and Georgia be at liberty to import. The western people are already calling out for slaves for their new lands and will fill that country with slaves if they can be got through South Carolina and Georgia. Slavery discourages arts and manufactures. The poor despise labor when performed by slaves. They prevent the immigration of whites, who really enrich and strengthen a country. They produce the most pernicious effect on manners. Every master of slaves is born a petty tyrant. They bring the judgment of heaven on a country. As nations cannot be rewarded or punished in the next world they must be in this. By an inevitable chain of causes and effects, providence punishes national sins by national calamities. He lamented that some of our eastern brethren had from a lust of gain embarked in this nefarious traffic. As to the states being in possession of the right to import, this was the case with many other rights now to be properly given up. He held it essential in every point of view that the general government should have power to prevent the increase of slavery.

Mr. ELLSWORTH, as he had never owned a slave, could not judge of the effects of slavery on character. He said, however, that if it was to be considered in a moral light we ought to go farther and free those already in the country. As slaves also multiply so fast in Virginia and Maryland that it is cheaper to raise than import them, while in the sickly rice swamps foreign supplies are necessary, if we go no farther than is urged, we shall be unjust towards South Carolina and Georgia. Let us not intermeddle. As population increases, poor laborers will be so plenty as to render slaves useless. Slavery in time will not be a speck in our country. Provision is already made in Connecticut for abolishing it. And the abolition has already taken place in Massachusetts. As to the danger of insurrections from foreign influence, that will become a motive to kind treatment of the slaves.

Mr. PINCKNEY. If slavery be wrong, it is justified by the example of all the world. He cited the case of Greece, Rome, and other ancient states; the sanction given by France, England, Holland, and other modern states. In all ages, one half of mankind have been slaves. If the southern states were let alone, they will probably of themselves stop importations. He would himself as a citizen of South Carolina vote for it. An attempt to take away the right as proposed will produce serious objections to the Constitution which he wished to see adopted.

Gen. PINCKNEY declared it to be his firm opinion that if himself and all his colleagues were to sign the Constitution and use their personal influence, it would be of no avail towards obtaining the assent of their constituents. South Carolina and Georgia cannot do without slaves. As to Virginia [whose delegates had been arguing against importing slaves], she will gain by stopping the importations. Her slaves will rise in value, and she has more than she wants. It would be unequal to require South Carolina and Georgia to confederate on such unequal terms. . . . He contended that the importation of slaves would be for the interest of the whole Union. The more slaves, the more produce to employ the carrying trade; the more consumption also, and the more of this, the more of revenue for the common treasury. He admitted it to be reasonable that slaves should be dutied like other imports, but should consider a rejection of the clause as an exclusion of South Carolina from the Union.

Mr. BALDWIN had conceived national objects alone to be before the Convention, not such as, like the present, were of a local nature. Georgia was decided on this point. That state has always hitherto supposed a general government to be the pursuit of the central states, who wished to have a vortex for everything; that her distance would preclude her from equal advantage; and that she could not prudently purchase it by yielding national powers. From this, it might be understood in what light she would view an attempt to abridge one of her favorite prerogatives. If left to herself, she may probably put a stop to the evil. . . .

Mr. WILSON observed that if South Carolina and Georgia were

themselves disposed to get rid of the importation of slaves in a short time, as had been suggested, they would never refuse to unite because the importation might be prohibited. As the section now stands, all articles imported are to be taxed. Slaves alone are exempt. This is in fact a bounty on that article.

Mr. GERRY thought we had nothing to do with the conduct of the states as to slaves but ought to be careful not to give any sanction to it.

Mr. DICKINSON considered it as inadmissible on every principle of honor and safety that the importation of slaves should be authorized to the states by the Constitution. The true question was whether the national happiness would be promoted or impeded by the importation, and this question ought to be left to the national government, not to the states particularly interested. If England and France permit slavery, slaves are at the same time excluded from both those kingdoms. Greece and Rome were made unhappy by their slaves. He could not believe that the southern states would refuse to confederate on the account apprehended, especially as the power was not likely to be immediately exercised by the general government.

Mr. WILLIAMSON stated the law of North Carolina on the subject, to wit, that it did not directly prohibit the importation of slaves. It imposed a duty of £5 on each slave imported from Africa, £10 on each from elsewhere, and £50 on each from a state licensing manumission. He thought the southern states could not be members of the Union if the clause should be rejected, and that it was wrong to force anything down not absolutely necessary and which any state must disagree to.

Mr. KING thought the subject should be considered in a political light only. If two states will not agree to the Constitution as stated on one side, he could affirm with equal belief on the other that great and equal opposition would be experienced from the other states. He remarked on the exemption of slaves from duty while every other import was subjected to it as an inequality that could not fail to strike the commercial sagacity of the northern and middle states.

Mr. LANGDON was strenuous for giving the power to the general government. He could not with a good conscience leave it with the states, who could then go on with the traffic without being restrained by the opinions here given that they will themselves cease to import slaves.

Gen. PINCKNEY thought himself bound to declare candidly that he did not think South Carolina would stop her importations of slaves in any short time, but only stop them occasionally as she now does. He moved to commit the clause that slaves might be made liable to an equal tax with other imports, which he thought right and which would remove one difficulty that had been started.

Mr. RUTLEDGE. If the Convention thinks that North Carolina, South Carolina, and Georgia will ever agree to the plan unless their right to import slaves be untouched, the expectation is vain. The people of those states will never be such fools as to give up so important an interest. He was strenuous against striking out the section and seconded the motion of General Pinckney for a commitment.

Mr. G. MORRIS wished the whole subject to be committed, including the clauses relating to taxes on exports and to a navigation act. These things may form a bargain among the northern and southern states.

Mr. BUTLER declared that he never would agree to the power of taxing exports.

Mr. SHERMAN said it was better to let the southern states import slaves than to part with them, if they made that a sine qua non. He was opposed to a tax on slaves imported as making the matter worse, because it implied they were property. He acknowledged that if the power of prohibiting the importation should be given to the general government that it would be exercised. He thought it would be its duty to exercise the power.

Mr. READ was for the commitment, provided the clause concerning taxes on exports should also be committed.

Mr. SHERMAN observed that that clause had been agreed to and therefore could not be committed.

Mr. RANDOLPH was for committing in order that some middle ground might, if possible, be found. He could never agree to the clause as it stands. He would sooner risk the Constitution. He dwelt on the dilemma to which the Convention was exposed. By agreeing to the clause, it would revolt the Quakers, the Methodists, and many others in the states having no slaves. On the other hand, two states might be lost to the Union. Let us then, he said, try the chance of a commitment.

On the question for committing the remaining part of Sections 4 and 5 of Article VII: Conn., N.J., Md., Va., N.C., S.C., Ga., aye 7; N.H., Pa., Del., no 3; Mass., abstain.

Mr. PINCKNEY and Mr. LANGDON moved to commit Section 6, as to navigation act by two-thirds of each house.

Mr. GORHAM did not see the propriety of it. Is it meant to require a greater proportion of votes? He desired it to be remembered that the eastern states had no motive to Union but a commercial one. They were able to protect themselves. They were not afraid of external danger and did not need the aid of the southern states.

Mr. WILSON wished for a commitment in order to reduce the proportion of votes required.

Mr. ELLSWORTH was for taking the plan as it is. This widening of opinions has a threatening aspect. If we do not agree on this middle and moderate ground, he was afraid we should lose two states with such others as may be disposed to stand aloof; should fly into a variety of shapes and directions; and most probably into several confederations, and not without bloodshed.

On question for committing section as to navigation act to a member from each state: N.H., Mass., Pa., Del., Md., Va., N.C., S.C., Ga., aye 9; Conn., N.J., no 2.

The committee appointed were Mr. Langdon, King, Johnson, Livingston, Clymer, Dickinson, L. Martin, Madison, Williamson, C. C. Pinckney, and Baldwin.

The Convention also referred unresolved portions of Article VII, Sections 4 and 5, to this eleven-member committee. Meanwhile, it continued to work through the twenty-three numbered articles in the Constitution drafted by the Committee of Detail. On August 23 it came to Article VIII: a supremacy clause based on the one approved by the Convention on July 17. The Committee of Detail had strengthened this clause slightly. Where Martin's version followed the New Jersey Plan by instructing state judges that congressional acts were "the supreme law of the several states" and thus preempted state laws, the new version stated that acts passed by Congress also preempted state constitutions. On this day John Rutledge, a plantation owner and London-trained lawyer, proposed adding "this Constitution" to the beginning of the article. His amendment, which passed, made it clear that the Constitution itself (as well as congressional acts) preempted state laws and constitutions.

On August 24, the eleven-member committee reported its recommendations to the Convention concerning the major outstanding issues relating to congres-

sional power over trade. With respect to the slave trade, it recommended a compromise forbidding Congress to ban the importation of slaves until 1800. The following day, Charles Cotesworth Pinckney of South Carolina moved that the date be changed to 1808. The Convention approved this motion, with New Jersey, Pennsylvania, Delaware, and Virginia voting no. With respect to statutes regulating international shipping, or "navigation acts," the committee recommended striking the southern-inspired restriction requiring a two-thirds majority in each house for their passage, and the Convention passed it on August 29.

On August 28, as a concession to the South, the Convention unanimously approved a requirement that fugitive slaves in any state "be delivered up to the person justly claiming their service or labor."

Thursday, August 30, 1787.
IN CONVENTION

The Convention reached Article XXI on August 30. This article and the next one, both dealing with the process for ratifying the Constitution, raised practical and theoretical concerns that occupied the delegates for parts of two days.

———

Article XXI taken up, viz., "The ratifications of the conventions of
_____ states shall be sufficient for organizing this Constitution."
. . .
Mr. RANDOLPH was for filling the blank with "nine," that being a respectable majority of the whole and being a number made familiar by the constitution of the existing Congress.
. . .
Mr. MADISON remarked that if the blank should be filled with "seven," "eight," or "nine," the Constitution as it stands might be put in force over the whole body of the people though less than a majority of them [measured by population] should ratify it.

Mr. WILSON. As the Constitution stands, the states only which ratify can be bound. We must, he said, in this case go to the original powers of society. The house on fire must be extinguished without a scrupulous regard to ordinary rights.

Mr. BUTLER was in favor of "nine." He revolted at the idea that one or two states should restrain the rest from consulting their safety.

Mr. CARROLL moved to fill the blank with "the thirteen," unanimity being necessary to dissolve the existing confederacy, which had been unanimously established.

Mr. KING thought this amendment [by Carroll] necessary, otherwise, as the Constitution now stands, it will operate on the whole though ratified by a part only.

Adjourned.

FRIDAY, AUGUST 31, 1787.
IN CONVENTION

Debate continued on Article XXI, "The ratifications of the conventions of _____ states shall be sufficient for organizing this Constitution."

———

Mr. KING moved to add to the end of Article XXI the words "between the said states," so as to confine the operation of the government to the states ratifying it. [King's motion passed with only Maryland opposed.]

. . .

Mr. G. MORRIS moved to strike out "conventions of the" after "ratifications," leaving the states to pursue their own modes of ratification.

. . .

Mr. KING thought that striking out "conventions" as the requisite mode was equivalent to giving up the business altogether. Conventions alone, which will avoid all the obstacles from the complicated formation of the legislatures, will succeed, and if not positively required by the plan, its enemies will oppose that mode.

Mr. G. MORRIS said he meant to facilitate the adoption of the plan by leaving the modes approved by the several state constitutions to be followed.

Mr. MADISON considered it best to require conventions; among other reasons for this, that the powers given to the general government being taken from the state governments, the [state] legislatures would be more disinclined than conventions composed in part at least of other men, and if disinclined, they could devise modes apparently promoting but really thwarting the ratification. . . . The people were, in fact, the fountain of all power, and by resorting to them, all difficulties were got over. They could alter constitutions as they pleased.

. . .

Mr. L. MARTIN insisted on a reference to the state legislatures. He urged the danger of commotions from a resort to the people and to first principles in which the governments might be on one side and the people on the other. He was apprehensive of no such consequences, however, in Maryland, whether the legislature or the people should be appealed to. Both of them would be generally against the Constitution. . . .

. . .

On Mr. Gouverneur Morris's motion to strike out "conventions of the," it was negatived: Conn., Pa., Md., Ga., aye 4; N.H., Mass., N.J., Del., Va., S.C., no 6.

On filling the blank in Article XXI with "thirteen" [i.e., ratifying the Constitution would have required the unanimous consent of the states], moved by Mr. Carroll and Martin: all no except Maryland.

. . .

On question for "nine": N.H., Mass., Conn., N.J., Pa., Del., Md., Ga., aye 8; Va., N.C., S.C., no 3.

Article XXI as amended was then agreed to by all the states, Maryland excepted. . . .

———

Article XXII taken up, to wit, "This Constitution shall be laid before the United States in Congress assembled for their approbation; and it is the opinion of this Convention that it should be afterwards submitted to a convention chosen in each state under the recommendation of its legislature, in order to receive the ratification of such convention."

Mr. G. MORRIS . . . [stressed] the necessity of calling conventions in order to prevent enemies to the plan from giving it the go by. When it first appears with the sanction of the Convention, the people will be favorable to it. By degrees, the state officers and those interested in the state governments will intrigue and turn the people against it.

Mr. L. MARTIN believed Mr. Morris to be right that after a while the people would be against it, but for a different reason from that alleged. He believed they would not ratify it unless hurried into it by surprise.

Mr. GERRY enlarged on the idea of Mr. L. Martin, in which he concurred, represented the system as full of vices and dwelt on the impropriety of destroying the existing confederation without the unanimous consent of the parties to it.

. . .

Mr. GERRY moved to postpone Article XXII.

Col. MASON seconded the motion, declaring that he would sooner chop off his right hand than put it to the Constitution as it now stands. He wished to see some points not yet decided brought to a decision before being compelled to give a final opinion on this article. Should these points be improperly settled, his wish would then be to bring the whole subject before another general convention.

Mr. G. MORRIS was ready for a postponement. He had long wished for another convention that will have the firmness to provide a vigorous government, which we are afraid to do.

Mr. RANDOLPH stated his idea to be, in case the final form of the Constitution should not permit him to accede to it, that the state conventions should be at liberty to propose amendments to be submitted to another general convention, which may reject or incorporate them as shall be judged proper.

On the question for postponing: N.J., Md., N.C., aye 3; N.H., Mass., Conn., Pa., Del., Va., S.C., Ga., no 8.

On the question on Article XXII: N.H., Mass., Conn., N.J., Pa., Del., Va., N.C., S.C., Ga., aye 10; Md., no 1.

After finishing its first run through the draft Constitution, the Convention revisited various unresolved issues that it had passed on to committees. The weary delegates seem to have relied heavily on the recommendations of these committees in the days that remained rather than discuss matters at length, though some of this impression might come from Madison's clearly diminishing enthusiasm for taking notes.

Among the unresolved issues, perhaps none was more tangled than how to choose the president. The committee revisiting this issue proposed that the president would serve for four-year terms and could run for reelection. It revived, in modified form, the scheme that the Convention had considered in July of having state electors vote for the president. Under the modified scheme, each state legislature would determine a method to choose a number of electors equal to the state's representation in Congress. Each elector would make two choices for president, one of whom would have to be from another state. The ballots would be sent to the Senate, which would tally them. The candidate with a majority of votes would become president; the second-place candidate would take the newly conceived office of vice president. If no candidate had a majority, which delegates assumed would typically be the case, the Senate would choose from the five candidates with the most votes. Candidates from large states would likely gain the most votes, but the large-state advantage in the electoral college would be absent in the Senate. By this point, most of the delegates had accepted the idea of presidential electors, but they worried that this cumbersome process might still give the Senate too much influence over the president.

WEDNESDAY, SEPTEMBER 5.
IN CONVENTION

. . .

The report made yesterday as to the appointment of the executive being taken up.

Mr. PINCKNEY renewed his opposition to the mode, arguing (1) that the electors will not have sufficient knowledge of the fittest men and will be swayed by an attachment to the eminent men of their respective states. Hence, secondly, the dispersion of the votes would leave the appointment with the Senate, and as the president's reappointment will thus depend on the Senate he will be the mere creature of that body. (3) He will combine with the Senate against the House of Representatives. (4) This change in the mode of election was meant to get rid of the ineligibility of the president a second time, whereby he will become fixed for life under the auspices of the Senate.

. . .

Col. MASON . . . would state his objections to the mode proposed by the committee. (1) It puts the appointment in fact into the hands of the Senate, as it will rarely happen that a majority of the whole votes will fall on any one candidate; and as the existing president will always be one of the five highest, his reappointment will of course depend on the Senate. (2) Considering the powers of the president and those of the Senate, if a coalition should be established between these two branches, they will be able to subvert the Constitution. The great objection with him would be removed by depriving the Senate of the eventual election. . . .

Mr. WILLIAMSON. . . . Referring the appointment to the Senate lays a certain foundation for corruption and aristocracy.

Mr. G. MORRIS thought the point of less consequence than it was supposed on both sides. It is probable that a majority of votes will fall on the same man. As each elector is to give two votes, more than one-fourth will give a majority. Besides, as one vote is to be given to a man out of the state and as this vote will not be thrown away, one-half [of] the votes will fall on characters eminent and generally known. Again, if the president shall have given satisfaction, the votes will turn on him, of course, and a majority of them will reappoint him, without resort to the Senate. If he should be disliked, all disliking him would take care to unite their votes so as to ensure his being supplanted.

Col. MASON. Those who think there is no danger of there not being a majority for the same person in the first instance ought to give up the point to those who think otherwise.

Mr. SHERMAN reminded the opponents of the new mode proposed that if the small states had the advantage in the Senate's deciding among the five highest candidates, the large states would have in fact the nomination of these candidates.

. . .

Mr. WILSON moved to strike out "Senate" and insert the word "Legislature."

Mr. MADISON considered it as a primary object to render an eventual resort to any part of the legislature improbable. He was apprehensive that the proposed alteration would turn the attention of the large states too much to the appointment of candidates instead of aiming at an effectual appointment of the officer, as the large states would predominate in the legislature, which would have the final choice out of the candidates. Whereas if the Senate, in which the small states predominate, should have this final choice, the concerted effort of the large states would be to make the appointment in the first instance conclusive.

Mr. RANDOLPH. We have in some revolutions of this plan made a bold stroke for monarchy. We are now doing the same for an aristocracy. He dwelt on the tendency of such an influence in the Senate over the election of the president, in addition to its other powers, to convert that body into a real and dangerous aristocracy.

Mr. DICKINSON was in favor of giving the eventual election to the legislature instead of the Senate. It was too much influence to be super-added to that body.

On the question moved by Mr. Wilson: Pa., Va., S.C., aye 3; Mass., Conn., N.J., Del., Md., N.C., Ga., no 7; N.H., divided.

. . .

Mr. WILLIAMSON. There are seven states which do not contain one-third of the people. If the Senate are to appoint, less than one-sixth of the people will have the power.

. . .

Col. MASON. As the mode of appointment is now regulated, he could not forbear expressing his opinion that it is utterly inadmissible. He would prefer the government of Prussia to one which will put all power into the hands of seven or eight men and fix an aristocracy worse than absolute monarchy. . . .

The house adjourned.

THURSDAY, SEPTEMBER 6.
IN CONVENTION

The debate over how to choose the president continued. The Convention ultimately decided to have the House of Representatives, voting by state, elect the president from the top five candidates if no candidate achieved a majority of the electoral vote. The Senate thus lost its role in choosing the president. Large states, however, whose candidates were most likely to do well in the electoral college, lost the voting advantage that they otherwise enjoyed in the House of Representatives.

———

Mr. WILSON said that he had weighed carefully the report of the committee for remodeling the constitution of the executive, and on combining it with other parts of the plan, he was obliged to consider the whole as having a dangerous tendency to aristocracy, as throwing a dangerous power into the hands of the Senate. They will have, in fact, the appointment of the president, and through his dependence on them, the virtual appointment to offices; among others, the offices of the judiciary department. They are to make treaties and they are to try all impeachments. In allowing them thus to make the executive and judiciary appointments, to be the court of impeachments, and to make treaties which are to be laws of the land, the legislative, executive, and judiciary powers are all blended in one branch of the government. The power of making treaties involves the case of subsidies, and here, as an additional evil, foreign influence is to be dreaded. According to the plan as it now stands, the president will not be the man of the people as he ought to be, but the minion of the Senate. He cannot even appoint a tide-waiter without the Senate. . . .

Mr. G. MORRIS. . . . The Senate, he observed, had a voice in appointing the president out of all the citizens of the United States; by this they were limited to five candidates previously nominated to them, with a probability of being barred altogether by the successful ballot of the electors. Here surely was no increase of power. They are now to appoint judges nominated to them by the president. Before they had the appointment without any agency whatever of the president. Here again surely no additional power. If they are to make treaties as the plan now stands, the power was the same in the printed plan. If they are to try impeachments, the judges must have been triable by them before. Wherein then lay the dangerous tendency of the innovations to establish an aristocracy in the Senate?

. . .

Mr. HAMILTON said that he had been restrained from entering into the discussions by his dislike of the scheme of government in general; but as he meant to support the plan to be recommended as better than nothing, he wished in this place to offer a few remarks. . . . Considering the different views of different states, and the different districts, northern, middle, and southern, he concurred with those who thought that the votes would not be concentered [that is, that no presidential candidate would get a majority of the electors' votes] and that the appointment would consequently in the present mode devolve on the Senate. The nomination to offices will give great weight to the president. Here then is a mutual connection and influence that will perpetuate the president and aggrandize both him and the Senate.

What is to be the remedy? He saw none better than to let the highest number of ballots, whether a majority or not, appoint the president. What was the objection to this? Merely that too small a number might appoint. But as the plan stands, the Senate may take the candidate having the smallest number of votes and make him president.

. . .

Mr. WILLIAMSON suggested as better than an eventual choice by the Senate that this choice should be made by the legislature, voting by states and not per capita.

Mr. SHERMAN suggested the House of Representatives as preferable to the legislature and moved, accordingly, to strike out the words "the Senate shall immediately choose," etc., and insert "the House of Representatives shall immediately choose by ballot one of them for president, the members from each state having one vote."

Col. MASON liked the latter mode best as lessening the aristocratic influence of the Senate.

On the motion of Mr. Sherman: N.H., Mass., Conn., N.J., Pa., Md., Va., N.C., S.C., Ga., aye 10; Del., no.

. . .

FRIDAY, SEPTEMBER 7.
IN CONVENTION

Having settled on a means of selecting the president and particulars as to the president's term, the delegates moved on to unresolved aspects of the executive branch, including the post of vice president. Hugh Williamson observed that the vice president "was introduced merely for the sake of a valuable mode of election, which required the two to be chosen at the same time." The Convention made the vice president the presiding officer of the Senate because, as Roger Sherman put it, otherwise "he would be without employment." In a significant expansion of the president's powers, a committee recommended shifting the powers to make treaties and appoint ambassadors and judges from the Senate to the president, subject to "the advice and consent of the Senate." It was a sign of how much the Convention's conception of the presidency had grown that the only recommendation that sparked protracted debate was the committee's proposal that treaties require a two-thirds majority in the Senate for passage.

Section 4. "The president by and with the advice and consent of the Senate shall have power to make treaties"—"But no treaty shall be made without the consent of two-thirds of the members present"—this last being before the house.

Mr. WILSON thought it objectionable to require the concurrence of two-thirds, which puts it in nineteen [senators], the power of a minority, to control the will of a majority.

Mr. KING concurred in the objection, remarking that as the executive was here joined in the business, there was a check which did not exist in Congress, where the concurrence of two-thirds was required.

Mr. MADISON moved to insert after the word "treaty" the words "except treaties of peace," allowing these to be made with less difficulty than other treaties. It was agreed to nem. con.

Mr. MADISON then moved to authorize a concurrence of two-thirds of the Senate to make treaties of peace, without the concurrence of the president. The president, he said, would necessarily derive so much power and importance from a state of war that he might be tempted, if authorized, to impede a treaty of peace.

Mr. BUTLER seconded the motion.

Mr. GORHAM thought the precaution unnecessary, as the means of carrying on the war would not be in the hands of the president but of the legislature.

Mr. G. MORRIS thought the power of the president in this case harmless, and that no peace ought to be made without the concurrence of the president, who was the general guardian of the national interests.

Madison's second motion lost (3 aye to 8 no) and the proposed text as amended passed (8 aye to 3 no). The next day, the delegates reconsidered and rejected Madison's amendment relating to treaties of peace. The Convention again increased the president's authority on September 14 when it transferred the power to appoint the government's treasurer from Congress to the president.

MONDAY, SEPTEMBER 10.
IN CONVENTION

Reaching the final articles of the Committee of Detail's draft document, the Convention took up issues of amending and ratifying the Constitution.

———

Mr. GERRY moved to reconsider Article XIX, viz., "On the application of the legislatures of two-thirds of the states in the Union for an amendment of this Constitution, the legislature of the United States shall call a convention for that purpose." This Constitution, he said, is to be paramount to the state constitutions. It follows, hence, from this article that two-thirds of the states may obtain a convention, a majority of which can bind the Union to innovations that may subvert the state constitutions altogether. He asked whether this was a situation proper to be run into.

Mr. HAMILTON seconded the motion, but, he said, with a different view from Mr. Gerry.... The state legislatures will not apply for alterations but with a view to increase their own powers. The national legislature will be the first to perceive and will be most sensible to the necessity of amendments, and ought also to be empowered, whenever two-thirds of each branch should concur, to call a convention. There could be no danger in giving this power, as the people would finally decide in the case.

. . .

Mr. MADISON moved to postpone the consideration of the amended proposition in order to take up the following.

"The legislature of the United States whenever two-thirds of both houses shall deem necessary, or on the application of two-thirds of the legislatures of the several states, shall propose amendments to this Constitution, which shall be valid to all intents and purposes as part thereof, when the same shall have been ratified by three-fourths at least of the legislatures of the several states, or by conventions in three-fourths thereof, as one or the other mode of ratification may be proposed by the legislature of the United States."

Mr. HAMILTON seconded the motion.

Mr. RUTLEDGE said he never could agree to give a power by which the articles relating to slaves might be altered by the states not interested in that property and prejudiced against it. In order to obviate this objection, these words were added to the proposition: "provided that no amendments which may be made prior to the year 1808 shall in any manner affect the fourth and fifth sections of the VII article." The postponement being agreed to.

On the question on the proposition of Mr. Madison and Mr. Hamilton as amended: Mass., Conn., N.J., Pa., Md., Va., N.C., S.C., Ga., aye 9; Del., no 1; N.H., divided.

———

Mr. GERRY moved to reconsider Articles XXI and XXII [relating to the process for ratifying the Constitution], from the latter of which "for the approbation of Congress" had been struck out. He objected to proceeding to change the government without the approbation of [the Confederation] Congress as being improper and giving just umbrage to that body. He repeated his objections also to an annulment of the confederation with so little scruple or formality.

Mr. HAMILTON concurred with Mr. Gerry as to the indecorum of not requiring the approbation of [the Confederation] Congress. He considered this as a necessary ingredient in the transaction. He thought it wrong also to allow nine states, as provided by Article XXI, to institute a new government on the ruins of the existing one.

. . .

Mr. RANDOLPH declared if no change should be made in this part of the plan, he should be obliged to dissent from the whole of it. He had from the beginning, he said, been convinced that radical changes in the system of the Union were necessary. Under this conviction, he had brought forward a set of republican propositions as the basis and outline of a reform. These republican propositions had, however, much to his regret, been widely and, in his opinion, irreconcilably departed from. In this state of things, it was his idea, and he accordingly meant to propose, that the state conventions should be at liberty to offer amendments to the plan, and that these should be submitted to a second general convention with full power to settle the Constitution finally. He did not expect to succeed in this proposition, but the discharge of his duty in making the attempt would give quiet to his own mind.

. . .

Mr. GERRY urged the indecency and pernicious tendency of dissolving in so slight a manner the solemn obligations of the Articles of Confederation. If nine out of thirteen can dissolve the compact, six out of nine will be just as able to dissolve the new one hereafter.

. . .

Mr. WILSON . . . declared it to be worse than folly to rely on the concurrence of the Rhode Island members of [the Confederation] Congress in the plan. Maryland has voted on this floor for requiring the unanimous assent of the thirteen states to the proposed change in the federal system. New York has not been represented for a long time past in the Convention. Many individual deputies from other states have spoken much against the plan. Under these circumstances, can it be safe to make the assent of [the Confederation] Congress necessary? After spending four or five months in the laborious and arduous task of forming a government for our country, we are ourselves at the close throwing insuperable obstacles in the way of its success.

. . .

Mr. WILLIAMSON and Mr. GERRY moved to reinstate the words "for the approbation of Congress" in Article XXII which was disagreed to nem. con.

Having worked through the Committee of Detail's draft Constitution and made various amendments to it, the Convention referred the entire document on September 10 to a Committee of Style and Arrangement to polish the text. The committee consisted of five members, all noted for their drafting skills: William Samuel Johnson, Alexander Hamilton, Gouverneur Morris, James Madison, and Rufus King. On September 12, the committee submitted its finished product to the Convention (see Appendix D, the final version of the Constitution, but for the most part identical to this draft). The document opened with the bold and lyrical preamble that has become the Constitution's hallmark ("We the People of the United States, in order to form a more perfect Union . . .") and consolidated the twenty-three articles approved by the Convention into the seven more comprehensive ones that we know today. Having worked through the material three times—once as a Committee of the Whole, once in Convention considering the Virginia Plan as amended by the Committee of the Whole, and again in Convention considering the Committee of Detail's draft Constitution—and with many of the delegates eager to go home, only four days were spent reviewing and revis-

ing this final document. Few amendments were proposed and fewer accepted, but the Convention still made some important decisions in the course of its discussions.

WEDNESDAY, SEPTEMBER 12.
IN CONVENTION

After the Committee of Style presented its draft Constitution, the Convention reconsidered the clause in Article I, Section 7, requiring a three-fourths majority to override a presidential veto.

———

Dr. JOHNSON from the Committee of Style and Arrangement reported a digest of the plan, of which printed copies were ordered to be furnished to the members....

Mr. WILLIAMSON moved to reconsider the clause requiring three-fourths of each house to overrule the negative of the president, in order to strike out three-fourths and insert two-thirds. He had, he remarked, himself proposed three-fourths instead of two-thirds, but he had since been convinced that the latter proportion was the best. The former puts too much in the power of the president.

Mr. SHERMAN was of the same opinion, adding that the states would not like to see so small a minority and the president prevailing over the general voice. In making laws, regard should be had to the sense of the people, who are to be bound by them, and it was more probable that a single man should mistake or betray this sense than the legislature.

Mr. G. MORRIS. Considering the difference between the two proportions numerically, it amounts in one house to two members only, and in the other to not more than five, according to the numbers of which the legislature is at first to be composed. It is the interest, moreover, of the distant states to prefer three-fourths as they will be oftenest absent and need the interposing check of the president. The excess rather than the deficiency of laws was to be dreaded. The example of New York shows that two-thirds is not sufficient to answer the purpose.

. . .

Mr. WILLIAMSON was less afraid of too few than of too many laws. He was most of all afraid that the repeal of bad laws might be rendered too difficult by requiring three-fourths to overcome the dissent of the president.

. . .

Mr. PINCKNEY was warmly in opposition to three-fourths as putting a dangerous power in the hands of a few senators headed by the president.

Mr. MADISON. When three-fourths was agreed to, the president was to be elected by the legislature and for seven years. He is now to be elected by the people and for four years. . . . We must compare the danger from the weakness of two-thirds with the danger from the strength of three-fourths. He thought on the whole the former was the greater. As to the difficulty of repeals, it was probable that in doubtful cases the policy would soon take place of limiting the duration of laws so as to require renewal instead of repeal.

The reconsideration being agreed to. On the question to insert "two-thirds" in place of "three-fourths": Conn., N.J., Md., N.C., S.C., Ga., aye 6; Mass., Pa., Del., Va., no 4; N.H., divided.

Article III, Section 2, allowed for jury trials for criminal cases in federal courts, but not for civil cases. This absence led Elbridge Gerry and George Mason to make a broader motion for the preparation of a Bill of Rights. The motion was quickly dismissed as unnecessary, a dismissal that would almost sink the Constitution in the state ratifying conventions.

Mr. WILLIAMSON observed to the house that no provision was yet made for juries in civil cases and suggested the necessity of it.

Mr. GORHAM. It is not possible to discriminate equity cases from those in which juries are proper. The representatives of the people may be safely trusted in this matter.

Mr. GERRY urged the necessity of juries to guard against corrupt judges. He proposed that the committee last appointed should be directed to provide a clause for securing the trial by juries.

Col. MASON perceived the difficulty mentioned by Mr. Gorham. The jury cases cannot be specified. A general principle laid down on this and some other points would be sufficient. He wished the plan had been prefaced with a Bill of Rights and would second a motion if made for the purpose. It would give great quiet to the people, and with the aid of the state declarations, a bill might be prepared in a few hours.

Mr. GERRY concurred in the idea and moved for a committee to prepare a Bill of Rights.

Col. MASON seconded the motion.

Mr. SHERMAN was for securing the rights of the people where requisite. The state declarations of rights are not repealed by this Constitution and, being in force, are sufficient. There are many cases where juries are proper which cannot be discriminated. The legislature may be safely trusted.

Col. MASON. The laws of the United States are to be paramount to state bills of rights.

On the question for a committee to prepare a Bill of Rights: N.H., Conn., N.J., Pa., Del., Md., Va., N.C., S.C., Ga., no 10; Mass., absent.

. . .

SATURDAY, SEPTEMBER 15.
IN CONVENTION

On their last working day, the delegates made a variety of corrections and changes to the Constitution. Incorporating provisions approved by the Convention, the Constitution gave Congress the power "to lay and collect taxes, duties, imposts, and excises" and "to regulate commerce with foreign nations." It specifically barred states from laying duties on imports or exports without congressional consent. A proposal to qualify this restriction led to a brief exchange between Gouverneur Morris and James Madison on the negative reach of congressional power to regulate commerce. The extent of that power would become a significant and much litigated issue in American constitutional law.

———

Mr. MCHENRY and Mr. CARROLL moved that "no state shall be restrained from laying duties of tonnage for the purpose of clearing harbors and erecting lighthouses."

Col. MASON, in support of this, explained and urged the situation of the Chesapeake, which peculiarly required expenses of this sort.

Mr. G. MORRIS. The states are not restrained from laying tonnage as the Constitution now stands. The exception proposed will imply the contrary and will put the states in a worse condition than the gentleman wishes.

Mr. MADISON. Whether the states are now restrained from laying tonnage duties depends on the extent of the power "to regulate commerce." These terms are vague but seem to exclude this power of the states. They may certainly be restrained by treaty. He observed that there were other objects for tonnage duties as the support of seamen. He was more and more convinced that the regulation of commerce was in its nature indivisible and ought to be wholly under one authority.

Mr. SHERMAN. The power of the United States to regulate trade being supreme can control interferences of the state regulations when such interferences happen, so that there is no danger to be apprehended from a concurrent jurisdiction.

Mr. LANGDON insisted that the regulation of tonnage was an essential part of the regulation of trade and that the states ought to have nothing to do with it.

On motion "that no state shall lay any duty on tonnage without the consent of Congress": N.H., Mass., N.J., Del., Md., S.C., aye 6; Pa., Va., N.C., Ga., no 4; Conn., divided.

The Committee of Style's draft of the fugitive slave clause (Art. IV, Sec. 2, Par. 3) referred to persons "legally held to service or labor in one state." Delegates objected on this day that the adjective "legally" made it sound as if the Constitution was claiming that slavery was morally legal. Consequently, "under the laws thereof" was substituted for "legally" and placed after "state." This was the final expression of antislavery sentiment at the Convention.

With deliberations drawing to a close, George Mason made a last attempt to limit the legislature's power to restrict international shipping. When that failed, he joined Randolph and Gerry in voicing opposition to the overall Constitution. On the roll call, however, the states approved the Constitution unanimously.

Col. MASON, expressing his discontent at the power given to Congress by a bare majority to pass navigation acts, which, he said, would not only enhance the freight, a consequence he did not so much regard, but would enable a few rich merchants in Philadelphia, New York, and

Boston to monopolize the staples of the southern states and reduce their value perhaps 50 percent, moved a further proviso "that no law in nature of a navigation act be passed before the year 1808 without the consent of two-thirds of each branch of the legislature."

On this motion: Md., Va., Ga., aye 3; N.H., Mass., Conn., N.J., Pa., Del., S.C., no 7; N.C., absent.

———

Mr. RANDOLPH, animadverting on the indefinite and dangerous power given by the Constitution to Congress, expressing the pain he felt at differing from the body of the Convention on the close of the great and awful subject of their labors and anxiously wishing for some accommodating expedient which would relieve him from his embarrassments, made a motion importing "that amendments to the plan might be offered by the state conventions, which should be submitted to and finally decided on by another general convention." Should this proposition be disregarded, it would, he said, be impossible for him to put his name to the instrument. Whether he should oppose it afterwards he would not then decide, but he would not deprive himself of the freedom to do so in his own state, if that course should be prescribed by his final judgment.

Col. MASON seconded and followed Mr. Randolph in animadversions on the dangerous power and structure of the government, concluding that it would end either in monarchy or a tyrannical aristocracy—which, he was in doubt, but one or other, he was sure. This Constitution had been formed without the knowledge or idea of the people. A second convention will know more of the sense of the people and be able to provide a system more consonant to it. It was improper to say to the people, Take this or nothing. As the Constitution now stands, he could neither give it his support nor [his] vote in Virginia, and he could not sign here what he could not support there. With the expedient of another convention as proposed, he could sign.

Mr. PINCKNEY. These declarations from members so respectable at the close of this important scene give a peculiar solemnity to the present moment. He descanted on the consequences of calling forth the deliberations and amendments of the different states on the subject of government at large. Nothing but confusion and contrariety could spring from the experiment. The states will never agree in their plans, and the deputies to a second convention coming together under the discordant impressions of their constituents will never agree. Conventions are serious things and ought not to be repeated. He was not without objections as well as others to the plan. He objected to the contemptible weakness and dependence of the executive. He objected to the power of a majority only of Congress over commerce, but apprehending the danger of a general confusion and an ultimate decision by the sword, he should give the plan his support.

Mr. GERRY stated the objections which determined him to withhold his name from the Constitution: (1) the duration and reeligibility of the Senate; (2) the power of the House of Representatives to conceal their journals; (3) the power of Congress over the places of election; (4) the unlimited power of Congress over their own compensation; (5) Massachusetts has not a due share of representatives allotted to her; (6) three-fifths of the blacks are to be represented as if they were freemen; (7) under the power over commerce, monopolies may be established; (8) the vice president being made head of the Senate.

He could, however, he said, get over all these if the rights of the citizens were not rendered insecure (1) by the general power of the legislature to make what laws they may please to call necessary and proper, (2) raise armies and money without limit, (3) to establish a tribunal without juries, which will be a star-chamber as to civil cases. Under such a view of the Constitution, the best that could be done, he conceived, was to provide for a second general convention.

On the question on the proposition of Mr. Randolph: all the states answered no.

On the question to agree to the Constitution, as amended: all the states, aye.

The Constitution was then ordered to be engrossed.

And the house adjourned.

MONDAY, SEPTEMBER 17.
IN CONVENTION

The engrossed [or formal Convention-approved] Constitution being read.

Dr. FRANKLIN rose with a speech in his hand, which he had reduced to writing for his own convenience, and which Mr. Wilson read in the words following.

Mr. President, I confess that there are several parts of this Constitution which I do not at present approve, but I am not sure I shall never approve them, for having lived long, I have experienced many instances of being obliged by better information or fuller consideration to change opinions, even on important subjects, which I once thought right but found to be otherwise. It is, therefore, that the older I grow, the more apt I am to doubt my own judgment and to pay more respect to the judgment of others....

In these sentiments, sir, I agree to this Constitution with all its faults, if they are such, because I think a general government necessary for us, and there is no form of government but what may be a blessing to the people if well administered, and believe farther that this is likely to be well administered for a course of years, and can only end in despotism, as other forms have done before it, when the people shall become so corrupted as to need despotic government, being incapable of any other.

I doubt too whether any other convention we can obtain may be able to make a better Constitution. For when you assemble a number of men to have the advantage of their joint wisdom, you inevitably assemble with those men all their prejudices, their passions, their errors of opinion, their local interests, and their selfish views. From such an assembly can a perfect production be expected? It therefore astonishes me, sir, to find this system approaching so near to perfection as it does; and I think it will astonish our enemies, who are waiting with confidence to hear that our councils are confounded like those of the builders of Babel and that our states are on the point of separation, only to meet hereafter for the purpose of cutting one another's throats.

Thus I consent, sir, to this Constitution because I expect no better, and because I am not sure that it is not the best. The opinions I have had of its errors, I sacrifice to the public good. I have never whispered a syllable of them abroad. Within these walls they were born, and here they shall die. If every one of us in returning to our constituents were to report the objections he has had to it and endeavor to gain partisans in support of them, we might prevent its being generally received, and thereby lose all the salutary effects and great advantages resulting naturally in our favor, among foreign nations as well as among ourselves, from our real or apparent unanimity. Much of the strength and efficiency of any government in procuring and securing happiness to the people depends on opinion, on the general opinion of the goodness of the government as well as of the wisdom and integrity of its governors. I hope therefore that for our own sakes as a part of the people, and for the sake of posterity, we shall act heartily and unanimously in recommending this Constitution (if approved by [the Confederation] Congress and confirmed by the [state] conventions) wherever our influence may extend, and turn our future thoughts and endeavors to the means of having it well administered.

On the whole, sir, I cannot help expressing a wish that every member of the Convention who may still have objections to it would, with me, on this occasion doubt a little of his own infallibility, and to make manifest our unanimity put his name to this instrument.

—

He then moved that the Constitution be signed by the members and offered the following as a convenient form, viz., "Done in Convention by the unanimous consent of the states present the 17th of September, etc. In witness whereof we have hereunto subscribed our names."

This ambiguous form had been drawn up by Mr. Gouverneur Morris in order to gain the dissenting members, and put into the hands of Dr. Franklin that it might have the better chance of success.

Mr. GORHAM said if it was not too late he could wish, for the purpose of lessening objections to the Constitution, that the clause declaring "the number of representatives shall not exceed one for every forty thousand," which had produced so much discussion, might be yet reconsidered, in order to strike out "forty thousand" and insert "thirty thousand." This would not, he remarked, establish that as an absolute rule, but only give Congress a greater latitude which could not be thought unreasonable.

Mr. KING and Mr. CARROLL seconded and supported the idea of Mr. Gorham.

When the PRESIDENT [George Washington] rose for the purpose of putting the question, he said that although his situation had hitherto restrained him from offering his sentiments on questions depending in the house and, it might be thought, ought now to impose silence on him, yet he could not forbear expressing his wish that the alteration proposed might take place. It was much to be desired that the objections to the plan recommended might be made as few as possible. The smallness of the proportion of representatives had been considered by many members of the Convention an insufficient security for the rights and interests of the people. He acknowledged that it had always appeared to himself among the exceptionable parts of the plan, and, late as the present moment was for admitting amendments, he thought this of so much consequence that it would give much satisfaction to see it adopted.

No opposition was made to the proposition of Mr. Gorham and it was agreed to unanimously.

On the question to agree to the Constitution enrolled in order to be signed: it was agreed to, all the states answering aye.

. . .

On the motion of Dr. Franklin: N.H., Mass., Conn., N.J., Pa., Del., Md., Va., N.C., Ga., aye 10; S.C., divided.

. . .

The members then proceeded to sign the instrument.

While the last members were signing it, Dr. FRANKLIN, looking towards the president's chair, at the back of which a rising sun happened to be painted, observed to a few members near him that painters had found it difficult to distinguish in their art a rising from a setting sun. I have, said he, often and often in the course of the session, and the vicissitudes of my hopes and fears as to its issue, looked at that behind the president without being able to tell whether it was rising or setting. But now, at length, I have the happiness to know that it is a rising and not a setting sun.

The Constitution being signed by all the members except Mr. Randolph, Mr. Mason, and Mr. Gerry, who declined giving it the sanction of their names, the Convention dissolved itself by an adjournment sine die.

EPILOGUE
A POORLY KEPT SECRET

The delegates left the Constitutional Convention in September 1787 with a specific proposal for forging a stronger national union. In the words of its preamble, the purposes of the Constitution were to "establish justice, insure domestic tranquility, provide for the common defense, promote the general welfare, and secure the blessing of liberty." At a time of grave economic and political uncertainty, and given the failings of the Articles of Confederation on just these points, those goals were what many Americans wanted. But was the Constitution a cure that was worse than the disease?

Many people thought so. Critics of the proposed Constitution feared that it could lead to a central government that would be remote from the people, be controlled by an aristocracy, undermine state sovereignty, and endanger individual liberty. A strong national government would ultimately coalesce into a despotic regime, they warned, much as the Roman Republic descended into imperial rule. These critics wanted to keep a federation of states, as under the Articles of Confederation, perhaps with added powers given the central government. In a brilliant tactical move, the supporters of the Constitution co-opted the popular name "Federalists" for themselves (even though many of them favored a national over a federal government) and dismissed their opponents as "Antifederalists" (even though many of those opponents opposed the Constitution for being insufficiently federal).

The majority of voters probably were Antifederalists when the ratification process began, but the Federalists had the advantages of a positive agenda, excellent organization, and the towering prestige of men like George Washington and Benjamin Franklin. One by one, the states ratified the Constitution. The process took three years. First, the Confederation Congress, after a bitter debate, voted to send the document to the thirteen state legislatures with no recommendation but with the request that each of them submit it for ratification to a state convention elected for that purpose. The various state conventions began at different times. By the end of January 1788, Delaware, Pennsylvania, New Jersey, Georgia, and Connecticut had held their conventions and all five states had ratified the Constitution. The vote was unanimous in three of these conventions. In Pennsylvania, the sizable opposition never got a chance to organize, due to the speed with which the well-prepared Federalists moved.

The process proved more contentious in the next five states that ratified the document. The Massachusetts ratifying convention narrowly approved it in February 1788, but only after a compromise that resulted in the attachment of a number of recommended amendments, including the addition of a Bill of Rights. By mid-June 1788, Maryland, South Carolina, and New Hampshire had fallen into line—typically over vocal opposition and only after their conventions recommended further constitutional amendments. The 89 to 79 vote in Virginia's hard-fought convention on June 25, 1788, brought the total number of states ratifying the Constitution to ten, or one more than was required for it to take effect.

Federalists could hardly imagine an effective national government without New York, however. Anticipating stiff opposition there from Robert Yates, John Lansing, and other local Antifederalists, James Madison, Alexander Hamilton, and New York attorney John Jay, writing under the pseudonym "Publius," published a series of eighty-five newspaper essays explaining and defending the Constitution to "the People of the State of New York." Collectively known as *The Federalist,* these essays circulated in other states as well. Antifederalists countered in New York and elsewhere with newspaper essays of their own, often using similarly colorful pseudonyms, such as "Brutus" (Robert Yates or Thomas Treadwell) and "Federal Farmer" (perhaps the Revolutionary-era leader Richard Henry Lee of Virginia). In *Federalist No. 10,* Madison turned the Antifederalist claim that a republic could not rule over a large, widely scattered population on its head. Repeating an argument that he had made at the Constitutional Convention, Madison asserted that small republics were more vulnerable to becoming tyrannical than large ones. "Extend the sphere and you will take in a greater variety of parties and interests," he asserted. Diverse interests filtered through representative government provided a better foundation for protecting individual liberty than majority consensus. By a three-vote margin, the New York convention ratified the Constitution on July 26, 1788, pushed along by Federalist threats that New York City and its vicinity would break away if the state refused to join the new federal union. North Carolina ratified the Constitution in 1789, Rhode Island in 1790.

The Continental Congress received notice on July 2, 1788, that the Constitution was now in effect. In September, it arranged for the election of the first president to take place over the winter and set his inauguration for the following March. Congressional elections commenced in the fall of 1788, with the new Congress meeting for the first time in 1789. Responding to the requests of seven state conventions, that first Congress approved a series of constitutional amendments that became the Bill of Rights.

Although delegates returning from the Constitutional Convention played a decisive role in the ensuing state ratification efforts, events in Philadelphia did not become a major issue in the later process. Some Antifederalists attempted to discredit the Constitution by criticizing the Convention's secret meetings and unrepresentative composition, but the foreboding sectional divisions and bitter large-state/small-state differences that had darkened those proceedings went largely unmentioned during the ratification debates. Federalists wanted it that way. On its closing day, the Convention had voted to extend indefinitely the veil of secrecy over its proceedings. Fearing that if the journals of the Convention were made public "a bad use would be made of them by those who would wish to prevent the adoption of the Constitution," Rufus King moved that George Washington, as presiding officer, retain them, "subject to the order of Congress, if [one is] ever formed under the Constitution." Although this resolution did

not expressly cover private notes taken during the Convention, delegates more or less respected the rule of secrecy that applied to the
proceedings.

The public got its first extended insider's account of the Constitutional Convention in November 1787, when the disgruntled Anti-
federalist delegate Luther Martin of Maryland delivered his scathing
recollections of what had happened in Philadelphia to his state legislature. Hoping to derail the ratification effort, Martin published his report under the title *The Genuine Information . . . Relative to the Proceedings of
the General Convention*. Anticipating criticism for breaching the Convention's rule of secrecy, he began his recollections by stating, "No friend
to his country will think that they require an apology" because the
state legislature had requested them. The polemical nature of Martin's
report undermined its credibility from the outset, with Oliver Ellsworth taking the lead in disputing its accuracy. Historians agree: Martin's *Genuine Information* is unreliable. Although other delegates were
more circumspect than Martin in discussing the secret deliberations in
Philadelphia during the ratifying process, many of them alluded to
their own personal sense of the framers' intentions in the course of
arguing for or against ratification. Hamilton did so in *Federalist No. 33*,
for example, as did many other delegates in their essays, letters, and
speeches. Although it was widely known at the time that Madison,
Yates, and other delegates kept notes during the Convention and that
there was an official journal or record of votes cast on the various motions, none of these documents were made public until decades later.

By its nature, the Constitution is a concise document that includes
many ambiguous provisions. What does it mean for the president to
make treaties or appoint judges "with the advice and consent of the
Senate," for example, or to give Congress the power "to make all laws
which shall be necessary and proper" to regulate international or interstate commerce? What constitutes "advice" in treaty making or "necessity" in a commercial law? Returning delegates could not resist the
temptation to offer their interpretation on such matters based on their
recollections of debates at the Constitutional Convention. Madison,
Edmund Randolph, and George Mason did so at Virginia's contentious
ratifying convention, for example, and King, Elbridge Gerry, and Caleb
Strong did so at the convention in Massachusetts. At New York's divisive convention, Hamilton and Lansing contested the Constitution's

meaning by invoking conflicting memories of the deliberations in Philadelphia.

Selective political use of the "secret" history of the Constitutional Convention continued following ratification. During 1791, for example, in heated congressional debates over legislation to create a national bank that would oversee the nation's money supply, Virginia representative James Madison (who opposed the bill) complained that the Convention had expressly rejected a motion to give Congress the power to incorporate such an institution. As a result, he argued, the legislation was unconstitutional. Massachusetts representative Elbridge Gerry (who supported the bill) shot back, "No motion was made in that convention and, therefore, none could have been rejected for establishing a national bank." The rejected motion referred to creating commercial corporations in general, Gerry explained, not a national bank in particular, which he saw as being "necessary" to regulate interstate commerce. In his view, the legislation was constitutional.

After the bank bill passed but before he signed it, President Washington requested the advice of his cabinet regarding its constitutionality. Attorney General Edmund Randolph argued that chartering a national bank fell within the government's power to regulate interstate commerce. As to Madison's claim that the Convention's secret history demonstrated the bill's unconstitutionality, Randolph asked rhetorically, "Ought not the Constitution be decided on by the import of its own expressions? What may not be the consequences if an almost unknown history should govern the construction?" In his opinion to the president, Secretary of State Thomas Jefferson (who opposed the bank) countered Randolph by reiterating Madison's argument that the Constitution did not empower Congress to incorporate a national bank because the Convention had defeated a proposition granting such authority to Congress. Bank supporter Alexander Hamilton, then serving as Washington's secretary of the treasury, fired back, "What was the precise nature or extent of this proposition, or what were the reasons for refusing it, is not ascertained by any authentic document, or even by accurate recollection. . . . The secretary of state will not deny that, whatever may have been the intentions of the framers of the Constitution, or of a law, that intention is to be sought for in the instrument itself," not in the deliberations surrounding its drafting or enactment. In the end, Washington signed the bill into law. Convention history would never become the principal guiding light for interpreting the Constitution, but that did not make it meaningless.

Late in his second term, Washington himself drew on Convention history to defend his actions as president. Faced with congressional criticism over how his administration had negotiated Jay's Treaty with Britain, Washington summarily deposited the Convention's entire official journal with the State Department and then cited it in support of his treaty-making power. "If other proofs than these and the plain letter of the Constitution itself be necessary to ascertain the point under consideration, they may be found in the Journal of the General Convention, which I have deposited in the office of the Department of State," Washington declared. Thereafter, the Convention's official journal, which mainly recorded attendance, motions, and votes, was available for reference by members of Congress. As edited and compiled by then–Secretary of State John Quincy Adams, Congress published the journal in 1819. Although he had had his own transcribed copy of the official journal since 1789, Madison used the published version (as well as his transcribed copy) to correct and amplify his still-private notes. They would be published after his death, Madison decided.

With most of the delegates dead and the official journal published, an edited version of Yates's Convention notes was published in 1821— the first public account that purported to report actual debates from the proceedings. Madison denounced them as biased and inaccurate, but continued to insist on posthumous publication for his own version of the deliberations at Philadelphia. By this time, Madison valued his own notes primarily as a documentary record of a signal historical event rather than a guide to interpret the Constitution. Following the death of Madison in 1836, the last Convention delegate to die, Congress purchased the notes from his widow for the then-princely sum of $30,000 and published them in 1840. They immediately became the most widely trusted record of the proceedings and have remained so ever since. The notes of other delegates became public at various times during the nineteenth century. Yale University historian Max Farrand compiled the official journal and all of the available delegate notes into his 1911 masterpiece, *The Records of the Federal Convention of 1787.* As revised by Farrand in 1937, this four-volume set serves as the definitive record of the Constitutional Convention.

Farrand viewed Madison's notes as a rich resource for historians, the best report of deliberations at the Constitutional Convention, against which "all other records paled into insignificance." Among note takers at the Convention, only Madison attended every session and heard virtually every speech. Sitting in front of the presiding officer, he took detailed notes that he transcribed each evening on writing paper that still survives and is reliably dated to the time of the Convention. They are original writings, not later recollections (as some of Madison's partisan opponents later charged). When delegates gave prepared speeches at the Convention, Madison sought out copies and grafted them into his notes. He compared his records of votes on motions with those of the official journal and corrected his notes where appropriate. To the extent that Madison's notes overlap with those of other delegates, there is essential agreement on the course of deliberations at the Convention. In short, Madison's notes can be trusted so far as they go. He did not claim to transcribe the entire proceedings, however. He summarizes most speeches and may have omitted some of them altogether. His own remarks are given far more prominence than other note takers gave them. They must have been recorded after the fact, because Madison could not have spoken and taken notes at the same time and he never prepared his speeches in advance. Library of Congress archivist James Huston estimates that, on average, Madison recorded less than 10 percent of each hour's proceedings. Yet it is by far the best record we have and historians have made extensive use of it. Madison's notes remain *the* record of the Constitutional Convention.

The inestimable value of Madison's notes is self-evident to historians. Constitutional-law scholars, on the other hand, have been more dubious about the intrinsic value of records of the Convention for their purposes. Some object to using Madison's notes to interpret the Constitution because they were kept secret at the time. Therefore, they could not have affected the intentions or understandings of the state-convention delegates, who alone gave legal significance to the Constitution by ratifying it. It is the ratifiers' intentions or understandings that should matter, not those of the framers, these scholars argue. Others object to using the Convention record because it is incomplete, and therefore incapable of exposing fine distinctions in meaning that only a comprehensive transcript could possibly reveal. Still others suggest that by voting to make the Convention record secret, the framers expressed their intent that their deliberations should not be used to interpret the Constitution.

At a minimum, however, to the extent that delegate notes and the official journal provide a reliable (albeit partial) record of deliberations at the Constitutional Convention, they can help jurists, attorneys, and constitutional-law scholars to understand how the words that appear in the Constitution itself were commonly used and understood in 1787. The back-and-forth debates in Philadelphia exemplify conventional usage of terms in the document that are now obscure or ambiguous. From the time that Madison's notes became public, courts have drawn on them in interpreting problematic passages in the constitutional text. In 1854, for example, the Supreme Court used Madison's notes to limit the reach of the constitutional bar against ex post facto law to criminal cases. Judicial use of the Convention record has continued ever since. Indeed, in a 1949 opinion, Chief Justice Fred Vincent suggested that the "propriety of considering the proposals and debates of the Constitutional Convention" to understand the Constitution was long established.

Madison's notes, in short, are the best available record of one of the most critical episodes in American history and law. His account of what delegates said and did behind the closed doors of the Pennsylvania State House during the late spring and summer of 1787 still holds significance for anyone interested in what those delegates accomplished, or failed to accomplish, and how their efforts shaped, and continue to shape, the United States of America.

Biographical Notes on Delegates Speaking in This Record

ABRAHAM BALDWIN (1754–1807). Baldwin, the son of a blacksmith, was born in Connecticut and graduated from Yale in 1772. He returned to Yale three years later to serve as a minister and tutor before becoming a chaplain in the Continental Army. After the war, Baldwin became a lawyer and moved to Georgia, where he served in the state assembly and the Confederation Congress. Not a major figure at the Constitutional Convention, Baldwin's most important action was to drop his initial opposition to the Great Compromise on representation in Congress. Baldwin subsequently served in the House of Representatives and Senate as a Democratic Republican and was one of the founders of the University of Georgia.

GUNNING BEDFORD, JR. (1747–1812). Bedford roomed with James Madison at the College of New Jersey (hereafter referred to by its subsequent name, Princeton). A lawyer, he served in the Confederation Congress from 1783 to 1786 and thereafter became Delaware's attorney general. He was chosen as a delegate to the Annapolis Convention but never attended. Bedford defended the small states vociferously at the Constitutional Convention. Washington appointed him a federal judge in 1789.

DAVID BREARLY or BREARLEY(1745–1790). Brearly attended Princeton and became a lawyer. He was a member of the New Jersey state constitutional convention and rose to the rank of colonel in the state militia during the Revolutionary War. After the war, he became the chief justice of the New Jersey Supreme Court. Brearly supported the New Jersey Plan but otherwise did not play an important role at the Constitutional Convention. Washington made him a federal judge in 1789.

JACOB BROOM (1752–1810). The son of a blacksmith and farmer, Broom became a merchant and surveyor. In 1776, he started a long career of service in the Wilmington, Delaware, municipal government. His participation in the Revolutionary War was minimal, although he did make maps for the Patriot Army. Broom was a member of the Delaware state legislature in the 1780s. He was chosen as a delegate to the Annapolis Convention, although he did not attend. Broom played only a minor role at the Constitutional Convention.

PIERCE BUTLER (1744–1822). Butler was born in Ireland, the youngest son of a baronet. While a major in a British regiment, Butler was posted to Boston in 1768. He married a wealthy South Carolina woman in 1771 and resigned his commission. Butler served in the South Carolina militia during the Revolutionary War, rising to the rank of adjunct general, but lost most of his wealth in the conflict. Butler served in the Confederation Congress. At the Constitutional Convention, he was an ardent nationalist and defender of slavery. Subsequently, Butler was elected a senator from South Carolina. He served three separate terms and did not adhere consistently to either the Federalists or the Democratic Republicans.

DANIEL CARROLL (1730–1796). Offspring of a prominent Maryland Catholic family, Carroll received a Jesuit education in Europe. Fearing mob rule and the loss of the family's wealth, Carroll only reluctantly supported the Patriot cause during the Revolution. He served in the Continental Congress and the Maryland Senate before attending the Constitutional Convention as a strong nationalist. Carroll was elected to the House of Representatives in 1788, where he served one term. He later became a business partner of George Washington.

GEORGE CLYMER (1739–1813). A wealthy Philadelphia merchant, Clymer was active in the resistance movement against Great Britain and, as a member of the Continental Congress, signed the Declaration of Independence. After the war, he served in the Pennsylvania legislature. Clymer was a conscientious and respected delegate at the Constitutional Convention, but spoke rarely. He subsequently served briefly in the House of Representatives and retired from government service in 1796 to pursue his business and philanthropic interests.

WILLIAM DAVIE (1756–1820). Born in England and graduated from Princeton in 1776, Davie served as a colonel with the Patriot Army during the Revolutionary War. He was wounded in combat. After the war, Davie became a lawyer and was elected to the North Carolina legislature. At the Constitutional Convention, Davie urged his delegation to support the Great Compromise on representation in Congress. He left in the middle of August but fought hard for ratification in North Carolina. Davie subsequently helped to found the University of North Carolina and served as governor of that state.

JONATHAN DAYTON (1760–1824). As the teenaged son of a New Jersey merchant, Dayton graduated from Princeton in 1776 and joined the Patriot Army. He earned a captain's commission and was briefly a British prisoner. Dayton became a lawyer after the war. Twenty-seven years old at the time of the Constitutional Convention, he had served in the New Jersey assembly for only one year when he was chosen to take the place of his father as one of his state's delegates to the event. Dayton served in the House of Representatives from 1791 to 1799 as a Federalist. He was indicted but not prosecuted for treason for his involvement in Aaron Burr's conspiracy in 1806.

JOHN DICKINSON (1732–1808). Dickinson was the son of a prosperous Maryland judge. After studying law in Philadelphia and London, he became a prominent pamphleteer for the colonists in their struggles with the British Parliament during the 1760s and 1770s. Dickinson served in the Stamp Act Congress and the Continental Congress, but he opposed the Declaration of Independence, believing that it was premature. Dickinson wrote the original draft of the Articles of Confederation in 1776. He served as president (or governor) of both

Pennsylvania and Delaware in the 1780s and chaired the Annapolis Convention. He was one of the leading delegates at the Constitutional Convention.

OLIVER ELLSWORTH (1745–1807). Ellsworth was born in Connecticut, attended Yale and Princeton, and became a lawyer. He served in the Connecticut state government during the Revolutionary War. At the Constitutional Convention, Ellsworth was a key figure in working out the Great Compromise on representation. He left the Convention early but worked for ratification in his home state. Ellsworth became a Federalist in the 1790s and served as senator from Connecticut, chief justice of the United States Supreme Court, and commissioner to France.

THOMAS FITZSIMONS (1741–1811). Born in Ireland, Fitzsimons came to Philadelphia in the early 1760s and prospered as a merchant. In the Revolution, he commanded a militia company and helped supply the army. He served in the Continental Congress. Fitzsimons played a minor role at the Constitutional Convention. In the 1790s, he became a Federalist and represented Pennsylvania in the House of Representatives.

BENJAMIN FRANKLIN (1706–1790). Born in Boston to a candle maker, Franklin grew wealthy as a printer in Philadelphia. Through his scientific discoveries, technological inventions, civic activities, and popular writings, he became one of the most famous men of his time. As a delegate to the Continental Congress, Franklin served on the committee that drafted the Declaration of Independence. During the Revolution, he did invaluable service as a diplomat to France and negotiator of the peace treaty with Britain. After the war, Franklin served as president (or governor) of Pennsylvania. The oldest delegate at the Constitutional Convention, Franklin's most important substantive contribution was to make the proposal that became the Great Compromise while serving on the committee assigned the task of wrestling with representation. Fellow delegate William Pierce wrote of him, "He is no speaker, nor does he seem to let politics engage his attention. He is, however, a most extraordinary man, and tells a story in a style more engaging than anything I ever heard. . . . He is eighty-two years old, and possesses an activity of mind equal to a youth of twenty-five years of age."

ELBRIDGE GERRY (1744–1814). Gerry was the son of a wealthy Massachusetts merchant and joined his father's business after graduating from Harvard. He was an agitator before the Revolution and served in both the Continental and Confederation Congresses. Very active at the Constitutional Convention, Gerry did not sign the final document and fought against its ratification. He later served in the United States Congress and as commissioner to France. After a number of attempts, Gerry became the Democratic Republican governor of Massachusetts in 1810, where his enthusiasm for drawing up partisan redistricting lines gave the English language the verb "to gerrymander." Gerry was elected vice president under James Madison in 1812 and died in that office.

NATHANIEL GORHAM (1738–1796). Gorham was a self-made merchant who served in the Massachusetts government both before and during the Revolutionary War. He served in the Confederation Congress after the war, including a stint as its president. Gorham was appointed a state judge in 1785, a position he held to the end of his life. At the Constitutional Convention, Gorham fought for a strong central government while predicting that the country would fall apart within 150 years.

ALEXANDER HAMILTON (1755–1804). Born out of wedlock to British colonists living on the West Indies island of Nevis, Hamilton was reared by his impoverished mother and, after her death, her relatives. Brilliant, handsome, and engaging, the young Hamilton won friends who sent him to preparatory school in New Jersey and King's College (now Columbia University) in New York City during the 1770s. He became an aide-de-camp to Washington during the Revolutionary War and married into one of New York's wealthiest families. Hamilton was a determined nationalist and was active in the scheming and planning that led to the Constitutional Convention. He was outnumbered by antinationalists in the New York delegation at the Convention, however, and played only a minor role at the Convention itself. Hamilton's political and rhetorical skills (famously displayed in his coauthoring of *The Federalist Papers*) helped to secure New York's ratification of the Constitution, a critical step in bringing the new government into being. At the Convention, delegate William Pierce was impressed with Hamilton's intellect but noted that "his manners are tinctured with stiffness, and sometimes with a degree of vanity that is highly disagreeable." Following an enormously influential but profoundly controversial tenure as Washington's secretary of the treasury and his open feud with President John Adams, which divided the Federalist Party, Hamilton died in an 1804 duel with his chief New York political rival, Vice President Aaron Burr.

WILLIAM SAMUEL JOHNSON (1727–1819). Johnson was born in Connecticut to the prominent and controversial Anglican clergyman of the same name. Johnson received his B.A. from Yale and his M.A. from Harvard and became a wealthy lawyer. He received honorary degrees from Oxford University in 1765 and 1766. Johnson attended the Stamp Act Congress in 1765, but while he disapproved of British policy, he refused to join the independence movement, preferring to try to work as a peacemaker. Suspicious Connecticut Patriots detained him briefly in 1779. After the war, Johnson served in the Confederation Congress. At the Constitutional Convention, Johnson played an important role by advocating the Great Compromise on representation and serving as the chair of the Committee of Style, which drafted the final document. According to fellow delegate William Pierce, Johnson "engages the hearts of men by the sweetness of his temper and that affectionate style of address with which he accosts his acquaintance." Johnson served as one of Connecticut's first senators, but resigned in 1791 to take on the presidency of Columbia College (formerly King's College and currently Columbia University), where his father had served as president.

RUFUS KING (1755–1827). Son of a prosperous farmer and merchant who defended Britain in its escalating conflict with the colonies, King graduated from Harvard in 1777. A lawyer, he served in the Massachusetts assembly and the Confederation Congress. King was a vocal, active nationalist at the Constitutional Convention. Moving to New York

State, he was elected to the United States Senate and served as the nation's ambassador to Great Britain. King gained the Federalist Party nomination for president in 1816 but lost the election to James Monroe. He subsequently returned to the Senate and, consistent with the antislavery views he expressed at the Constitutional Convention, denounced the Missouri Compromise.

JOHN LANGDON (1741–1819). Langdon, the son of a farmer and without any formal education, grew wealthy as a New Hampshire merchant. Langdon supported the Patriot cause financially and by military service while increasing his own wealth through the risky business of financing privateers. Langdon served in the Continental Congress, in the New Hampshire legislature, and as New Hampshire governor before coming to the Constitutional Convention as a nationalist in mid-July. New Hampshire only sent its two-person delegation to Philadelphia because Langdon paid the expenses. Afterward he served in the Senate and again as governor of New Hampshire. Initially in the 1790s he was a supporter of Hamilton, but he later drifted to the Democratic Republicans.

JOHN LANSING, JR. (1754–1829). Lansing served in the military and the New York assembly during the Revolutionary War and subsequently in the Confederation Congress. An antinationalist, Lansing left the Constitutional Convention early and opposed the Constitution's ratification in New York. He thereafter had a long tenure on the New York Supreme Court. Lansing disappeared without a trace in 1829 after leaving a New York City hotel to post letters.

JAMES MADISON, JR. (1751–1836). Madison came from a Virginia planter family and was educated at Princeton. An active, although bookish, Patriot during the Revolutionary War, he served in the Virginia legislature and the Continental Congress and helped write the Virginia state constitution. During the 1780s, Madison became increasingly involved in the effort to strengthen the federal government. As a thirty-six-year-old Virginia delegate to the Constitutional Convention, he drew on his study of history and political theory to work out the basic ideas of the Virginia Plan. Fellow delegate William Pierce wrote of

Madison, "What is very remarkable, every person seems to acknowledge his greatness." Elected to the first United States House of Representatives in 1789, Madison proposed a series of amendments to the Constitution that formed the basis of the Bill of Rights. He helped found the Democratic Republican Party during his years in Congress and served two terms as president of the United States, from 1809 to 1817.

LUTHER MARTIN (1748–1826). Martin was a bad-mannered, slovenly, heavy-drinking Princeton graduate who succeeded as a lawyer in Maryland. He was active in the independence movement and became the state's attorney general in 1778. Martin's opposition to the Constitution caused him to leave the Convention early and oppose its ratification. Fellow delegate William Pierce grumbled that Martin "never speaks without tiring the patience of all who hear him." Martin's hatred for Thomas Jefferson prompted him to join the Federalist Party in the early 1790s. Martin won an acquittal for his friend Supreme Court Justice Samuel Chase in the latter's impeachment trial in 1805, and he served as one of the defense attorneys for Aaron Burr in his trial for treason in 1807. Alcohol abuse and paralysis left Martin in poverty in his old age, and he was buried in an unmarked grave in New York City.

GEORGE MASON (1725–1792). Mason was a wealthy Virginia planter. He wrote against the Stamp Act in 1765 and was active in the Patriot movement. Mason wrote the bill of rights for the Virginia state constitution. At the Constitutional Convention, Mason was one of the most frequent speakers and an influential participant. He refused to sign the final document, however, primarily because it did not include a bill of rights. Mason campaigned unsuccessfully against Virginia's ratification of the Constitution.

JAMES MCHENRY (1735–1816). McHenry was born in Ireland, came to America in 1771, and studied medicine in Philadelphia with famed physician Benjamin Rush. During the Revolution, he worked as a military surgeon and eventually joined Washington's staff. He served in Congress from 1783 to 1786. McHenry contributed little to the Constitutional Convention, in part because a brother's illness kept him away for most of it. Washington appointed him secretary of war in 1796, a position he held under John Adams as well.

JOHN MERCER (1759–1821). Born into a Virginia planter family, Mercer attended the College of William and Mary and joined the army in 1778. After training as a lawyer in Delaware, he attended the Continental Congress. Mercer moved to Maryland in 1785 and attended the Constitutional Convention as a Maryland delegate. The second youngest delegate, Mercer opposed the Constitution and left the Convention early. Mercer subsequently served in the House of Representatives as a Democratic Republican, but moved to the Federalists and served as governor of Maryland from 1801 to 1803.

THOMAS MIFFLIN (1744–1800). From a wealthy Pennsylvania Quaker family, Mifflin was educated at the College of Philadelphia. A successful merchant, he became an ardent Patriot during the years leading up to the Revolution. After serving in the First and Second Continental Congresses, in 1776 Mifflin accepted a commission as a major in the Continental Army, for which the pacifist Quakers expelled him. Mifflin rose to the rank of brigadier general and later returned to the Continental Congress. Following the Constitutional Convention, in which Mifflin played only a small role, he became governor of Pennsylvania. He gradually aligned himself with the emerging Democratic Republican Party during his long tenure in that office, from 1790 to 1799. While an able governor, Mifflin handled his personal affairs badly and died penniless and hounded by creditors.

GOUVERNEUR MORRIS (1752–1816). From a wealthy background, Morris went to King's College (later Columbia University) and became a lawyer. He was active in the independence movement, helped to draft the New York state constitution, and served in the Continental Congress. Morris moved to Philadelphia and became Robert Morris's assistant in handling the Continental Congress's tangled finances. Morris was one of the most important men at the Constitutional Convention, giving many speeches and writing much of the final document. According to fellow delegate William Pierce, Morris "winds through all the mazes of rhetoric and throws around him such a glare that he charms, captivates, and leads away the senses of all who hear him." Morris later became a Federalist, but he avoided political office save for a single term in the United States Senate. He was famed for his flamboyant style, wooden leg, and amorous adventures.

WILLIAM PATERSON (1745–1806). Paterson was born in Ireland but came to America when he was two. After an education at Princeton, Paterson became a lawyer. He served in the New Jersey government during the Revolutionary War. An ardent defender of the interests of the small states, Paterson wrote and introduced the New Jersey Plan at the Constitutional Convention. Delegate William Pierce noted of him, "Mr. Paterson is one of those kind of men whose powers break in upon you, and create wonder and astonishment." Paterson later became a United States senator, New Jersey governor, and United States Supreme Court justice.

WILLIAM LEIGH PIERCE (c. 1740–1789). Little is known about Pierce's early life. He fought bravely in the Revolutionary War and reached the rank of major. After the war, he became a merchant in Savannah, Georgia, and served as a member of the Confederation Congress and the Georgia legislature. Although Pierce was not a major figure at the Constitutional Convention, he wrote useful character sketches of the other delegates. Pierce went bankrupt shortly after returning to Georgia and died two years later, deeply in debt.

CHARLES PINCKNEY (1757–1824). Pinckney came from a wealthy South Carolina planter family. During the Revolutionary War, he served in the Continental Congress, the army (and was briefly a British prisoner), and the South Carolina state legislature. Pinckney took an extremely active role at the Constitutional Convention as a nationalist and protector of slavery and submitted a draft constitution of his own. Not a modest man, Pinckney later claimed that he was the most influential delegate at the Convention. He gradually aligned himself with the Democratic Republicans in the 1790s and served as governor of South Carolina, a member of Congress, and United States ambassador to Spain.

CHARLES COTESWORTH (General) PINCKNEY (1746–1825). From a prominent South Carolina family and the cousin of fellow delegate Charles Pinckney, Charles Cotesworth Pinckney was educated at Oxford and trained for the law at London's Middle Temple. Active in the independence movement, he joined the army, was briefly held by the British, and ultimately rose to the rank of general. Pinckney resumed his law practice after the war. He took an active role at the Constitutional Convention as a nationalist and defender of slavery. Pinckney ran as the Federalist vice-presidential candidate in 1800 and its presidential candidate in 1804 and 1808, losing to Madison in the later election—the only time two Constitutional Convention delegates faced off in a presidential election.

EDMUND RANDOLPH (1753–1813). Randolph came from a wealthy Virginia planter family. He was educated at the College of William and Mary and trained as a lawyer. While Randolph's loyalist parents and sisters went to England at the start of the Revolutionary War, Randolph served briefly as an aide-de-camp to George Washington and then returned to Virginia, where he became the state's attorney general and a representative to the Continental Congress. Randolph became governor of Virginia in 1786. As titular head of the Virginia delegation to the Constitutional Convention, Governor Randolph formally introduced the Virginia Plan, but he grew increasingly dissatisfied with the Convention's direction. Although he refused to sign the final document, he ultimately supported it at the Virginia ratifying convention. Randolph served as Washington's attorney general and secretary of state, but retired from politics in 1795.

GEORGE READ (1733–1798). Son of a prosperous Delaware farmer, Read became a successful lawyer. He was a moderate opponent of British measures from the Stamp Act onward. As a delegate to the Continental Congress, he initially voted against independence, but later signed the Declaration of Independence. Active in Delaware politics, Read presided over the state constitutional convention, and he served as a delegate to the Annapolis Convention. He was a strong nationalist at the Constitutional Convention even while he defended the interests of the small states. Read's most notable proposal at the Convention was that the United States be divided up into new, equally sized states. Read served in the first United States Senate as a Federalist but resigned to become chief justice of the Delaware Supreme Court in 1793.

JOHN RUTLEDGE (1739–1800). Son of a South Carolina physician, Rutledge trained for the law at London's Middle Temple. He represented South Carolina in the Stamp Act Congress of 1765 and was a moderate in the First Continental Congress. He helped to write the South Carolina state constitution and was elected governor of the state in 1779. Rutledge subsequently served in the Confederation Congress and the South Carolina legislature. At the Constitutional Convention, Rutledge was a nationalist and vehement protector of South Carolina's interests. He later served as chief justice of the South Carolina Supreme Court and on the United States Supreme Court.

ROGER SHERMAN (1721–1793). Unlike most of the other leading men at the Convention, Sherman was a self-made autodidact. Born in Connecticut, his father taught him the cobbler's trade, but he became a lawyer, shopkeeper, and politician. In the Continental Congress, Sherman served on the committees that drafted the Declaration of Independence and Articles of Confederation, both of which he signed. Sherman came to the Constitutional Convention wanting only to amend the Articles of Confederation. At the Convention, he was an active and well-respected, if singular, participant. Fellow delegate William Pierce said of him, "The oddity of his address, the vulgarisms that accompany his public speaking, and that strange New England cant which runs through his public as well as his private speaking make everything that is connected with him grotesque and laughable. And yet he deserves infinite praise; no man has a better heart or a clearer head." In the few remaining years of his life, Sherman represented Connecticut in the United States House of Representatives and Senate.

RICHARD DOBBS SPAIGHT (1758–1802). Spaight was born in North Carolina, where his father was the colony's treasurer, but he went to live with his Irish relatives after his parents died in 1767. Spaight returned to North Carolina in 1778 to fight for the Patriot cause and subsequently served in the state legislature and Confederation Congress. After the Constitutional Convention, Spaight played a major role in the protracted effort to ratify the Constitution in North Carolina. He served as governor of North Carolina and in the House of Representatives. A Democratic Republican, Spaight died in a duel with a Federalist political opponent in 1802.

GEORGE WASHINGTON (1732–1799). From a prominent Virginia planter family, Washington was largely self-taught. As a colonel in the Virginia militia, his military blunders while asserting Virginia land claims in the Ohio valley helped to trigger the French and Indian War (1756–1763). Washington married a wealthy widow, Martha Custis, in 1759 and inherited his family's Mount Vernon plantation two years later. Washington served in the Virginia assembly during the following decade and joined in the protests against British policies. The Continental Congress appointed him commander in chief of the Patriot Army in 1775. Against formidable odds, Washington fashioned and held together a force capable of holding its own against the British. Washington resigned his commission when the war ended in 1783 and returned to Mount Vernon as the most widely admired man in the United States. Washington believed strongly in the need for a more effective national government than was provided under the Articles of Confederation. His willingness to attend the Constitutional Convention and serve as the first president of the new national government were major factors in the success of the Constitution.

HUGH WILLIAMSON (1735–1819). Williamson graduated from the College of Philadelphia (later incorporated into the University of Pennsylvania). He was licensed as a Presbyterian minister, but he took a medical degree at the University of Utrecht and set up as a physician. A keen amateur scientist, Williamson was known internationally for his astronomical skills. Abroad when independence was declared, Williamson returned to settle in North Carolina, where he worked as a merchant and doctor. He served in the Confederation Congress, in the North Carolina state assembly, and as a delegate to the Annapolis Convention. At the Constitutional Convention, Williamson played an important role in the Great Compromise on representation in Congress. In 1793, after serving two terms in the United States House of Representatives from North Carolina, Williamson moved to New York City to pursue his scientific and philanthropic interests.

JAMES WILSON (1742–1798). Wilson was born and educated in Scotland and came to Pennsylvania in 1765, where he prospered as a lawyer. As a delegate to the Continental Congress, Wilson signed the Declaration of Independence. He opposed Pennsylvania's radical state government and was a close business associate of Robert Morris. Serving in the Confederation Congress during the 1780s, Wilson pushed to have its powers strengthened. Well versed in political theory, Wilson played a major role at the Constitutional Convention. "All the political institutions of the world he knows in detail," wrote his awed fellow delegate William Pierce, "and can trace the causes and effects of every revolution from the earliest stages of the Grecian commonwealth down to the present time." Washington appointed Wilson to the United States Supreme Court in 1789. As a result of disastrous large-scale land speculation, Wilson died in flight from creditors eleven years later.

ROBERT YATES (1738–1801). Yates, a lawyer, was deeply involved in the independence movement in New York. He drafted the New York state constitution and joined the New York Supreme Court in 1777, where he stayed until 1798. Yates left the Constitutional Convention early in protest of the power it was giving the new national government and unsuccessfully fought against the Constitution's ratification by New York State. His private notes of the proceedings in Philadelphia were published after his death.

APPENDIX A
THE VIRGINIA PLAN

Introduced by Edmund Randolph on May 29, 1787
AS RECORDED IN MADISON'S NOTES OF THE CONVENTION

1. Resolved that the Articles of Confederation ought to be so corrected and enlarged as to accomplish the objects proposed by their institution; namely, "common defense, security of liberty and general welfare."

2. Resolved therefore that the rights of suffrage in the National Legislature ought to be proportioned to the quotas of contribution or to the number of free inhabitants, as the one or the other rule may seem best in different cases.

3. Resolved that the National Legislature ought to consist of two branches.

4. Resolved that the members of the first branch of the National Legislature ought to be elected by the people of the several States every _____ for the term of _____ ; to be of the age of _____ years at least, to receive liberal stipends by which they may be compensated for the devotion of their time to public service; to be ineligible to any office established by a particular State or under the authority of the United States (except those peculiarly belonging to the functions of the first branch) during the term of service and for the space of _____ after its expiration; to be incapable of reelection for the space of _____ after the expiration of their term of service; and to be subject to recall.

5. Resolved that the members of the second branch of the National

Legislature ought to be elected by those of the first, out of a proper number of persons nominated by the individual legislatures; to be of the age of _____ years at least; to hold their offices for a term sufficient to ensure their independency; to receive liberal stipends, by which they may be compensated for the devotion of their time to public service; and to be ineligible to any office established by a particular State or under the authority of the United States (except those peculiarly belonging to the functions of the second branch) during the term of service and for the space of _____ after the expiration thereof.

6. Resolved that each branch ought to possess the right of originating acts; that the National Legislature ought to be empowered to enjoy the legislative rights vested in Congress by the Confederation and moreover to legislate in all cases to which the separate States are incompetent or in which the harmony of the United States may be interrupted by the exercise of individual legislation; to negative all laws passed by the several States contravening in the opinion of the National Legislature the Articles of Union; and to call forth the force of the Union against any member of the Union failing to fulfill its duty under the articles thereof.

7. Resolved that a National Executive be instituted to be chosen by the National Legislature for the term of _____ years; to receive punctually at stated times a fixed compensation for the services rendered, in which no increase or diminution shall be made so as to affect the magistracy existing at the time of increase or diminution; and to be ineligible a second time; and that besides a general authority to execute the national laws, it ought to enjoy the Executive rights vested in Congress by the Confederation.

8. Resolved that the Executive and a convenient number of the National Judiciary ought to compose a council of revision with authority to examine every act of the National Legislature before it shall operate and every act of a particular legislature before a negative thereon shall be final; and that the dissent of the said council shall amount to a rejection unless the act of the National Legislature be again passed, or that of a particular legislature be again negatived by _____ of the members of each branch.

9. Resolved that a National Judiciary be established to consist of one or more supreme tribunals, and of inferior tribunals to be chosen by the National Legislature; to hold their offices during good behav-

ior; and to receive punctually at stated times fixed compensation for their services, in which no increase or diminution shall be made so as to affect the persons actually in office at the time of such increase or diminution; that the jurisdiction of the inferior tribunals shall be to hear and determine in the first instance, and of the supreme tribunal to hear and determine in the dernier resort, all piracies and felonies on the high seas; captures from an enemy; cases in which foreigners or citizens of other States applying to such jurisdictions may be interested; or which respect the collection of the national revenue, impeachments of any national officers, and questions which may involve the national peace and harmony.

10. Resolved that provision ought to be made for the admission of States lawfully arising within the limits of the United States, whether from a voluntary junction of government and territory or otherwise, with the consent of a number of voices in the National Legislature less than the whole.

11. Resolved that a republican government and the territory of each State (except in the instance of a voluntary junction of government and territory) ought to be guarantied by the United States to each State.

12. Resolved that provision ought to be made for the continuance of Congress and their authorities and privileges until a given day after the reform of the Articles of Union shall be adopted, and for the completion of all their engagements.

13. Resolved that provision ought to be made for the amendment of the Articles of Union whensoever it shall seem necessary, and that the assent of the National Legislature ought not to be required thereto.

14. Resolved that the Legislative, Executive, and Judiciary powers within the several States ought to be bound by oath to support the Articles of Union.

15. Resolved that the amendments which shall be offered to the Confederation by the Convention ought at a proper time, or times, after the approbation of Congress to be submitted to an assembly or assemblies of representatives, recommended by the several legislatures to be expressly chosen by the people, to consider and decide thereon.

APPENDIX B
THE NEW JERSEY PLAN

Introduced by William Paterson on June 15, 1787
AS RECORDED IN MADISON'S NOTES OF THE CONVENTION

1. Resolved that the Articles of Confederation ought to be so revised, corrected, and enlarged as to render the federal Constitution adequate to the exigencies of government and the preservation of the Union.

2. Resolved that in addition to the powers vested in the United States in Congress by the present existing Articles of Confederation, they be authorized to pass acts for raising a revenue by levying a duty or duties on all goods or merchandise of foreign growth or manufacture imported into any part of the United States; by stamps on paper, vellum, or parchment; and by a postage on all letters or packages passing through the general post office, to be applied to such federal purposes as they shall deem proper and expedient; to make rules and regulations for the collection thereof; and the same from time to time to alter and amend in such manner as they shall think proper; to pass acts for the regulation of trade and commerce as well with foreign nations as with each other, provided that all punishments, fines, forfeitures, and penalties to be incurred for contravening such acts, rules, and regulations shall be adjudged by the common law judiciaries of the State in which any offense contrary to the true intent and meaning of such acts, rules, and regulations shall have been committed or perpetrated, with liberty of commencing in the first instance all suits and prosecutions for that purpose in the superior common law judiciary in such State, subject nevertheless, for the correction of all errors (both in

law and fact in rendering judgment) to an appeal to the Judiciary of the United States.

3. Resolved that whenever requisitions shall be necessary, instead of the rule for making requisitions mentioned in the Articles of Confederation, the United States in Congress be authorized to make such requisitions in proportion to the whole number of white and other free citizens and inhabitants of every age, sex, and condition (including those bound to servitude for a term of years) and three fifths of all other persons not comprehended in the foregoing description, except Indians not paying taxes; that if such requisitions be not complied within the time specified therein, to direct the collection thereof in the non-complying States and for that purpose to devise and pass acts directing and authorizing the same; provided that none of the powers hereby vested in the United States in Congress shall be exercised without the consent of at least _____ States, and in that proportion if the number of confederated States should hereafter be increased or diminished.

4. Resolved that the United States in Congress be authorized to elect a federal Executive to consist of _____ persons, to continue in office for the term of _____ years, to receive punctually at stated times a fixed compensation for their services, in which no increase or diminution shall be made so as to affect the persons composing the Executive at the time of such increase or diminution, to be paid out of the federal treasury; to be incapable of holding any other office or appointment during their time of service and for _____ years thereafter; to be ineligible a second time, and removable by Congress on application by a majority of the executives of the several States; that the executives besides their general authority to execute the federal acts ought to appoint all federal officers not otherwise provided for, and to direct all military operations; provided that none of the persons composing the federal Executive shall on any occasion take command of any troops so as personally to conduct any enterprise as general or in other capacity.

5. Resolved that a federal Judiciary be established to consist of a supreme tribunal the judges of which to be appointed by the Executive, and to hold their offices during good behaviour, to receive punctually at stated times a fixed compensation for their services in which no increase or diminution shall be made so as to affect the persons ac-

tually in office at the time of such increase or diminution; that the Judiciary so established shall have authority to hear and determine in the first instance on all impeachments of federal officers and by way of appeal in the dernier resort in all cases touching the rights of ambassadors, in all cases of captures from an enemy, in all cases of piracies and felonies on the high seas, in all cases in which foreigners may be interested, in the construction of any treaty or treaties, or which may arise on any of the acts for regulation of trade, or the collection of the federal revenue; that none of the Judiciary shall during the time they remain in office be capable of receiving or holding any other office or appointment during their time of service, or for _____ thereafter.

6. Resolved that all acts of the United States in Congress made by virtue and in pursuance of the powers hereby and by the Articles of Confederation vested in them, and all treaties made and ratified under the authority of the United States, shall be the supreme law of the respective States so far forth as those acts or treaties shall relate to the said States or their citizens, and that the judiciary of the several States shall be bound thereby in their decisions, any thing in the respective laws of the individual States to the contrary notwithstanding; and that if any State, or any body of men in any State, shall oppose or prevent carrying into execution such acts or treaties, the federal Executive shall be authorized to call forth the power of the Confederated States or so much thereof as may be necessary to enforce and compel an obedience to such acts or an observance of such treaties.

7. Resolved that provision be made for the admission of new States into the Union.

8. Resolved the rule for naturalization ought to be the same in every State.

9. Resolved that a citizen of one State committing an offense in another State of the Union shall be deemed guilty of the same offense as if it had been committed by a citizen of the State in which the offense was committed.

APPENDIX C

COMMITTEE OF DETAIL DRAFT CONSTITUTION

As Recorded in Madison's Notes of the Convention [*]
AUGUST 6, 1787

We the people of the States of New Hampshire, Massachusetts, Rhode-Island and Providence Plantations, Connecticut, New-York, New-Jersey, Pennsylvania, Delaware, Maryland, Virginia, North-Carolina, South-Carolina, and Georgia, do ordain, declare, and establish the following Constitution for the Government of Ourselves and our Posterity.

ARTICLE I

The stile of the Government shall be, "The United States of America."

ARTICLE II

The Government shall consist of supreme legislative, executive, and judicial powers.

ARTICLE III

The legislative power shall be vested in a Congress, to consist of two separate and distinct bodies of men, a House of Representatives and a

---

[*]Reprinted without modification from the printed version submitted by the Committee of Detail as corrected by Madison.

Senate; each of which shall in all cases have a negative on the other. The Legislature shall meet on the first Monday in December in every year.

[ARTICLE] IV

Sect. 1. The members of the House of Representatives shall be chosen every second year, by the people of the several States comprehended within this Union. The qualifications of the electors shall be the same, from time to time, as those of the electors in the several States, of the most numerous branch of their own legislatures.

Sect. 2. Every member of the House of Representatives shall be of the age of twenty five years at least; shall have been a citizen in the United States for at least three years before his election; and shall be, at the time of his election, a resident of the State in which he shall be chosen.

Sect. 3. The House of Representatives shall, at its first formation, and until the number of citizens and inhabitants shall be taken in the manner herein after described, consist of sixty five Members, of whom three shall be chosen in New-Hampshire, eight in Massachusetts, one in Rhode-Island and Providence Plantations, five in Connecticut, six in New-York, four in New-Jersey, eight in Pennsylvania, one in Delaware, six in Maryland, ten in Virginia, five in North-Carolina, five in South-Carolina, and three in Georgia.

Sect. 4. As the proportions of numbers in different States will alter from time to time; as some of the States may hereafter be divided; as others may be enlarged by addition of territory; as two or more States may be united; as new States will be erected within the limits of the United States, the Legislature shall, in each of these cases, regulate the number of representatives by the number of inhabitants, according to the provisions herein after made, at the rate of one for every forty thousand.

Sect. 5. All bills for raising or appropriating money, and for fixing the salaries of the officers of Government, shall originate in the House of Representatives, and shall not be altered or amended by the Senate.

No money shall be drawn from the Public Treasury, but in pursuance of appropriations that shall originate in the House of Representatives.

Sect. 6. The House of Representatives shall have the sole power of impeachment. It shall choose its Speaker and other officers.

Sect. 7. Vacancies in the House of Representatives shall be supplied by writs of election from the executive authority of the State in the representation from which they shall happen.

ARTICLE V

Sect. 1. The Senate of the United States shall be chosen by the Legislatures of the several States. Each Legislature shall chuse two members. Vacancies may be supplied by the Executive until the next meeting of the Legislature. Each member shall have one vote.

Sect. 2. The Senators shall be chosen for six years; but immediately after the first election they shall be divided, by lot, into three classes, as nearly as may be, numbered one, two and three. The seats of the members of the first class shall be vacated at the expiration of the second year, of the second class at the expiration of the fourth year, of the third class at the expiration of the sixth year, so that a third part of the members may be chosen every second year.

Sect. 3. Every member of the Senate shall be of the age of thirty years at least; shall have been a citizen in the United States for at least four years before his election; and shall be, at the time of his election, a resident of the State for which he shall be chosen.

Sect. 4. The Senate shall choose its own President and other officers.

ARTICLE VI

Sect. 1. The times and places and manner of holding the elections of the members of each House shall be prescribed by the Legislature of each State; but their provisions concerning them may, at any time be altered by the Legislature of the United States.

Sect. 2. The Legislature of the United States shall have authority to establish such uniform qualifications of the members of each House, with regard to property, as to the said Legislature shall seem expedient.

Sect. 3. In each House a majority of the members shall constitute a quorum to do business; but a smaller number may adjourn from day to day.

Sect. 4. Each House shall be the judge of the elections, returns and qualifications of its own members.

Sect. 5. Freedom of speech and debate in the Legislature shall not be impeached or questioned in any Court or place out of the Legislature; and the members of each House shall, in all cases, except treason, felony and breach of the peace, be privileged from arrest during their attendance at Congress, and in going to and returning from it.

Sect. 6. Each House may determine the rules of its proceedings; may punish its members for disorderly behaviour; and may expel a member.

Sect. 7. The House of Representatives, and the Senate, when it shall be acting in a legislative capacity, shall keep a journal of their proceedings, and shall, from time to time, publish them: and the yeas and nays of the members of each House, on any question, shall at the desire of one-fifth part of the members present, be entered on the journal.

Sect. 8. Neither House, without the consent of the other, shall adjourn for more than three days, nor to any other place than that at which the two Houses are sitting. But this regulation shall not extend to the Senate, when it shall exercise the powers mentioned in the _____ article.

Sect. 9. The members of each House shall be ineligible to, and incapable of holding any office under the authority of the United States, during the time for which they shall respectively be elected: and the members of the Senate shall be ineligible to, and incapable of holding any such office for one year afterwards.

Sect. 10. The members of each House shall receive a compensation for their services, to be ascertained and paid by the State, in which they shall be chosen.

Sect. 11. The enacting stile of the laws of the United States shall be "Be it enacted by the Senate and Representatives in Congress assembled."

Sect. 12. Each House shall possess the right of originating bills, except in the cases before mentioned.

Sect. 13. Every bill, which shall have passed the House of Representatives and the Senate, shall, before it becomes a law, be presented to the President of the United States for his revision: if, upon such revision, he approve of it, he shall signify his approbation by signing it: But if, upon such revision, it shall appear to him improper for being passed into a law, he shall return it, together with his objections against it, to that House in which it shall have originated, who shall enter the objections at large on their journal and proceed to reconsider the bill. But if after such reconsideration, two thirds of that House shall, notwithstanding the objections of the President, agree to pass it, it shall together with his objections, be sent to the other House, by which it shall likewise be reconsidered, and if approved by two thirds of the other House also, it shall become a law. But in all such cases, the votes of both Houses shall be determined by yeas and nays; and the names of the persons voting for or against the bill shall be entered on the journal of each House respectively. If any bill shall not be returned by the President within seven days after it shall have been presented to him, it shall be a law, unless the legislature, by their adjournment, prevent its return; in which case it shall not be a law.

ARTICLE VII

Sect. 1. The Legislature of the United States shall have the power to lay and collect taxes, duties, imposts and excises;

To regulate commerce with foreign nations, and among the several States;

To establish an uniform rule of naturalization throughout the United States;

To coin money;

To regulate the value of foreign coin;

To fix the standard of weights and measures;

To establish Post-offices;

To borrow money, and emit bills on the credit of the United States;

To appoint a Treasurer by ballot;

To constitute tribunals inferior to the Supreme Court;

To make rules concerning captures on land and water;

To declare the law and punishment of piracies and felonies committed on the high seas, and the punishment of counterfeiting the coin of the United States, and of offenses against the law of nations;

To subdue a rebellion in any State, on the application of its legislature;

To make war;

To raise armies;

To build and equip fleets;

To call forth the aid of the militia, in order to execute the laws of the Union, enforce treaties, suppress insurrections, and repel invasions;

And to make all laws that shall be necessary and proper for carrying into execution the foregoing powers, and all other powers vested, by this Constitution, in the government of the United States, or in any department or office thereof.

Sect. 2. Treason against the United States shall consist only in levying war against the United States, or any of them; and in adhering to the enemies of the United States, or any of them. The Legislature of the United States shall have power to declare the punishment of treason. No person shall be convicted of treason, unless on the testimony of two witnesses. No attainder of treason shall work corruption of blood, nor forfeiture, except during the life of the person attainted.

Sect. 3. The proportions of direct taxation shall be regulated by the whole number of white and other free citizens and inhabitants of every age, sex and condition, including those bound to servitude for a term of years, and three fifths of all other persons not comprehended in the foregoing description, (except Indians not paying taxes) which number shall, within six years after the first meeting of the Legislature, and within the term of every ten years afterwards, be taken in such a manner as the said Legislature shall direct.

Sect. 4. No tax or duty shall be laid by the Legislature on articles exported from any State; nor on the migration or importation of such persons as the several States shall think proper to admit; nor shall such migration or importation be prohibited.

Sect. 5. No capitation tax shall be laid, unless in proportion to the Census hereinbefore directed to be taken.

Sect. 6. No navigation act shall be passed without the assent of two thirds of the members present in the House.

Sect. 7. The United States shall not grant any title of Nobility.

ARTICLE VIII

The Acts of the Legislature of the United States made in pursuance of this Constitution, and all treaties made under the authority of the United States shall be the supreme law of the several States, and of their citizens and inhabitants; and the judges in the several States shall be bound thereby in their decisions; any thing in the Constitutions or laws of the several States to the contrary notwithstanding.

ARTICLE IX

Sect 1. The Senate of the United States shall have power to make treaties, and to appoint Ambassadors, and Judges of the Supreme Court.

Sect. 2. In all disputes and controversies now subsisting, or that may hereafter subsist between two or more States, respecting jurisdiction or territory, the Senate shall possess the following powers. Whenever the Legislature, or the Executive authority, or lawful agent of any State, in controversy with another, shall by memorial to the Senate, state the matter in question, and apply for a hearing; notice of such memorial and application shall be given by order of the Senate, to the Legislature or the Executive authority of the other State in Controversy. The Senate shall also assign a day for the appearance of the parties, by their agents, before that House. The Agents shall be directed to appoint, by joint consent, commissioners or judges to constitute a Court for hearing and determining the matter in question. But if the Agents cannot agree, the Senate shall name three persons out of each of the several States; and from the list of such persons each party shall alternately strike out one, until the number shall be reduced to thirteen; and from that number not less than seven nor more than nine names, as the Senate shall direct, shall in their presence, be drawn out by lot; and the persons whose names shall be so drawn, or any five of them shall be commissioners or Judges to hear and finally determine the controversy; provided a majority of the Judges, who shall hear the cause, agree in the determination. If either party shall neglect to attend at the day assigned, without shewing sufficient reasons for not attending, or being present shall refuse to strike, the Senate shall proceed to nominate three persons out of each State, and the Clerk of the Senate shall strike in behalf of the party absent or refusing. If any of the parties shall refuse to submit to the authority of such Court; or shall not appear to prosecute or defend their claim or cause, the Court shall nevertheless proceed to pronounce judgment. The judgment shall be final and conclusive. The proceedings shall be transmitted to the President of the Senate, and shall be lodged among the public records, for the security of the parties concerned. Every Commissioner shall, before he sit in judgment, take an oath, to be administered by one of the Judges of the Supreme or Superior Court of the State where the cause shall be tried, "well and truly to hear and determine the matter in question according to the best of his judgment, without favour, affection, or hope of reward."

Sect. 3. All controversies concerning lands claimed under different grants of two or more States, whose jurisdictions, as they respect such lands shall have been decided or adjusted subsequently to such grants, or any of them, shall, on application to the Senate, be finally determined, as near as may be, in the same manner as is before prescribed for deciding controversies between different States.

ARTICLE X

Sect. 1. The Executive Power of the United States shall be vested in a single person. His stile shall be, "The President of the United States of America;" and his title shall be, "His Excellency." He shall be elected by ballot by the Legislature. He shall hold his office during the term of seven years; but shall not be elected a second time.

Sect. 2. He shall, from time to time, give information to the Legislature, of the state of the Union: he may recommend to their consideration such measures as he shall judge necessary, and expedient: he may convene them on extraordinary occasions. In case of disagreement between the two Houses, with regard to the time of adjournment, he may adjourn them to such time as he thinks proper: he shall take care that the laws of the United States be duly and faithfully executed: he shall commission all the officers of the United States; and shall appoint officers in all cases not otherwise provided for by this Constitution. He shall receive Ambassadors, and may correspond with the supreme Executives of the several States. He shall have power to grant reprieves and pardons; but his pardon shall not be pleadable in bar of an impeachment. He shall be commander in chief of the Army and Navy of the United States, and of the Militia of the several States. He shall, at stated times, receive for his services, a compensation, which shall neither be increased nor diminished during his continuance in office. Before he shall enter on the duties of his department, he shall take the following oath or affirmation, "I _____ solemnly swear, (or affirm) that I will faithfully execute the office of President of the United States of America." He shall be removed from his office on impeachment by the House of Representatives, and conviction in the supreme Court, of treason, bribery, or corruption. In case of his removal as aforesaid, death, resignation, or disability to discharge the powers and duties of his office, the President of the Senate shall exercise those powers and duties, until another President of the United States be chosen, or until the disability of the President be removed.

ARTICLE XI

Sect. 1. The Judicial Power of the United States shall be vested in one Supreme Court, and in such inferior Courts as shall, when necessary, from time to time, be constituted by the Legislature of the United States.

Sect. 2. The Judges of the Supreme Court, and of the Inferior Courts, shall hold their offices during good behaviour. They shall, at stated times, receive for their services, a compensation, which shall not be diminished during their continuance in office.

Sect. 3. The Jurisdiction of the Supreme Court shall extend to all cases arising under laws passed by the Legislature of the United States; to all cases affecting Ambassadors, other Public Ministers and Consuls; to the trial of impeachments of officers of the United States; to all cases of Admiralty and maritime jurisdiction; to controversies between two or more States, (except such as shall regard Territory or Jurisdiction) between a State and Citizens of another State, between Citizens of different States, and between a State or the Citizens thereof and foreign States, citizens or subjects. In cases of impeachment, cases affecting Ambassadors, other Public Ministers and Consuls, and those in which a State shall be party, this jurisdiction shall be original. In all the other cases beforementioned, it shall be appellate, with such exceptions and under such regulations as the Legislature shall make. The Legislature may assign any part of the jurisdiction abovementioned (except the trial of the President of the United States) in the manner, and under the limitations which it shall think proper, to such Inferior Courts, as it shall constitute from time to time.

Sect. 4. The trial of all criminal offences (except in cases of impeachments) shall be in the State where they shall be committed; and shall be by Jury.

Sect. 5. Judgment, in cases of Impeachment, shall not extend further than to removal from office, and disqualification to hold and enjoy any office of honour, trust or profit, under the United States. But the party convicted shall nevertheless be liable and subject to indictment, trial, judgment and punishment according to law.

ARTICLE XII

No State shall coin money; nor grant letters of marque and reprisal; nor enter into any Treaty, alliance, or confederation; nor grant any title of Nobility.

ARTICLE XIII

No State, without the consent of the Legislature of the United States, shall emit bills of credit, or make any thing but specie a tender in payment of debts; nor lay imposts or duties on imports; nor keep troops or ships of war in time of peace; nor enter into any agreement or compact with another State, or with any foreign power; nor engage in any war, unless it shall be actually invaded by enemies, or the danger of invasion be so imminent, as not to admit of delay, until the Legislature of the United States can be consulted.

ARTICLE XIV

The Citizens of each State shall be entitled to all privileges and immunities of citizens in the several States.

ARTICLE XV

Any person charged with treason, felony or high misdemeanor in any State, who shall flee from justice, and shall be found in any other State, shall, on demand of the Executive power of the State from which he fled, be delivered up and removed to the State having jurisdiction of the offence.

ARTICLE XVI

Full faith shall be given in each State to the acts of the Legislatures, and to the records and judicial proceedings of the Courts and magistrates of every other State.

ARTICLE XVII

New States lawfully constituted or established within the limits of the United States may be admitted, by the Legislature, into this Government; but to such admission the consent of two thirds of the members present in each House shall be necessary. If a new State shall arise within the limits of any of the present States, the consent of the Legislatures of such States shall be also necessary to its admission. If the admission be consented to, the new States shall be admitted on the same terms with the original States. But the Legislature may make conditions with the new States, concerning the public debt which shall be then subsisting.

ARTICLE XVIII

The United States shall guaranty to each State a Republican form of Government; and shall protect each State against foreign invasions, and, on the application of its Legislature, against domestic violence.

ARTICLE XIX

On the application of the Legislatures of two thirds of the States in the Union, for an amendment of this Constitution, the Legislature of the United States shall call a Convention for that purpose.

ARTICLE XX

The members of the Legislatures, and the Executive and Judicial officers of the United States, and of the several States, shall be bound by oath to support this Constitution.

ARTICLE XXI

The ratifications of the Conventions of _____ States shall be sufficient for organizing this Constitution.

ARTICLE XXII

This Constitution shall be laid before the United States in Congress assembled, for their approbation; and it is the opinion of this Convention, that it should be afterwards submitted to a Convention chosen in each State under the recommendation of its legislature, in order to receive the ratification of such Convention.

ARTICLE XXIII

To introduce this government, it is the opinion of this Convention, that each assenting Convention should notify its assent and ratification to the United States in Congress assembled; that Congress, after receiving the assent and ratification of the Conventions of _____ States, should appoint and publish a day, as early as may be, and appoint a place for commencing proceedings under this Constitution; that after such publication, the Legislatures of the several States should elect members of the Senate, and direct the election of members of the House of Representatives; and that the members of the Legislature should meet at the time and place assigned by Congress, and should, as soon as may be, after their meeting, choose the President of the United States, and proceed to execute this Constitution.

APPENDIX D

CONSTITUTION OF THE UNITED STATES OF AMERICA

*As Approved by the Constitutional Convention**
SEPTEMBER 17, 1787

We the People of the United States, in Order to form a more perfect Union, establish Justice, insure domestic Tranquility, provide for the common defence, promote the general Welfare, and secure the Blessings of Liberty to ourselves and our Posterity, do ordain and establish this Constitution for the United States of America.

ARTICLE. I.

Section. 1. All legislative Powers herein granted shall be vested in a Congress of the United States, which shall consist of a Senate and House of Representatives.

Section. 2. The House of Representatives shall be composed of Members chosen every second Year by the People of the several States, and the Electors in each State shall have the Qualifications requisite for Electors of the most numerous Branch of the State Legislature.

No Person shall be a Representative who shall not have attained to the Age of twenty five Years, and been seven Years a Citizen of the

---

*Reprinted without modification from the printed version approved by the Convention except for the addition of the word "Section" before section numbers throughout.

United States, and who shall not, when elected, be an Inhabitant of that State in which he shall be chosen.

Representatives and direct Taxes shall be apportioned among the several States which may be included within this Union, according to their respective Numbers, which shall be determined by adding to the whole Number of free Persons, including those bound to Service for a Term of Years, and excluding Indians not taxed, three fifths of all other Persons. The actual Enumeration shall be made within three Years after the first Meeting of the Congress of the United States, and within every subsequent Term of ten Years, in such Manner as they shall by Law direct. The Number of Representatives shall not exceed one for every thirty Thousand, but each State shall have at Least one Representative; and until such enumeration shall be made, the State of New Hampshire shall be entitled to chuse three, Massachusetts eight, Rhode-Island and Providence Plantations one, Connecticut five, New-York six, New Jersey four, Pennsylvania eight, Delaware one, Maryland six, Virginia ten, North Carolina five, South Carolina five, and Georgia three.

When vacancies happen in the Representation from any State, the Executive Authority thereof shall issue Writs of Election to fill such Vacancies.

The House of Representatives shall chuse their Speaker and other Officers; and shall have the sole Power of Impeachment.

Section. 3. The Senate of the United States shall be composed of two Senators from each State, chosen by the Legislature thereof, for six Years; and each Senator shall have one Vote.

Immediately after they shall be assembled in Consequence of the first Election, they shall be divided as equally as may be into three Classes. The Seats of the Senators of the first Class shall be vacated at the Expiration of the second Year, of the second Class at the Expiration of the fourth Year, and of the third Class at the Expiration of the sixth Year, so that one third may be chosen every second Year; and if Vacancies happen by Resignation, or otherwise, during the Recess of the Legislature of any State, the Executive thereof may make temporary Appointments until the next Meeting of the Legislature, which shall then fill such Vacancies.

No Person shall be a Senator who shall not have attained to the Age of thirty Years, and been nine Years a Citizen of the United States, and who shall not, when elected, be an Inhabitant of that State for which he shall be chosen.

The Vice President of the United States shall be President of the Senate, but shall have no Vote, unless they be equally divided.

The Senate shall chuse their other Officers, and also a President pro tempore, in the Absence of the Vice President, or when he shall exercise the Office of President of the United States.

The Senate shall have the sole Power to try all Impeachments. When sitting for that Purpose, they shall be on Oath or Affirmation. When the President of the United States is tried, the Chief Justice shall preside: And no Person shall be convicted without the Concurrence of two thirds of the Members present.

Judgment in Cases of Impeachment shall not extend further than to removal from Office, and disqualification to hold and enjoy any Office of honor, Trust or Profit under the United States: but the Party convicted shall nevertheless be liable and subject to Indictment, Trial, Judgment and Punishment, according to Law.

Section. 4. The Times, Places and Manner of holding Elections for Senators and Representatives, shall be prescribed in each State by the Legislature thereof; but the Congress may at any time by Law make or alter such Regulations, except as to the Places of chusing Senators.

The Congress shall assemble at least once in every Year, and such Meeting shall be on the first Monday in December, unless they shall by Law appoint a different Day.

Section. 5. Each House shall be the Judge of the Elections, Returns and Qualifications of its own Members, and a Majority of each shall constitute a Quorum to do Business; but a smaller Number may adjourn from day to day, and may be authorized to compel the Attendance of absent Members, in such Manner, and under such Penalties as each House may provide.

Each House may determine the Rules of its Proceedings, punish its Members for disorderly Behaviour, and, with the Concurrence of two thirds, expel a Member.

Each House shall keep a Journal of its Proceedings, and from time to time publish the same, excepting such Parts as may in their Judgment require Secrecy; and the Yeas and Nays of the Members of either House on any question shall, at the Desire of one fifth of those Present, be entered on the Journal.

Neither House, during the Session of Congress, shall, without the Consent of the other, adjourn for more than three days, nor to any other Place than that in which the two Houses shall be sitting.

Section. 6. The Senators and Representatives shall receive a Compensation for their Services, to be ascertained by Law, and paid out of the Treasury of the United States. They shall in all Cases, except Treason, Felony and Breach of the Peace, be privileged from Arrest during their Attendance at the Session of their respective Houses, and in going to and returning from the same; and for any Speech or Debate in either House, they shall not be questioned in any other Place.

No Senator or Representative shall, during the Time for which he was elected, be appointed to any civil Office under the Authority of the United States, which shall have been created, or the Emoluments whereof shall have been encreased during such time; and no Person holding any Office under the United States, shall be a Member of either House during his Continuance in Office.

Section. 7. All Bills for raising Revenue shall originate in the House of Representatives; but the Senate may propose or concur with Amendments as on other Bills.

Every Bill which shall have passed the House of Representatives and the Senate, shall, before it become a Law, be presented to the President of the United States; If he approve he shall sign it, but if not he shall return it, with his Objections to that House in which it shall have originated, who shall enter the Objections at large on their Journal, and proceed to reconsider it. If after such Reconsideration two thirds of that House shall agree to pass the Bill, it shall be sent, together with the Objections, to the other House, by which it shall likewise be reconsidered, and if approved by two thirds of that House, it shall become a Law. But in all such Cases the Votes of both Houses shall be determined by yeas and nays, and the Names of the Persons voting for and against the Bill shall be entered on the Journal of each House respectively. If any Bill shall not be returned by the President within ten Days (Sundays excepted) after it shall have been presented to him, the

Same shall be a Law, in like Manner as if he had signed it, unless the Congress by their Adjournment prevent its Return, in which Case it shall not be a Law.

Every Order, Resolution, or Vote to which the Concurrence of the Senate and House of Representatives may be necessary (except on a question of Adjournment) shall be presented to the President of the United States; and before the Same shall take Effect, shall be approved by him, or being disapproved by him, shall be repassed by two thirds of the Senate and House of Representatives, according to the Rules and Limitations prescribed in the Case of a Bill.

Section. 8. The Congress shall have Power To lay and collect Taxes, Duties, Imposts and Excises, to pay the Debts and provide for the common Defence and general Welfare of the United States; but all Duties, Imposts and Excises shall be uniform throughout the United States;

To borrow Money on the credit of the United States;

To regulate Commerce with foreign Nations, and among the several States, and with the Indian Tribes;

To establish an uniform Rule of Naturalization, and uniform Laws on the subject of Bankruptcies throughout the United States;

To coin Money, regulate the Value thereof, and of foreign Coin, and fix the Standard of Weights and Measures;

To provide for the Punishment of counterfeiting the Securities and current Coin of the United States;

To establish Post Offices and post Roads;

To promote the Progress of Science and useful Arts, by securing for limited Times to Authors and Inventors the exclusive Right to their respective Writings and Discoveries;

To constitute Tribunals inferior to the supreme Court;

To define and punish Piracies and Felonies committed on the high Seas, and Offences against the Law of Nations;

To declare War, grant Letters of Marque and Reprisal, and make Rules concerning Captures on Land and Water;

To raise and support Armies, but no Appropriation of Money to that Use shall be for a longer Term than two Years;

To provide and maintain a Navy;

To make Rules for the Government and Regulation of the land and naval Forces;

To provide for calling forth the Militia to execute the Laws of the Union, suppress Insurrections and repel Invasions;

To provide for organizing, arming, and disciplining, the Militia, and for governing such Part of them as may be employed in the Service of the United States, reserving to the States respectively, the Appointment of the Officers, and the Authority of training the Militia according to the discipline prescribed by Congress;

To exercise exclusive Legislation in all Cases whatsoever, over such District (not exceeding ten Miles square) as may, by Cession of particular States, and the Acceptance of Congress, become the Seat of the Government of the United States, and to exercise like Authority over all Places purchased by the Consent of the Legislature of the State in which the Same shall be, for the Erection of Forts, Magazines, Arsenals, dock-yards, and other needful Buildings;—And

To make all Laws which shall be necessary and proper for carrying into Execution the foregoing Powers, and all other Powers vested by this Constitution in the Government of the United States, or in any Department or Officer thereof.

Section. 9. The Migration or Importation of such Persons as any of the States now existing shall think proper to admit, shall not be prohibited by the Congress prior to the Year one thousand eight hundred and eight, but a Tax or duty may be imposed on such Importation, not exceeding ten dollars for each Person.

The Privilege of the Writ of Habeas Corpus shall not be suspended, unless when in Cases of Rebellion or Invasion the public Safety may require it.

No Bill of Attainder or ex post facto Law shall be passed.

No Capitation, or other direct, Tax shall be laid, unless in Proportion to the Census or Enumeration herein before directed to be taken.

No Tax or Duty shall be laid on Articles exported from any State.

No Preference shall be given by any Regulation of Commerce or Revenue to the Ports of one State over those of another; nor shall Vessels bound to, or from, one State, be obliged to enter, clear, or pay Duties in another.

No Money shall be drawn from the Treasury, but in Consequence of Appropriations made by Law; and a regular Statement and Account of the Receipts and Expenditures of all public Money shall be published from time to time.

No Title of Nobility shall be granted by the United States: And no Person holding any Office of Profit or Trust under them, shall, without the Consent of the Congress, accept of any present, Emolument, Office, or Title, of any kind whatever, from any King, Prince, or foreign State.

Section. 10. No State shall enter into any Treaty, Alliance, or Confederation; grant Letters of Marque and Reprisal; coin Money; emit Bills of Credit; make any Thing but gold and silver Coin a Tender in Payment of Debts; pass any Bill of Attainder, ex post facto Law, or Law impairing the Obligation of Contracts, or grant any Title of Nobility.

No State shall, without the Consent of the Congress, lay any Imposts or Duties on Imports or Exports, except what may be absolutely necessary for executing its inspection Laws; and the net Produce of all Duties and Imposts, laid by any State on Imports or Exports, shall be for the Use of the Treasury of the United States; and all such Laws shall be subject to the Revision and Control of the Congress.

No State shall, without the Consent of Congress, lay any Duty of Tonnage, keep Troops, or Ships of War in time of Peace, enter into any Agreement or Compact with another State, or with a foreign Power, or engage in War, unless actually invaded, or in such imminent Danger as will not admit of delay.

ARTICLE. II.

Section. 1. The executive Power shall be vested in a President of the United States of America. He shall hold his Office during the Term of four Years, and, together with the Vice President, chosen for the same Term, be elected, as follows:

Each State shall appoint, in such Manner as the Legislature thereof may direct, a Number of Electors, equal to the whole Number of Senators and Representatives to which the State may be entitled in the Congress: but no Senator or Representative, or Person holding an Office of Trust or Profit under the United States, shall be appointed an Elector.

The Electors shall meet in their respective States, and vote by Ballot for two Persons, of whom one at least shall not be an Inhabitant of the same State with themselves. And they shall make a List of all the Persons voted for, and of the Number of Votes for each; which List they shall sign and certify, and transmit sealed to the Seat of the Government of the United States, directed to the President of the Senate. The President of the Senate shall, in the Presence of the Senate and House of Representatives, open all the Certificates, and the Votes shall then be counted. The Person having the greatest Number of Votes shall be the President, if such Number be a Majority of the whole Number of Electors appointed; and if there be more than one who have such Majority, and have an equal Number of Votes, then the House of Representatives shall immediately chuse by Ballot one of them for President; and if no Person have a Majority, then from the five highest on the List the said House shall in like Manner chuse the President. But in chusing the President, the Votes shall be taken by States, the Representation from each State having one Vote; a quorum for this Purpose shall consist of a Member or Members from two thirds of the States, and a Majority of all the States shall be necessary to a Choice. In every Case, after the Choice of the President, the Person having the greatest Number of Votes of the Electors shall be the Vice President. But if there should remain two or more who have equal Votes, the Senate shall chuse from them by Ballot the Vice President.

The Congress may determine the Time of chusing the Electors, and the Day on which they shall give their Votes; which Day shall be the same throughout the United States.

No Person except a natural born Citizen, or a Citizen of the United States, at the time of the Adoption of this Constitution, shall be eligible to the Office of President; neither shall any Person be eligible to that Office who shall not have attained to the Age of thirty five Years, and been fourteen Years a Resident within the United States.

In Case of the Removal of the President from Office, or of his Death, Resignation, or Inability to discharge the Powers and Duties of the said Office, the Same shall devolve on the Vice President, and the Congress may by Law provide for the Case of Removal, Death, Resignation or Inability, both of the President and Vice President, declaring what Officer shall then act as President, and such Officer shall act accordingly, until the Disability be removed, or a President shall be elected.

The President shall, at stated Times, receive for his Services, a Compensation, which shall neither be increased nor diminished during the Period for which he shall have been elected, and he shall not receive within that Period any other Emolument from the United States, or any of them.

Before he enter on the Execution of his Office, he shall take the following Oath or Affirmation:—"I do solemnly swear (or affirm) that I will faithfully execute the Office of President of the United States, and will to the best of my Ability, preserve, protect and defend the Constitution of the United States."

Section. 2. The President shall be Commander in Chief of the Army and Navy of the United States, and of the Militia of the several States, when called into the actual Service of the United States; he may require the Opinion, in writing, of the principal Officer in each of the executive Departments, upon any Subject relating to the Duties of their respective Offices, and he shall have Power to grant Reprieves and Pardons for Offences against the United States, except in Cases of Impeachment.

He shall have Power, by and with the Advice and Consent of the Senate, to make Treaties, provided two thirds of the Senators present concur; and he shall nominate, and by and with the Advice and Consent of the Senate, shall appoint Ambassadors, other public Ministers and Consuls, Judges of the supreme Court, and all other Officers of the United States, whose Appointments are not herein otherwise provided for, and which shall be established by Law: but the Congress may by Law vest the Appointment of such inferior Officers, as they think proper, in the President alone, in the Courts of Law, or in the Heads of Departments.

The President shall have Power to fill up all Vacancies that may happen during the Recess of the Senate, by granting Commissions which shall expire at the End of their next Session.

Section. 3. He shall from time to time give to the Congress Information of the State of the Union, and recommend to their Consideration such Measures as he shall judge necessary and expedient; he may, on extraordinary Occasions, convene both Houses, or either of them, and in Case of Disagreement between them, with Respect to the Time of Adjournment, he may adjourn them to such Time as he shall think proper; he shall receive Ambassadors and other public Ministers; he shall take Care that the Laws be faithfully executed, and shall Commission all the Officers of the United States.

Section. 4. The President, Vice President and all civil Officers of the United States, shall be removed from Office on Impeachment for, and Conviction of, Treason, Bribery, or other high Crimes and Misdemeanors.

ARTICLE. III.

Section. 1. The judicial Power of the United States shall be vested in one supreme Court, and in such inferior Courts as the Congress may from time to time ordain and establish. The Judges, both of the supreme and inferior Courts, shall hold their Offices during good Behaviour, and shall, at stated Times, receive for their Services a Compensation, which shall not be diminished during their Continuance in Office.

Section. 2. The judicial Power shall extend to all Cases, in Law and Equity, arising under this Constitution, the Laws of the United States, and Treaties made, or which shall be made, under their Authority;— to all Cases affecting Ambassadors, other public Ministers and Consuls;—to all Cases of admiralty and maritime Jurisdiction;—to Controversies to which the United States shall be a Party;—to Controversies between two or more States;—between a State and Citizens of another State;—between Citizens of different States;—between Citizens of the same State claiming Lands under Grants of different States, and between a State, or the Citizens thereof, and foreign States, Citizens or Subjects.

In all Cases affecting Ambassadors, other public Ministers and Consuls, and those in which a State shall be Party, the supreme Court shall have original Jurisdiction. In all the other Cases before mentioned, the supreme Court shall have appellate Jurisdiction, both as to Law and Fact, with such Exceptions, and under such Regulations as the Congress shall make.

The Trial of all Crimes, except in Cases of Impeachment, shall be by Jury; and such Trial shall be held in the State where the said Crimes shall have been committed; but when not committed within any State, the Trial shall be at such Place or Places as the Congress may by Law have directed.

Section. 3. Treason against the United States shall consist only in levying War against them, or in adhering to their Enemies, giving them Aid and Comfort. No Person shall be convicted of Treason unless on the Testimony of two Witnesses to the same overt Act, or on Confession in open Court.

The Congress shall have Power to declare the Punishment of Treason, but no Attainder of Treason shall work Corruption of Blood, or Forfeiture except during the Life of the Person attainted.

ARTICLE. IV.

Section. 1. Full Faith and Credit shall be given in each State to the public Acts, Records, and judicial Proceedings of every other State. And the Congress may by general Laws prescribe the Manner in which such Acts, Records and Proceedings shall be proved, and the Effect thereof.

Section. 2. The Citizens of each State shall be entitled to all Privileges and Immunities of Citizens in the several States.

A Person charged in any State with Treason, Felony, or other Crime, who shall flee from Justice, and be found in another State, shall on Demand of the executive Authority of the State from which he fled, be delivered up, to be removed to the State having Jurisdiction of the Crime.

No Person held to Service or Labour in one State, under the Laws thereof, escaping into another, shall, in Consequence of any Law or Regulation therein, be discharged from such Service or Labour, but shall be delivered up on Claim of the Party to whom such Service or Labour may be due.

Section. 3. New States may be admitted by the Congress into this Union; but no new State shall be formed or erected within the Jurisdiction of any other State; nor any State be formed by the Junction of two or more States, or Parts of States, without the Consent of the Legislatures of the States concerned as well as of the Congress.

The Congress shall have Power to dispose of and make all needful Rules and Regulations respecting the Territory or other Property belonging to the United States; and nothing in this Constitution shall be so construed as to Prejudice any Claims of the United States, or of any particular State.

Section. 4. The United States shall guarantee to every State in this Union a Republican Form of Government, and shall protect each of them against Invasion; and on Application of the Legislature, or of the Executive (when the Legislature cannot be convened), against domestic Violence.

ARTICLE. V.

The Congress, whenever two thirds of both Houses shall deem it necessary, shall propose Amendments to this Constitution, or, on the Application of the Legislatures of two thirds of the several States, shall call a Convention for proposing Amendments, which, in either Case, shall be valid to all Intents and Purposes, as Part of this Constitution, when ratified by the Legislatures of three fourths of the several States, or by Conventions in three fourths thereof, as the one or the other Mode of Ratification may be proposed by the Congress; Provided that no Amendment which may be made prior to the Year One thousand eight hundred and eight shall in any Manner affect the first and fourth Clauses in the Ninth Section of the first Article; and that no State, without its Consent, shall be deprived of its equal Suffrage in the Senate.

ARTICLE. VI.

All Debts contracted and Engagements entered into, before the Adoption of this Constitution, shall be as valid against the United States under this Constitution, as under the Confederation.

This Constitution, and the Laws of the United States which shall be made in Pursuance thereof; and all Treaties made, or which shall be made, under the Authority of the United States, shall be the supreme Law of the Land; and the Judges in every State shall be bound thereby, any Thing in the Constitution or Laws of any State to the Contrary notwithstanding.

The Senators and Representatives before mentioned, and the Members of the several State Legislatures, and all executive and judicial Officers, both of the United States and of the several States, shall be bound by Oath or Affirmation, to support this Constitution; but no religious Test shall ever be required as a Qualification to any Office or public Trust under the United States.

ARTICLE. VII.

The Ratification of the Conventions of nine States, shall be sufficient for the Establishment of this Constitution between the States so ratifying the Same.

The Word, "the," being interlined between the seventh and eighth Lines of the first Page, The Word "Thirty" being partly written on an Erazure in the fifteenth Line of the first Page, The Words "is tried" being interlined between the thirty second and thirty third Lines of the first Page and the Word "the" being interlined between the forty third and forty fourth Lines of the second Page.

Attest William Jackson
Secretary

done in Convention by the Unanimous Consent of the States present the Seventeenth Day of September in the Year of our Lord one thousand seven hundred and Eighty seven and of the Independence of the United States of America the Twelfth In witness whereof We have hereunto subscribed our Names,

Go. WASHINGTON—Presidt and deputy from Virginia

New Hampshire: JOHN LANGDON, NICHOLAS GILMAN

Massachusetts: NATHANIEL GORHAM, RUFUS KING

Connecticut: WM. SAML. JOHNSON, ROGER SHERMAN

New York: ALEXANDER HAMILTON

New Jersey: WIL: LIVINGSTON, DAVID BREARLEY. WM. PATERSON, JONA: DAYTON

Pennsylvania: B FRANKLIN, THOMAS MIFFLIN, ROBT MORRIS, GEO. CLYMER, THOS. FITZ SIMONS, JARED INGERSOLL, JAMES WILSON, GOUV MORRIS

Delaware: GEO: READ, GUNNING BEDFORD jun, JOHN DICKINSON, RICHARD BASSETT, JACO: BROOM

Maryland: JAMES MCHENRY, DAN OF ST THOS. JENIFER, DANL CARROLL

Virginia: JOHN BLAIR, JAMES MADISON jr

North Carolina: WM. BLOUNT, RICHD. DOBBS SPAIGHT, HU WILLIAMSON

South Carolina: J. RUTLEDGE, CHARLES COTESWORTH PINCKNEY, CHARLES PINCKNEY, PIERCE BUTLER

Georgia: WILLIAM FEW, ABR BALDWIN

In Convention Monday, September 17th, 1787.

Present: The States of New Hampshire, Massachusetts, Connecticut, Mr. Hamilton from New York, New Jersey, Pennsylvania, Delaware, Maryland, Virginia, North Carolina, South Carolina and Georgia.

Resolved,

That the preceeding Constitution be laid before the United States in Congress assembled, and that it is the Opinion of this Convention, that it should afterwards be submitted to a Convention of Delegates, chosen in each State by the People thereof, under the Recommendation of its Legislature, for their Assent and Ratification; and that each Convention assenting to, and ratifying the Same, should give Notice thereof to the United States in Congress assembled. Resolved, That it is the Opinion of this Convention, that as soon as the Conventions of nine States shall have ratified this Constitution, the United States in Congress assembled should fix a Day on which Electors should be appointed by the States which have ratified the same, and a Day on which the Electors should assemble to vote for the President, and the Time and Place for commencing Proceedings under this Constitution. That after such Publication the Electors should be appointed, and the Senators and Representatives elected: That the Electors should meet on the Day fixed for the Election of the President, and should transmit their Votes certified, signed, sealed and directed, as the Constitution requires, to the Secretary of the United States in Congress assembled, that the Senators and Representatives should convene at the Time and Place assigned; that the Senators should appoint a President of the Senate, for the sole purpose of receiving, opening and counting the Votes for President; and, that after he shall be chosen, the Congress, together with the President, should, without Delay, proceed to execute this Constitution.

By the Unanimous Order of the Convention

Go. WASHINGTON—Presidt.
W. JACKSON Secretary.

SUGGESTIONS FOR FURTHER READING

Our book provides a highly edited version of Madison's notes on the Constitutional Convention with a narrative context. Readers may want to fill in the ellipses at various points in the debates. This is easily done. Several Internet sites provide the entire text of Madison's notes along with related material. We recommend Yale Law School's Avalon Project website at http://www.yale.edu/lawweb/avalon/constpap.htm, which includes a rich array of documents relating to the American Constitution, going back to the Magna Carta and forward through the ratification process. Perhaps the most user-friendly Internet access to Madison's notes is found on the Constitution Society's webpage at http://www.constitution.org/dfc/dfc_0000.htm. As noted in the epilogue, the definitive print source for documents of the Constitutional Convention is Max Farrand's four-volume *The Records of the Federal Convention of 1787,* 2nd ed. (1937), together with James H. Huston's *Supplement to Max Farrand's The Records of the Federal Convention of 1787* (1987). The standard one-volume edition of Madison's notes is Adrienne Koch, ed., *Notes of Debates on the Federal Convention of 1787* (1966).

Numerous books rely heavily on Madison's notes to retell the story of the Constitutional Convention. We recommend starting with Max Farrand, *The Framing of the Constitution of the United States* (1913). Other notable works are Charles Warren, *The Making of the Constitution* (1923);

Catherine Drinker Bowen, *Miracle at Philadelphia: The Story of the Constitutional Convention* (1966); Clinton Rossiter, *1787: The Grand Convention* (1966); and Carol Berkin, *A Brilliant Solution: Inventing the American Constitution* (2002).

The Constitutional Convention was the product of a convulsive revolutionary process that stretched back to the first colonial protests against the British government during the 1760s. For two fine overviews of that process, see John Ferling, *A Leap in the Dark: The Struggle to Create the American Republic* (2003), and Gordon S. Wood, *The Radicalism of the American Revolution* (1992). There are many other excellent works dealing with this critical period in American history.

Modern historical study of the making of the Constitution began with Charles Beard, *Economic Interpretation of the Constitution* (1913). Beard investigated the financial holdings of the delegates to the Constitutional Convention, which were heavily tilted toward western lands, loans, and war bonds, and argued that the delegates designed the Constitution to protect their investments. Beard's thesis dominated scholarly understanding of the Constitution for half a century. Forrest McDonald, *We the People: The Economic Origins of the Constitution* (1958), was sympathetic to Beard's reduction of politics to economic self-interest, but he demonstrated that there was no obvious correlation between investments and positions on the Constitution. For a recent reevaluation of the role economic self-interest played in delegates' votes at the Constitutional Convention and state ratifying conventions, see Robert A. McGuire, *To Form a More Perfect Union: A New Economic Interpretation of the United States Constitution* (2003).

With Beard's thesis in disarray by the 1960s, a brilliant book by Gordon S. Wood, *The Creation of the American Republic, 1776–1787* (1969), provided a fresh start for scholarship on the roots of the Constitution. Wood traces the complex relationship between political events and political ideas during the Revolutionary era. For him, the founders were not so much aggressive capitalists as they were frightened aristocrats, rethinking their traditional but decaying eighteenth-century understanding of politics and government in the face of a rising tide of democracy. Following Wood's book, there has been much intensive investigation into the intellectual world of the founding fathers, including Forrest McDonald, *Novus Ordo Seclorum: The Intellectual*

Origins of the Constitution (1985), and Jack N. Rakove, *Original Meanings: Politics and Ideas in the Making of the Constitution* (1996).

In addition to these three broadly conceived works, many specialized studies ably explore various facets of the complex interaction between ideas, interests, and politics that led to the American Constitution. Cathy D. Matson and Peter S. Onuf, *A Union of Interests: Political and Economic Thought in Revolutionary America* (1990), investigates the developing relationship between growing economic regionalism and understandings of the role of a national government. Peter S. Onuf, *The Origins of the Federal Republic: Jurisdictional Controversies in the United States, 1775–1787* (1983), looks at how disputes between the states spurred the development of a national government. Roger H. Brown, *Redeeming the Republic: Federalists, Taxation, and the Origins of the Constitution* (1993), illumines the role of state tax policies in the drive toward the Constitution. Two good collections of essays in this respect are Richard Beeman, Stephen Botein, and Edward C. Carter II, eds., *Beyond Confederation: Origins of the Constitution and American National Identity* (1987), and Leonard Levy and Dennis J. Mahoney, eds., *The Framing and Ratification of the Constitution* (1987). For a thorough quantitative study of shifting voting alliances at the Constitutional Convention, see Calvin C. Jillson, *Constitution Making: Conflict and Consensus in the Federal Convention of 1787* (1988).

Two recent studies have broken significant new ground for understanding the origins of the American Constitution. Max Edling, *A Revolution in Favor of Government: Origins of the U.S. Constitution and the Making of the American State* (2003), argues that the most important concern of most nationalists was to create a government that was powerful enough to stand against European powers. Christopher Collier, *All Politics Is Local: Family, Friends, and Provincial Interests in the Creation of the Constitution* (2003), provides a detailed study of the impact of specific local political, social, and economic circumstances on both how Connecticut's individual delegates voting at the Convention acted and how the finished document was received in their home state. Both works should influence the next generation of historical scholarship on the Constitution.

The literature on the struggle to ratify the Constitution is extensive. We cannot begin to do it justice here. For a vivid description of the process, see Forrest McDonald's sometimes speculative but always engaging *E Pluribus Unum: The Formation of the American Republic, 1776–1790* (1965). Insightful analysis of the ratification debates appears in Gordon S. Wood, *The Creation of the American Republic, 1776–1787* (1969), and Jack N. Rakove, *Original Meanings: Politics and Ideas in the Making of the Constitution* (1996). The classic source for the records of these debates is Jonathan Elliot's *The Debates in the Several State Conventions, On the Adoption of the Federal Constitution, as Recommended by the General Convention at Philadelphia, in 1787* (1817, 1828, and 1830), commonly referred to as simply *Elliot's Debates*. For a more recent collection of these records, see the multivolume set, *Documentary History of the Ratification of the Constitution* (1976–84), with various volumes edited by John P. Kaminski, Merrill Jensen, and Gaspare J. Saladino. Extended discussion of objections to the ratification of the Constitution appears in Herbert J. Storing, *What the Anti-Federalists Were For* (1981), and Saul Cornell, *Other Founders: Anti-Federalism and the Dissenting Tradition in America, 1788–1828* (1999). Along with his book, Storing also published an impressive seven-volume collection of documents written in opposition to ratification, *The Complete Anti-Federalist* (1981). On the winning side, *The Federalist Papers* are available in many editions.

Readers may wish to dig deeper into the individual biographies of various delegates. The choices here are legion. Books about Washington could fill a small library, as could ones about Franklin. For Washington, one good place to start is James Thomas Flexner, *Washington: The Indispensable Man* (1974). Two notable new biographies of Washington are Joseph J. Ellis's *His Excellency: George Washington* (2004) and Henry Wiencek's *An Imperfect God: George Washington, His Slaves, and the Creation of America* (2003). Among the many recent Franklin biographies are Walter Isaacson's *Benjamin Franklin: An American Life* (2003), Gordon S. Wood's *The Americanization of Benjamin Franklin* (2004), and Edmond S. Morgan's *Benjamin Franklin* (2002). For Madison, we recommend starting with either Lance Banning, *The Sacred Fire of Liberty: James Madison and the Founding of the Federal Republic* (1995), or, for a shorter work, Jack Rakove, *James Madison and the Founding of the Federal Republic* (1990). The most recent biography of Hamilton is Ron Chernow's *Alexander Hamilton* (2004)—a delightful read.

To learn more about other delegates, the decision facing readers is less which biography than which delegate. Many of the delegates are the subject of at least one major biography. For the delegates who stand out in our reading of the Convention, we recommend beginning with the following books. On other delegates from Virginia, see Helen Hill Miller, *George Mason: Gentleman Revolutionary* (1975), and John J. Reardon, *Edmund Randolph: A Biography* (1974). For two of the outstanding delegates from Pennsylvania, see William Howard Adams, *Gouverneur Morris: An Independent Life* (2003), and Charles Page Smith, *James Wilson: Founding Father, 1742–1798* (1956). Other notable biographies include George Athan Billias, *Elbridge Gerry: Founding Father and Republican Statesman* (1976); Christopher Collier, *Roger Sherman's Connecticut: Yankee Politics and the American Revolution* (1971); Milton E. Flower, *John Dickinson: Conservative Revolutionary* (1983); Elizabeth P. McCaughey, *From Loyalist to Founding Father: The Political Odyssey of William Samuel Johnson* (1980); and John E. O'Connor, *William Paterson: Lawyer and Statesman, 1745–1806* (1979).

For the most part, the legal discussion over what role Madison's notes and Convention history should play in construing the Constitution's current meaning is nestled obscurely in law review articles and judicial opinions. This narrow discussion is related to, but not determined by, the wider debate over the proper role of original intent and textualism in constitutional interpretation. Partisans on various sides of the originalist debate take differing positions on how the deliberations in Philadelphia should impact constitutional law today. For an introduction to this narrow issue, we recommend beginning with Philip Bobbitt, *Constitutional Fate: Theory of the Constitution* (1982); H. Jefferson Powell, "The Original Understanding of Original Intent," *Harvard Law Review*, 98 (1985), 885; Akhil Reed Amar, "Our Forgotten Constitution: A Bicentennial Comment," *Yale Law Journal*, 97 (1987), 281; Larry Kramer, "Fidelity to History—And Through It," *Fordham Law Review*, 65 (1997), 1627; and Vesan Kesavan and Michael Stokes Paulsen, "The Interpretive Force of the Constitution's Secret Drafting History," *Georgetown Law Journal*, 91 (2003), 1113. The wider debate over originalism is beyond the scope of this bibliographic essay.

Within the legal community, we find that some people still wonder about the criticisms of Madison's notes leveled two generations ago by University of Chicago constitutional law professor William W. Crosskey. In *Politics and the Constitution in the History of the United States* (1953) and elsewhere, Crosskey denounced Madison as a forger who tampered with his notes of the Constitutional Convention to serve his own partisan purposes. Crosskey's criticisms are perhaps best answered and the integrity of Madison's notes most ably defended in James H. Hutson, "The Creation of the Constitution: The Integrity of the Documentary Record," *Texas Law Review*, 65 (1986), 1. In the debate between Crosskey and Hutson, we side with Hutson—as do virtually all historians and constitutional-law scholars.

INDEX

EDWARD J. LARSON is the Russell Professor of History and Talmadge Professor of Law at the University of Georgia. He is the recipient of multiple awards for teaching and writing, including the 1998 Pulitzer Prize in History for his book *Summer for the Gods: The Scopes Trial and America's Continuing Debate Over Science and Religion.* His most recent book is *Evolution: The Remarkable History of a Scientific Theory* (Modern Library, 2004). His articles have appeared in dozens of journals, including *The Atlantic Monthly, Nature, The Nation, Science,* and *Scientific American.*

MICHAEL P. WINSHIP is the E. Merton Coulter Professor of History at the University of Georgia. He has written numerous articles and books on early American history.

A NOTE ON THE TYPE

The principal text of this Modern Library edition
was set in a digitized version of Janson, a typeface that
dates from about 1690 and was cut by Nicholas Kis,
a Hungarian working in Amsterdam. The original matrices have
survived and are held by the Stempel foundry in Germany.
Hermann Zapf redesigned some of the weights and sizes for
Stempel, basing his revisions on the original design.

MODERN LIBRARY IS ONLINE AT
WWW.MODERNLIBRARY.COM

MODERN LIBRARY ONLINE IS YOUR GUIDE TO CLASSIC LITERATURE ON THE WEB

THE MODERN LIBRARY E-NEWSLETTER

Our free e-mail newsletter is sent to subscribers, and features sample chapters, interviews with and essays by our authors, upcoming books, special promotions, announcements, and news. To subscribe to the Modern Library e-newsletter, visit **www.modernlibrary.com**

THE MODERN LIBRARY WEBSITE

Check out the Modern Library website at
www.modernlibrary.com for:

- The Modern Library e-newsletter
- A list of our current and upcoming titles and series
- Reading Group Guides and exclusive author spotlights
- Special features with information on the classics and other paperback series
- Excerpts from new releases and other titles
- A list of our e-books and information on where to buy them
- The Modern Library Editorial Board's 100 Best Novels and 100 Best Nonfiction Books of the Twentieth Century written in the English language
- News and announcements

Questions? E-mail us at **modernlibrary@randomhouse.com**.
For questions about examination or desk copies, please visit
the Random House Academic Resources site at
www.randomhouse.com/academic